Acclaim
for the *Penny Pinching* editions!

"Loaded with savvy tips on everything from cutting your food bills to keeping your utility expenses under control to vacationing in style without regrets when the bills come in."

—*Detroit Free Press*

"A no-nonsense, no-frills compendium, conveniently organized by subject. There's advice on everything from cutting grocery bills to investing in mutual funds."

—*Kiplinger's Personal Finance Magazine*

"The perfect '90s pocket book for people who want to keep more than pocket change."

—*The Atlanta Journal*

Featured on *Oprah!*

Now updated to include more than a hundred money-saving Internet sources, this fifth completely revised edition of *Penny Pinching* is bigger and better than ever!

For busy, successful people who want to live well, care about quality, and prefer not to cut back on the luxuries they enjoy right now, here is the book that offers hundreds of ways you can do what you want to do, eat what you want to eat, wear the clothes you want to wear, and live the way you always have—but for less money than you're spending now.

PENNY
PINCHING

Lee and Barbara Simmons

BANTAM BOOKS
NEW YORK • TORONTO • LONDON • SYDNEY • AUCKLAND

PENNY PINCHING
A Bantam Book

PUBLISHING HISTORY
Bantam first edition / September 1991
Bantam fifth edition / January 1999

ISBN 0-553-57367-5

Published simultaneously in the United States and Canada

Bantam Books are published by Bantam Books, a division of Random House, Inc. Its trademark, consisting of the words "Bantam
Books" and the portrayal of a rooster, is Registered in U.S. Patent
and Trademark Office and in other countries. Marca Registrada.
Bantam Books, 1540 Broadway, New York, New York 10036.

PRINTED IN THE UNITED STATES OF AMERICA

WCD   10 9 8 7 6 5 4 3 2 1

CONTENTS

Introduction: No Pain, Much Gain

This is the fifth revised, completely updated edition of a book first published in September 1991.

It is filled with dozens of completely new tips and many more that have been extensively revised because of changes in the consumer environment. It includes many new sources, telephone numbers, and Internet addresses that will be invaluable to any penny pincher with access to a computer and a modem.

We had no idea when we started working on the first edition back in 1990 that it would soon be followed by a flood of other books and newsletters filled with advice from self-proclaimed tightwads, skinflints, cheapskates, and other promoters of frugal living. But the reason why so many of these newsletters and books were successful is clear. In the 1990s, cutting costs became a necessity for millions of beleaguered middle-class American consumers.

For the husband-and-wife authors of this book, that

wasn't bad news at all. Long before the recession of the early 1990s, when a change in jobs in 1988 sharply reduced our income, we began to learn, test, develop, and live with many of the penny-pinching strategies you will find in the following pages. Our goal: to reduce our expenses without lowering our standard of living. We didn't want to buy cheap substitutes for the kind of food and clothing we had always enjoyed. We didn't want to spend hours of extra time each week doing things like bartering cents-off coupons or washing and saving old aluminum foil.

We still don't. That's why *Penny Pinching* is different from most of the books on the subject that followed our first edition. This is *not* the book for you if you think you might want to save money by:

- identifying reusable food in Dumpsters.
- buying a goat to mow your lawn.
- rinsing coffee filters for reuse.
- baking your own dog biscuits.
- cutting wide rubber bands in half lengthwise so you'll have two for the price of one.

We watch with both amazement and amusement as rival frugality newsletters try to outdo each other with advice like the above—all actual examples. But we have no intention of trying to compete.

As we told Oprah Winfrey when we appeared on her show to discuss defensive shopping in supermarkets, we are serious about saving money and reducing waste, but we aren't crazed coupon-clippers or anti–brand name fanatics. Life is too short to devote it entirely to pinching every last penny.

"Penny pinching" is, after all, a term that has been passed down from a time when a penny was actually worth something. It's still a useful description of a worthwhile discipline, but we concentrate on pinching dollars, not cents. Of course, if it is easy to take advantage of a 25-cents-off coupon on a $1 purchase, we do it. If we can easily save a few cents by switching to a product of equal quality, we do that, too. Cents still add up to dollars. But the operative words are "easy" and "quality"; we insist on both. So this book is for busy, successful people who want to live well, care about quality, don't want to sacrifice a lot of precious leisure time, and prefer not to cut back on the luxuries they enjoy right now. What they need are ways to do what they do, eat what they eat, wear the clothes they want to wear, and live the way they always have—but for less money than it is costing them now.

How can you cut your weekly grocery bill by 10 to 15 percent without changing your family's eating habits? What are the no-pain ways to cut heating expenses? How do you buy the cheapest airline ticket possible? How can virtually anyone save up to 10 percent on automobile insurance even without changing insurance companies?

This book has some answers. You'll find money-saving tips on everything from cabbages and lightbulbs to designer clothes and treasury bills. How much can they save you? Perhaps hundreds, perhaps even thousands of dollars a year. For most people, changing just a few habits can lead to very substantial savings. What's more, although effective penny pinching requires a more organized approach than most people take in managing their money, many penny-pinching strategies will in the end actually save you time as well as money.

IT'S YOU AGAINST THEM

To be a successful penny pincher, you must understand that you live in a society dominated by marketers who have devised countless sophisticated techniques to sell you what they want you to buy, when they want you to buy it, at the prices they want you to pay. They have created powerful brand images that persuade people to pay $1.50 for Soap A, which is identical except for packaging to 50-cent Soap B. They advertise "enormous savings" when things are priced at a normal markup and don't advertise at all when the same things are really on sale. They invent products you don't need but soon want.

There's nothing wrong with any of this. Selling, merchandising, advertising, and marketing are essential to a healthy national economy. But your own financial health depends on knowing when to turn off the sell messages and what tactics to employ when confronted with various purchase decisions.

Will anyone who reads this book want to or be able to use all of its strategies and tips? No. In fact, we've included quite a few ideas we can't or don't choose to use ourselves. Nevertheless, they have proved their usefulness with penny-pinching friends and readers who have shared them with us.

Are you already likely to be aware of some of the ideas it recommends? Certainly. We debated including some of them because they seem to turn up in every magazine article about saving money. But if everyone knows that a cheap, homemade window-washing mixture is just as effective as the expensive brand-name products, how come tens of millions of dollars' worth of those products are still sold year after year?

Even people who already are successfully pinching pennies are bound to find a couple of new ways to save money—at least enough to pay for this book a few times over.

THE PENNY PINCHER'S BEST FRIENDS

There are constant references throughout this book to libraries, 800 numbers, and Internet web sites. Pinching pennies would be far more difficult without them. That's because saving money is most often a matter of having the right information. Even the smallest public libraries have reference books and magazines that can help. A lot of people are nervous about doing "research" in a library because they never learned how or have forgotten what they learned in school. Don't let that stop you. Good librarians enjoy helping you get started. Tell them what your question is, and chances are they will immediately tell you where to find the answer.

The most useful telephone number for a penny pincher is 1-800-555-1212. That's directory assistance for the toll-free 800-888 system. It doesn't cost a penny to call it in most areas of the country. Thousands of companies and organizations have set up 800 and 888 numbers because they want you to call for information or service. You can get free brochures and booklets, advice on how to fix just about anything, and competitive prices on virtually every product made. All without leaving home, all at no cost.

Finally, although the Internet has been a part of our lives for only a brief period of time, it has already revolutionized the way we communicate and get information. As we head toward the year 2000 and beyond, the Internet has already become the single most powerful penny-pinching resource available. If you don't have access to a computer and a modem, this book will still be as helpful as it has ever been. If you do, you'll find more than 150 suggestions about Internet sites to visit that will make penny pinching easier than ever before.

Whether you use the Internet or not, we hope you'll find enough penny-pinching tips and strategies in these pages to help you live the good life for a lot less money.

§1§

Slashing Food and Grocery Bills

Have you ever given much thought to how a modern supermarket is organized? Probably not. But the corporations that own the supermarkets sure have, and so have Procter & Gamble, RJR Nabisco, Coca-Cola, and the other giant package-goods companies that make and market what's on the shelves.

After billions of dollars and hours spent on continuing research and consumer testing, they have learned to stack the supermarket deck to accomplish one basic goal: to separate you from as much of your money as possible every time you set foot in a store.

Every element of a supermarket's design and floor plan is carefully set up to encourage as much unplanned "impulse" buying as possible. That's why the staple items needed by most shoppers are strategically spread all over the store—you are forced to walk through as many aisles as possible to get to them. That's also why you'll nearly always find pretzels near the beer shelves;

maybe you just went in for a six-pack but you'll leave with more than that.

Does that enormous display of one product at the end of an aisle signal a great bargain? Probably not. Often, the product is reaching its expiration date, but not on sale. Or the display is there because the product's distributor "rented" the space for a period of time from the supermarket.

The only way for you to win is to change the rules of the game so it is played your way, not theirs. The supermarket marketers want you to wander through their aisles making last-minute decisions about tonight's dinner. Don't do it. Some of the strategies and tips in this chapter help you cut your grocery bills by avoiding impulse shopping. If you adopt most of them, annual savings of 15 percent or even more are a realistic goal. What's more, by cutting down on the number of extra trips you make to the supermarket, you'll save time and a lot of aggravation as well.

The highest profits made by the giant food companies and supermarkets are in products that cost more because they promise to save you time and effort. To achieve maximum savings in your weekly food bill, cut out convenience foods altogether.

That's easier said than done, of course. It is cheaper to make your own soups than to buy cans, to bake a cake from scratch than to buy one from a bakery, to prepare a homemade chicken pot pie than to buy a frozen one. But few people these days have either the time or the inclination to do such things very often. It is worth paying for convenience—in some food categories, some of the time.

What is not worth paying for is the marketing ingenuity that has extended the convenience-food concept to laughable extremes. Only a few of the more outrageous or pervasive examples are cited in the tips that follow. They will help you avoid some obvious rip-offs, but you can easily find hundreds more if you keep just a few rules of thumb in mind about shopping and paying for "convenience."

- The more removed from the original basic ingredients and the effort needed to prepare them, the more expensive the convenience product. For instance, making pancakes from flour, milk, eggs, baking powder, salt, sugar, and cooking oil is cheaper than buying a package of pancake mix; which is cheaper than frozen, premixed pancake batter; which is cheaper than frozen pancakes; which are cheaper than (the most recent gimmick) frozen, *microwavable* pancakes. Estimated cost of quality ingredients to make one dozen 4-inch pancakes from scratch: 40 cents. Cost of the same number of frozen microwave pancakes: $2.59.

- In any blind taste test, which kind of pancakes do you think would win? The addition of convenience characteristics nearly always means some loss of freshness, taste, texture, etc.

- Avoid convenience that is only a matter of smart packaging. Example: a can of chow mein vegetables sold in the same box with a pouch of soy sauce. Buy them separately. This kind of packaging provides no meaningful added convenience, just higher prices.

- Convenience is most expensive in small packages. Food marketers know that, as a group, busy single people are most likely to want no-hassle ways to prepare a meal. They charge especially high prices for "individual servings."

Prices used in this chapter were actual store prices at the time this book was going to press. Although the prices you will see on many items will no doubt be different, the price ratios between competitive choices probably won't change much at all.

▶ SHOP ONCE A WEEK

If you remember that impulse buying is the enemy, it makes sense to limit the number of times you face temptation. Besides, think of all the time (and gasoline and shoe leather) you waste by running to the supermarket for three or four items at a time.

You have to break this rule when you eat fresh fish or other highly perishable foods. But the principle is still sound: Try to buy everything you can on a once-a-week basis, and head right to the fish counter, the fresh bread case, or the fruit-and-vegetable section when you have to make a special trip.

▶ SHOP ALONE

Watch the next time you see a couple doing their weekly shopping together. The odds are good that she's filling her shopping basket with exactly the items on her checklist. He's roaming the aisles, reading the labels on all sorts of exotic stuff, and idly slipping jars of gourmet mustard and salsa into the basket. Kids are just as big a problem, and harder to argue with when they simply must have the new super-sugared Technicolor cereal they just saw on TV.

▶ BEND AND STRETCH

Supermarkets tend to display the most expensive and/or fastest-moving merchandise at eye level, encouraging impulse buying by making it easy. You will often find better buys higher or lower on the shelves.

▶ DON'T SHOP WHEN YOU'RE HUNGRY

You'll be far less likely to buy foods impulsively if you shop on a full stomach, not an empty one.

▶ USE UNIT PRICING

Most states now require "unit price" information to be displayed on supermarket shelves, along with the price of the item. Especially given the often deceptive packaging practices of some food companies, unit price information is extremely helpful to consumers who want to know exactly how much they are getting for their money.

Example: Package A, priced at $1.50, sits right next to a competing brand of the same product, Package B, priced at $1.60. They are in exactly the same size package. Is A a better buy? No, because A contains only 6 ounces and B 8 ounces. In a unit price state, the unit price per quart or pound as well as the price of the package must be displayed under each product: $4 a pound for A ($1.50 divided by 6 ounces = 25 cents per ounce; 25 cents × 16 = $4.00), and $3.20 a pound for B ($1.60 divided by 8 ounces = 20 cents per ounce; 20 cents × 16 = $3.20).

It isn't difficult to do your own unit pricing if your state doesn't mandate it. Use a pocket calculator. When you are deciding between competitive packages, read the small print that tells you how much is inside. It will take a couple of seconds to divide the price by its weight or volume, as we did in the paragraph above, to come up with a unit price.

▶ **START WITH A LIST**

There is no way to avoid making a few lists if you're serious about saving money. Grocery lists are probably the lists you'll use most often, and good ones can save you hundreds of dollars a year. The important impulse-avoiding rule is: *Never* shop without a grocery list in hand.

One way to have an efficient list each week is to first write down categories of food and groceries on a sheet or two of paper, *in the same order that your supermarket's aisles are laid out.* This is important; if you just jot down things you need in no particular order, you will spend a lot of extra time doubling back through aisles you have been in before, thus increasing the likelihood of impulse buying.

Leave space under each category to write down the items you may need each week, and photocopy this basic list. Keep a few dozen copies on hand.

Then, each week, before you go to the market, plan your menus and check your supplies, with preprinted basic list in hand. Write down the items you need in each category. Include brand names if you have strong preferences.

Many families keep a preprinted basic list on the refrigerator and make it each person's responsibility to note when, say, the eggs are running low or the last of the tuna fish cans has been used.

▶ BUY DRY STAPLES IN BULK

All you need is adequate storage space (someplace dry and cool) to save from 10 to 30 percent a year on items like toilet paper, paper towels, diapers, pasta, soap and detergents, toothpaste, and canned goods. Moving from your kitchen shelves and laundry to linen closets and bathrooms, make a list of items you are positive you use in case quantities.

Properly stored dry spaghetti, for example, lasts at least eighteen months. If you use twenty-four 1-pound packages a year, it makes sense to buy a case at a time. Canned food is nearly always good for two years or so, but check the "best if used by" date before buying in bulk.

Some supermarkets quietly give regular customers a discount when they buy by the case. When you make up your first list, show it to the store manager and ask him what discounts he can offer. If necessary, you might politely suggest that you are prepared to go elsewhere for such discounts—and perhaps buy the rest of your groceries there, too. Since the list will probably represent quite a significant purchase, he'll want to keep you happy. Thereafter, when you may want to buy just a case at a time, remind him that he *always* gives you case discounts.

Whether or not you can get discounts on case purchases at your supermarket, if you have a warehouse club within driving distance, by all means check out prices there. It may be worth paying the annual membership fee most warehouse clubs charge and making a few special trips a year, if the discounts are better than your supermarket's. We saved 37 percent off the supermarket price of spaghetti recently by buying in bulk from our warehouse club.

Dividends: When you make special trips for bulk purchases, you'll be amazed at how much less you have to carry home from your weekly supermarket trip. And you will be far less likely to run out of the staple items you store in quantity.

▶ BUY SEASONALLY

Modern agriculture, transportation, and storage methods have made it possible to buy just about anything at any time of the year. But if you live in the Northeast, the $4-a-pint strawberries in December don't taste anywhere near as good as the 89-cent pint that's available in June. Anybody who eats corn on the cob except for the few weeks a year when locally grown corn is available is paying far too much for a vastly inferior vegetable. Penny-pinching corn-on-the-cob lovers gorge on it three or four times a week when it is at its best—and cheapest.

▶ BUY SEASONALLY FOR YOUR FREEZER

When your favorite berries are in season and at their cheapest and best, why not buy a few extra boxes and freeze them. It's easy to do, and the frozen berries are both cheaper and superior to the sugar-loaded commercially frozen products you might otherwise buy. Simply clean and dry the berries—blue, straw, black, or raspberries—put them in a single layer on a cookie sheet, and place that in the freezer. An hour or so later, move them a bit to prevent them from sticking or settling. When they are solidly frozen, within four hours, pour them into a freezer bag and seal. They will be good for months.

Sample saving: The April price of Birds Eye frozen strawberries in sugar syrup is $2.19 for a 10-ounce package. Since the price of a quart of fresh strawberries when they are in season in our area is about the same amount, we pay at least 50 percent less for berries that we think are 500 percent better.

▶ SOME ADS WILL SAVE YOU MONEY

At least once a week, your local newspaper probably includes an advertising insert listing dozens of items on sale at your supermarket. The same insert is always available in the store. It makes sense to use this ad when planning menus and making out your weekly grocery list. All supermarket chains make special quantity buys that allow them to price some items at genuinely lower prices than usual.

▶ GET A RAIN CHECK

Stores commonly run out of heavily advertised specials toward the end of the sale period. When they do, most will give you a "rain check"—an authorization that will allow you to buy the product at the sale price when it is back in stock. Often the rain check is good until months after the sale is over, so you can use it when you actually need more of the product.

▶ GENERIC VERSUS BRAND-NAME PRODUCTS

The standard advice about saving money on food and groceries involves substituting store brands and/or generics for national brands. The problem is, you prefer the taste or the quality of certain brands and don't want to give them up.

If you have a strong brand preference, one that you are sure of, stay with it and save in other ways. If you are not convinced about such a preference, though, experiment. Try the least expensive option first. If you like it, why not save money by using it thereafter? If you don't, move up in price until you find an acceptable choice.

In many cases, you'll be equally satisfied with two or three similarly priced brands. When one of them is on sale or you have cents-off coupons saved for it, stock up.

In the last few years, many supermarket chains have moved away from the idea of selling generics but have improved the quality and variety of foods offered under their store-brand names. If you haven't used them lately, you might want to try again. Many store-brand products are produced by major manufacturers whose own brands are made with the same ingredients in the same factories. Often the only differences are the labels and the prices.

▶ A FEW ALWAYS-BUY STORE BRANDS

We can't think of a single reason to buy brand-name packages of certain staples. Typical saving:

- Store-brand granulated sugar: 5 pounds, $2.29 cents (45.8 cents per pound). Domino brand: 5 pounds, $2.79 (55.8 cents per pound).
- Store-brand all-purpose, enriched, bleached flour: 5 pounds, $1.29 (25.8 cents per pound). Pillsbury brand: 5 pounds, $1.69 (33.8 cents per pound).
- Store-brand distilled white vinegar: 54.8 cents a quart. Heinz brand: $1.09.
- Store-brand ammonia: 67 cents a quart. Parsons brand: $1.25.
- Store-brand regular bleach: $1.19 for two quarts. Clorox brand: $1.39.
- Store-brand iodized salt: 30.2 cents a pound. Diamond Crystal brand: 40 cents. But the price of Morton's brand at our warehouse club was 79 cents for a 4-pound box (19.8 cents per pound). If bought in bulk quantities, similar savings on all of the staples cited in this tip are available at our warehouse club.

▶ THE TRUTH ABOUT COUPONS

Some people brag about saving thousands of dollars a year in grocery bills by using coupons. But unless you join a "trader's club" (or trade on-line; see next tip) and spend hours a week searching for, clipping, organizing, and trading coupons, that kind of saving is unlikely. In fact, what some obsessive coupon-clippers are doing is "saving" money on a lot of products they otherwise wouldn't have bought and in many instances won't ever use.

Nevertheless, coupons are an important part of any grocery-shopping strategy. They may not save you thousands a year, but they can definitely save you hundreds. You don't have to be obsessive about them, but you do have to manage and organize them properly.

There are two major sources of coupons—the manufacturers and the stores themselves. Actually, the stores use promotional money provided by manufacturers for their own special offers. Although some manufacturers have implemented plans to reduce their dependence on couponing and to switch instead to an "everyday low-price strategy," we expect couponing will continue to play an important role in every major package-goods company's marketing plans. Study after study proves that they increase sales, despite the fact that fewer than 10 percent of the coupons issued by manufacturers are ever redeemed. In-store coupons are far more profitable for stores than simply lowering the shelf price of a product. That's because at least four out of ten people buying a couponed product in the store won't bother to use the coupon and will pay full price.

So the first, obvious tip for any penny-pinching grocery shopper is to compare your shopping list with the store's special sales flyer before you start shopping. You may very well want to adjust your list to take advantage of a special. Also:

- Don't clip and use coupons for new products. You'll break this rule occasionally, but it is good advice ninety-nine times out of a hundred. All food manufacturers offer coupons to entice you to try their new products, but few new products—nearly always more expensive "convenience" foods—offer significant improvements over what's already available.
- Clip, save, and use coupons only for the brand names you normally buy or substitutes you know are acceptable. Do this on a regular weekly basis. It takes very little time to review the coupon advertising you re-

ceive when you look for and clip only the coupons for known, wanted brands. This way, you don't have to waste time reading the ads!

■ Very often, when a brand-name product is being "couponed," coupons appear in more than one place in a very brief period. Clip and save every coupon you see for a product you know you use. If it is for a perishable product, check the coupon expiration dates and use as many as feasible. If the product isn't perishable, use all the coupons you can and stock up.

■ Don't be in too great a hurry to redeem coupons. Supermarkets have been known to raise the prices of certain items the week after they are couponed. It is very possible that the same item will be "sale-priced" two weeks later, and your coupons will end up saving you even more.

■ Stores in some areas accept double coupons on certain products; that is, they allow two coupons to be used toward the purchase of a single item. If so, it may be worthwhile to buy another copy of the newspaper in which the coupon appears.

■ Stores in some areas sometimes honor a different kind of "double coupon" or even "triple coupon" by allowing a 25-cent coupon, for instance, to be redeemed for 50 or 75 cents.

■ Keep all the coupons you clip in one envelope or in an old checkbook cover. If this becomes unmanageable, divide the coupons by category into a few more envelopes.

■ It takes just a couple of seconds per coupon to mark the expiration date of each with a yellow grease pencil or felt-tip pen. Once you do, you'll spot that date whenever you look at the coupon. Missed a date? There are greater tragedies. Throw it away.

■ Review your coupons quickly before you make out your weekly shopping list. Then put an X next to each item you plan to buy for which you have a coupon. As you select each of these products, pull the coupons out of their storage envelopes and paper-clip them together for easy retrieval at the checkout counter.

■ Check the precoupon price before you buy a product. Sometimes, you may find that that price minus the coupon value is still higher than the price of the uncouponed but acceptable substitute right next to it.

▶ TRADE COUPONS ON-LINE

Visit *Coupon Net* (http://www.couponnet.com) and trade coupons with people nationwide. There is a big advantage to trading this way instead of locally in a "trader's club." Marketers tailor coupons to different regions of the country. One example: In some areas where double couponing is rare or nonexistent, marketers may issue 50- or 75-cent coupons instead of the 25-cent coupons for the same product issued in areas where double couponing is common. If you live in the double-couponing area and can get a 75-cent coupon for the product, you may be able to save $1.50 instead of 50 cents.

▶ GET COUPONS VIA E-MAIL

Supermarkets Online (http://www.valupage.com) lets you download manufacturers' coupons or, if you prefer, will send them to you weekly via E-mail. In fact, if you log on to this site and answer a few questions about your shopping habits, including your preferred supermarket, you will get only coupons that match your family's lifestyle and preferences. You will be giving up some privacy because marketers will have access to that information, but until proven otherwise we think the convenience outweighs the privacy concern.

▶ JOIN SUPERMARKET SHOPPER CLUBS—ALL OF THEM

Many supermarkets issue free cards that regular customers present at the checkout counter. Some cards give you special discounts; some give you "points" that you can accumulate and turn in for a free gift. In most cases, the cards are also supposed to guarantee you all the coupon savings offered that day by the store itself—without the hassle of cutting out the coupons.

As long as they are free, why not get cards even for supermarkets you use infrequently? Keep in mind that the cards that give you automatic savings do so only on the store's own coupons, not on those issued by manufacturers; you still have to clip those. Double-check your register receipts to make sure you really have gotten all the discounts you know are coming to you. Computers don't make mistakes, but the people responsible for updating them often do.

▶ CASH IN ON REFUND OFFERS

Coupons you redeem in stores save you money. Manufacturers' refund offers give you cash. For some reason, many people who use coupons in stores never take advantage of refund offers. Yet it is really quite an easy way to pick up a few extra dollars a month without much effort—perhaps as much as a few hundred a year, if you want to devote some extra time and energy to it.

You'll find refund offers in the same places as coupons, as well as on forms attached to the product itself. Because it costs you a first-class stamp to mail the refund form (along with proof of purchase—normally a specific panel from the product's label), it would be silly to return one to get a 40-cent check. Most manufacturers' refund offers are therefore for at least $1.00. Exchanging 32 cents for a dollar or two makes perfectly good sense to us, even taking into acount the typical eight-week delay until the manufacturer's check is sent to you.

▶ DON'T TRUST THE CHECKOUT SCANNER

Large supermarket chains typically make thousands of price changes every week. Mistakes are made by those who input the changes into the central computers as well as by those who don't update shelf price tags. One study of supermarkets using scanners at their checkout counters estimated that as many as 40 percent of customer bills contain some kind of error.

Not even a penny pincher wants to delay a checkout line interminably, and it is true that sometimes the mistakes are in your favor. But more often (no surprise) the errors are significantly in the store's favor. Your best defense is to write down the prices of items on your shopping list as you put them into your cart. Then monitor and compare the prices that appear on the scanner at the checkout counter. If one of them is incorrect, speak up immediately. The people behind you will understand and some stores will give you the item free if their scanners are wrong.

▶ ON SALE NEAR THE CHECKOUT COUNTER? BEWARE

Among the highest-margin items in the store are those such as gum, candy, batteries, and magazines displayed by the checkout counter line. Don't succumb to impulse shopping at the end of your shopping trip. Buy your batteries elsewhere for a lot less money.

▶ JOIN A WAREHOUSE CLUB

The giant warehouse clubs—Wal-Mart's *Sam's Club,* the merged *Price-Costco Club,* and the regional *B.J.'s Wholesale Club*—are now found in most parts of the country and as a group do well over $35 billion of business annually. Typically, they charge a membership fee of $25 to $35 a year and offer a hodgepodge of merchandise—including brand-name food and groceries—at deeply discounted prices.

Should you join a warehouse club? The best way to decide is to visit one first. Either call ahead to confirm that the club will allow you to look the place over before joining, or accompany a friend who is already a member. Before you make the trip, make a list of all of the staple grocery, food, drugstore, and hardware items you use in bulk or large quantities. Then go to your normal sources for these items, and price them. *Important:* Very often, warehouse clubs sell only larger packages that are not available in other retail stores, so make sure you note unit pricing of food and groceries (the cost per ounce, quart, or pound).

Have you also been considering buying a new small appliance of any kind? New tires? Sheets? Towels? A garden hose? A computer? You are likely to find just about anything for sale in a warehouse club, including major national brand names, but you won't find the variety of choices within product categories that you will in other stores. Knowing beforehand the competitive prices of anything you might purchase is important because incredible buys are likely to sit right next to items that can be purchased elsewhere for even less.

In our experience, however, it isn't likely that a careful shopper will make a big mistake at a warehouse club. Nearly all of the food and grocery prices we have checked at our warehouse club are at least competitive, and we save from 20 percent to as much as 60 percent on some items.

Warehouse clubs are profit-making businesses, not consumer clubs. Don't get carried away, buying things in bulk that will ultimately spoil or will never get used. Also, be wary of two or three disparate items shrink-wrapped together and sold for one price (a cookbook with a Teflon fry pan, for instance). This kind of merchandising is how the clubs enhance "perceived value," but do you really want both items? If not, the combined price is certainly not a bargain.

▶ SOME WAREHOUSE CLUB RECOMMENDATIONS

It is stupid to buy in bulk anything that won't get used in that quantity or that will go bad before it is used. But there are a number of food items that will last a very long time, so buying in what may seem to be too-large quantities can make sense. Five years ago, tempted by our warehouse club's extremely low price, we bought a two-bottle package of Worcestershire sauce. Two huge,

15-ounce bottles, in fact. We laughed about having a lifetime supply; as it turned out, it was only a five-year supply. We just bought two more bottles.

This is an extreme example, and we are not recommending you buy five-year supplies of many things. We have plenty of good, dry storage space, though, so if the price is right we buy the giant, warehouse club bottles or packages of the following long-lived items:

- Spices, including bay leaves, whole black pepper, cayenne pepper, chili powder, cinnamon, cumin, nutmeg, paprika, and rosemary.
- Vinegars and oils, including balsamic vinegar, white vinegar, white and red wine vinegar, vegetable oil, and sesame oil.
- Flour, granulated sugar, brown sugar, baking powder, baking soda, unsweetened cocoa, cornstarch, and cornmeal.
- Ketchup, chili sauce, Dijon mustard, soy sauce, and Worcestershire sauce.
- Pasta and rice.

► KEEP TRACK OF PRICES

The rise of wholesale clubs was a direct challenge to all kinds of retail stores, especially supermarkets. The giant supermarket chains have fought back with a vengeance, and now sometimes offer bulk quantities of some items at prices below those at wholesale clubs. This competition is terrific news for penny-pinching consumers, but it has also made shopping for the best price far more confusing.

Unless you want to check prices daily at every conceivable outlet for every item on your shopping list, it is virtually impossible to make certain you always get the best price. We carry a small pocket notebook in which we jot down the prices of items we know are likely to be on sale at different places in which we shop. That way, when we visit our wholesale club—usually every four to six weeks—we can compare prices with those at our supermarket, discount drugstore, and discount hardware store. We also check prices on-line from Net-Grocer and Wal-Mart (see next tip).

Do we always succeed? Of course not. Recently, the day after buying a case of paper towels at our wholesale club, our supermarket had a "warehouse sale" on the same brand for 10 percent less than we had paid. Nevertheless, the system works well most of the time and we think we buy at the lowest prices 90 percent of the time.

▶ CHECK OUT NETGROCER AND WAL-MART ON-LINE

Will you ever shop for groceries on-line? *NetGrocer* (http://www.netgrocer.com) is making a serious effort to persuade you to do just that. It offers more than four thousand popular nonperishable grocery products. Its web site is easy to navigate and FedEx delivers your order to your door within four days after you place it. Delivery costs just $2.99 for orders up to $50, and $4.99 for orders over that amount. *Wal-Mart* (http://www. wal-mart.com) also sells groceries on-line, with a usual delivery charge of just $3.

We regularly do some comparison shopping involving NetGrocer, Wal-Mart's web site, local supermarkets, and our warehouse club. On-line prices have been lower on some items, higher on others. If you don't have a warehouse club close by and like the idea of shopping from home, however, you can order from NetGrocer or Wal-Mart and feel confident that you are getting good, competitive prices overall.

▶ AVOID SUPERMARKETS FOR MOST NONFOOD ITEMS

As supermarkerts grow larger and stock a wider variety of products, you can get in the habit of using them to buy products that are cheaper elsewhere. In our area, discount drugstores always have lower prices on toothpaste and aspirin, for instance. Lightbulbs are cheaper at Home Depot. Diapers are much cheaper at Toys "R"

Us. Our wholesale club sells all of these things at lower prices than our supermarket. If we aren't able to buy in bulk there, we try to stock up on items sold in discount stores so we don't find ourselves "running out" and buying them one at a time from our supermarket.

▶ JOIN A FOOD CO-OP

There are more than five hundred food cooperatives (retail stores owned by co-op members) and more than thirty-five hundred cooperative buying clubs (groups formed to buy in bulk, then fill individual member orders) in the U.S. Many of them require members to donate a few hours a month in return for membership. Savings can be substantial—from 20 percent to 50 percent below normal supermarket prices—but in nearly all cases you will have to supplement what you can buy in a co-op with trips to a supermarket.

It is easy to investigate any co-ops that are active in your area. *The National Cooperative Business Association* (http://www.cooperative.org) will give you the 800 numbers of regional warehouses that supply co-ops. Call the warehouse that services your area to find out what clubs it supplies.

▶ START YOUR OWN FOOD CO-OP

We don't belong to a food co-op, but we have developed an informal co-op with four neighbors, all of whom shop at the same warehouse club. First, if we are low on one item that we normally buy in bulk from a warehouse club, we might check to see which of our friends has a visit scheduled next and ask her to buy that item for us. Because our club is ten miles away, a few phone calls a year save us all both time and the costs of gasoline.

Second, because many items in a warehouse club are sold only in quantities that none of us could individually justify buying, we agree to split up certain purchases. We get big savings this way, but nobody gets stuck with ten years' worth of pickles or pineapple chunks.

▶ USE PRODUCE DEPARTMENT SCALES

Don't use them just to weigh items sold by the pound. When lettuce is sold by the head, the weight difference among heads can amount to as much as 33 percent. "Five pound" bags of potatoes or apples don't all weigh exactly five pounds; why not buy the one that weighs nearly six?

▶ COMPARE LOOSE VERSUS "BY THE BAG" PRODUCE PRICES

Kept in a cool, dry place, potatoes will keep for about a month. If you will use 10 pounds in that time, buying a 10-pound bag (as we recently did for $3.99) beats buying loose (99 cents a pound). The loose potatoes were larger, but we don't find it inconvenient (at a saving of 59 cents a pound) to use an extra couple from the bag when we are baking them.

Yellow onions, which will keep for up to a month, were 59 cents a pound loose, $3.59 for a 10-pound bag. Per-pound difference: 23 cents.

▶ MAKE YOUR OWN BABY FOOD

Few parents would want to give up the convenience of prepared baby foods altogether, but you can save a significant amount of money, particularly when fresh fruits and vegetables are in abundant supply, by making baby meals from the same foods you'll be eating. Just put them in a mini–food processor after cooking. Use fresh foods, and don't mix two or more together—babies prefer single flavors. For some excellent recipes and advice on making and storing your own baby food, see *The Complete New Guide to Preparing Baby Foods* by Sue Castle ($4.99, Bantam Books).

▶ AND CHECK OUT TOYS "R" US

Competitive pricing is always subject to change, but Toys "R" Us does sell baby food, and the last time we checked its prices were 10 percent lower than our supermarket's for Gerber's prepared baby food and formula. Our wholesale club also often sells case quantities of baby food and formula at better-than-supermarket prices.

▶ SAVE WITH FRESH VERSUS CANNED OR FROZEN VEGETABLES

There's a reason to buy one can of mushrooms that will keep indefinitely and can be used at the last minute in an emergency. Otherwise, why not buy fresh? Price per pound: $2.49. Price for a 7-ounce jar (4 ounces drained) of Green Giant whole mushrooms, $1.49 ($5.96 a pound).

Not every example is as dramatic, and store-brand frozen green beans may not cost significantly more than fresh green beans at certain times of the year. But there's normally some kind of saving, and the extra time devoted to washing and cutting fresh beans always seems to us to pay off when they are served.

▶ CONVENIENCE RIP-OFFS: PRODUCE SECTION

- A 16-ounce cellophane package of chopped cabbage and a few bits of carrot labeled "Classic Cole Slaw." Price: $1.59. Three feet away: cabbages at 49 cents a pound. Estimated time to chop a pound of cabbage: 90 seconds. Hourly rate being charged: $44 for the convenience of prechopped greens that are usually dried out.
- A 10-ounce package of shredded carrots. Price: $1.29. Two feet away: a bunch of carrots (1½ pounds). Price: 79 cents. Weight after removal of tops and peeling off outer skin: 18 ounces. Adjusted price for 10 ounces: 43.8 cents. Estimated time to remove tops, peel, and shred 10 ounces of carrots: 3 minutes. Hourly rate: $17.
- A 16-ounce package of celery hearts. Price: $1.89. In the adjacent bin, bunches of celery (weight from 24

to 32 ounces) for 99 cents. Since all that distinguishes the two kinds of celery is a simple swipe of a chopping knife (removing the leafy top part of the celery; estimated time: 5 seconds), the price of convenience was at least $648 an hour.

▶ CONVENIENCE RIP-OFFS: SALAD AND FRUIT BARS

Salad and fruit bars that charge a set price per pound or ounce no matter what you put on your plate have become commonplace in supermarkets and many inexpensive restaurants, especially those catering to office workers looking for a quick, take-back-to-the-desk lunch. The price of convenience at all of them is very high, but it may be unavoidable if you insist on three varieties of lettuce and salad dressings, four different salad vegetables, and five different fruits—all on the same lunch plate.

If, however, you simply want a plate of three different fruits for a light lunch, you will probably save at least 80 percent by buying the individual fruits in the produce section and slicing them yourself. If you have coworkers who share your eating habits, you can multiply your choices and still save hundreds of dollars a year.

▶ CONVENIENCE RIP-OFFS: BABY FOOD

This is a section of the supermarket where the price of convenience and individual servings is particularly high. If you don't want to make a lot of your own baby food (although food processors, blenders, and food mills make it very simple with many foods), at least compare prices with what's offered in other sections. For instance, six 4-ounce jars of Gerber's apple juice cost $2.79 ($3.72 a quart). Store-brand apple juice was either 79 cents a quart (made from concentrate) or 99 cents a quart (not made from concentrate).

▶ CONVENIENCE RIP-OFFS: RICE, PASTA, CEREAL

- A 10-pound bag of Uncle Ben's converted rice cost $5.99 at a warehouse club ($7.49 at a supermarket). A 7-ounce package of the same rice in four "boil-in" bags cost $1.29. Per-pound premium for the convenience of boil-in bags: $2.35 (versus warehouse club), $2.20 (versus supermarket).

- Five pounds of macaroni cost $2.19 (44 cents a pound) at a warehouse club. The supermarket price of a 7 1/4-ounce package of Kraft's Macaroni and Cheese was 79 cents ($1.74 a pound). For the $1.30-per-pound difference, you can buy a lot more and a lot better cheese than the salty stuff inside the pouch included in the convenience package.

- Quaker Oats instant oatmeal comes in a box that includes ten pouches of different "with fruit" flavors. Total weight: 13.7 ounces. Price: $3.59, or 35.9 cents per average serving of 1.37 ounces. Quick Quaker Oats are $3.49 for 42 ounces. Add your own fruit and save 24.5 cents a serving.

- Any cereal with fruit in the box is invariably more expensive than the ingredients warrant, and the fruit is a pale imitation of the real thing. At least in our experience, the raisins in those cereal boxes are often hard and dry. We buy and add our own.

While we are on the subject of cereals, you should also check out prices at health-food stores. Very often, because they buy and sell bran and other cereals, grains, flours, beans, rice, pasta, and other staples generically and in bulk quantities, you'll find prices well below those in your supermarket. Also at least try supermarket store-brand cereals. The odds are good you won't be able to tell the difference between them and the expensive national brands.

▶ CONVENIENCE RIP-OFFS: FROZEN FOODS

The frozen-foods section of any supermarket is a virtual cornucopia of convenience rip-offs. Just a few:

- A 3.5-ounce "single serve" package of Ore-Ida microwave crinkle-cut french-fried potatoes. Price: 75 cents ($3.43 a pound). Price per pound of a 10-pound bag of russet potatoes: 25 cents. Price of a single pound of potatoes (if you cook only for yourself, you can't often buy in large quantities): 49 cents.
- Gorton's Microwave Baked Scrod with Bread Crumbs: $3.19 for a 6-ounce package, or $8.51 a pound. But since the bread crumbs, by our measure, amounted to about 2 ounces of the weight, the price for the frozen scrod was actually $12.76 per pound. Fresh scrod was priced at $5.99 a pound.
- Like buttered vegetables? Add the butter yourself. A 9-ounce package of frozen small peas in a pouch with butter was $1.79, 40 cents more than the same size package of butterless peas.

▶ PRICE CHEESE THREE WAYS

Depending on its size, your supermarket may sell cheese in even more than three locations. But most stores sell at least some cheeses in the dairy section, at the deli counter, and on a special cheese table. Prices for cheeses such as cheddar and Swiss will probably be lowest in the dairy section.

▶ BARGAIN AT THE FISH COUNTER LATE IN THE DAY

There is nothing in the store more perishable than fresh fish. Asking for a discount at the fish counter late in the day is often a successful strategy.

▶ RETURN CANS AND BOTTLES

This tip appeared for the first time in the third edition because it never occurred to us before then that anyone didn't return bottles and cans for the deposit on them. The results of a survey back in 1994 astonished us: At least one out of four buyers of beer and soda routinely throws returnable cans and bottles away. Not only are these people wasting money, they are also contributing to a growing environmental crisis.

If, like us, you hate the slow machines supermarkets make you use to get your nickel deposits, collect cans and bottles in a big plastic bag until you have enough to make a trip to a large beverage dealer worthwhile. At least in our area, they still take returns the old-fashioned way.

▶ SAVE ON MEAT AND POULTRY

There aren't many bargains in the meat and poultry cases of supermarkets. Many people save by joining a service that makes home deliveries of frozen meats, buying in quantity for storage in home freezers. We tried such a service years ago, didn't like the quality of the frozen food we got, and found we always had the wrong quantities of the wrong things. Also, like many people, we have cut back on the amount of meat we eat these days, so buying in large quantities doesn't make sense for us.

If you have a large family, though, you might want to check into such a service. Look in your Yellow Pages under "Food Plans" or get recommendations from friends. You should be able to save between 10 and 20 percent by buying this way.

You can also take advantage of seasonal fluctuations in the price of different cuts of meat. Steaks and chopped beef are more expensive in the summer months because people are grilling outside. Roasts tend to be less expensive in the summer because many people think of them as "winter" fare. Either buy in quantity in the off-season and freeze, or plan menus around "out of season" cuts.

We try not to pay for the convenience of easy butchering. Our supermarket, for instance, was recently selling "pork kabobs"—chunks of pork loin—for $4.99 per pound. The pork loin itself was $3.99. There are many other examples of this kind of convenience packaging in the meat case, and you'll have to decide if the convenience is worth the price in each individual case.

▶ BUY LARGE WHOLE TURKEYS AND CHICKENS

There is more meat per pound on a large whole roast chicken than on a small one. Buy a larger one than you need and use the leftovers for inexpensive second and third meals. There are a lot of great ways to use cooked chicken and turkey; see our cookbook recommendations later in this chapter.

▶ MARINATE LESS COSTLY CUTS OF MEAT

Substituting less expensive round steak for sirloin (just one example) doesn't have to mean giving up tenderness or flavor. Experiment with recipes that call for marinating the meat, and extend the length of marinating time called for in the recipe.

You can often cut down on the amount of liquid called for in a marinade, and therefore its cost, if you marinate in a self-closing plastic bag instead of an open, flat pan.

▶ MAKE YOUR OWN SALAD DRESSINGS

Homemade salad dressings, without chemicals and preservatives, taste better than brand-name prepared salad dressings. That's just an opinion, of course, but if you share it you can save from 25 to 90 percent on salad dressings without spending more than five extra minutes a week mixing your own. Try the recipes in any good general cookbook. Here are three that we use constantly:

- *Spicy sweet-and-sour dressing.* Mix 1 cup salad oil, 1/3 cup red wine vinegar, 1/4 cup chili sauce, 1/4 cup mayonnaise, 1 tablespoon sugar, 2 crushed garlic cloves, pinches of salt and cayenne pepper to taste. Shake all ingredients in a jar, chill well, and always shake before using. Will keep for a couple of weeks.
- *Sort-of-French dressing.* Mix 1/2 cup salad oil, 1/3 cup red wine vinegar, 1 teaspoon dry mustard, 1 teaspoon

sugar, 1 teaspoon dry basil or 2 teaspoons finely minced fresh basil, $1/2$ teaspoon freshly grated black pepper, $1/2$ teaspoon salt. Chill and shake well before using. Will keep for a couple of weeks.

- *Sort-of-Italian dressing.* Because it will keep for months, we make this in larger quantities. Mix $1^1/2$ cups salad oil, 1 cup white vinegar, $1/4$ cup sugar, $1/2$ cup finely minced onion, 3 teaspoons dry basil, 3 teaspoons oregano. Chill and shake well before using.

Storage: Use old glass jars and bottles that have clean lids that still close tightly. Sterilize first by simmering (just below boiling temperature) jars and lids separately in a large pot for fifteen minutes.

▶ USE A FOOD PROCESSOR

Why buy bread crumbs when you can make them in seconds from frozen crusts of stale bread you would otherwise have thrown out? A lot of the prepared and processed foods you may be buying now at your supermarket can be made for a lot less money with a food processor. Many processors come with free recipe books that explain how to buy foods when they are at their lowest prices, then process and freeze them for later use. Processors are also useful for converting leftovers into appetizing soups, sauces, and casseroles. A good blender will do practically the same job.

▶ START YOUR OWN CONTAINER GARDEN

Too many people think that vegetable gardening is an all-or-nothing proposition, that you can't have a garden unless you cultivate a large area and spend hours a week seeding, weeding, and spraying. Not so. Container gardening allows you to plant enough tomato plants in a half barrel to keep a family of four well supplied with delicious tomatoes for a few weeks—at one tenth the cost of store-bought. A container or windowsill herb garden is easy to tend and is a real money saver. And if you do not have a lot of land available but can devote a couple of hours a week to a small vegetable garden, even a hundred square feet is enough to save hundreds of dollars a year.

▶ DON'T TAKE OUT—COOK AHEAD

Anyone with a full-time job knows how tempting it is to stop by a take-out place on the way home from work, or to have dinner delivered. But these are expensive options. Instead, when you are in the mood to cook, prepare such things as casseroles and soups in quantity. Freeze them in portions just big enough for one meal, then bake or microwave a quick, no-fuss dinner whenever you don't feel like cooking.

▶ ASK FOR "COUPON PRICE" PIZZA

It works with a take-out pizza nearly every time, and it works fairly often at other take-out places as well. When you order, ask what the "coupon price" is. Most pizza places have some kind of dollars-off coupons in circulation at any given time. If they don't, they will usually match a competitor's coupon deal. You don't need to have an actual coupon to get the discounted price.

▶ CHANGE OFFICE EATING HABITS

How much do you spend a year on morning coffee and doughnuts? How much on take-out sandwiches you eat at your desk? If you work in an office in a big city, the answer could easily be as much as $30 a week—$1,500 a year. You can save at least 75 percent by making your own coffee (share a $19.95 coffeemaker and cleanup chores with two or three other penny pinchers in your office) and bringing lunch from home.

▶ INVEST IN A GOOD BASIC COOKBOOK

Many people who have grown up with prepared convenience foods think that cooking is terribly complicated and time-consuming. If you are one of them, a big basic cookbook, one that explains everything, including how to boil water, is likely to convince you otherwise.

Perhaps you'll go back to the convenience products, but with the step-by-step guidance in these books you can at least experiment. Especially with the labor-saving appliances now available, preparing and cooking foods is far less time-consuming now than it was a generation ago. And as convenience food marketers add gimmicks to their products, prices continue to escalate. A "back to the basics" approach will pay off in better-tasting, more nutritious, additive-free meals, in less environment-threatening packaging waste, and in lower food costs.

The book we turn to first for advice is the mammoth—984 pages long and truly comprehensive—*New Doubleday Cookbook* by Jean Anderson and Elaine Hanna (Doubleday, $35 list price). *The Joy of Cooking* and *The Good Housekeeping Cookbook* are other good choices.

▶ GET GREAT RECIPES FREE ON-LINE

One of our favorite web sites is *Epicurious* (http://www.epicurious.com), which offers thousands of recipes from two Conde Nast magazines, *Bon Appetit* and *Gourmet*. Best of all, you can access these recipes by providing a list of ingredients you have on hand. Last night, we had fresh basil and some mushrooms in the refrigerator and some chicken breasts in the freezer. When we asked Epicurious to search for recipes that included these ingredients, we were given a choice of over sixty of them.

We also have found good recipes on the Internet at *Digital Chef* (http://www.digitalchef.com), *Star Chefs* (http://www.starchefs.com), *Global Gourmet* (http://www.foodwine.com), and a Hearst magazine site, *Homearts* (http://www.homearts.com).

2

§ Holding Down Utility and House Expenses §

If you own an average-size home and haven't yet focused on saving energy, you should find it easy to lop a few hundred dollars a year off your energy bill. The first thing you should know is what your energy dollar buys. Based on national averages, the Department of Energy estimates that 46 percent of it goes to heat and/or cool your house. An additional 15 percent is spent on heating water. Refrigerators and freezers use 15 percent. Lighting, cooking, and running appliances account for the remaining 24 percent.

This chapter is filled with tips that will help you cut your costs in each one of these areas. It will also tell you where to go for more technical advice on major projects such as replacing heating equipment or installing solar energy. For tips about buying energy-saving appliances, see Chapter 5.

If you rent a home or apartment and pay utility bills, many of the energy-saving tips in this chapter will apply to you. If you don't pay for utilities, see what your land-lord thinks about a serious effort on your part to cut costs. Especially if your apartment is separately me-tered, you might be able to work out a way to share his or her savings.

Other tips in this chapter can be categorized as gen-eral "household hints." There are a number of good books, including those by Mary Ellen and Heloise, that list an astonishing array of hints on everything from treating diaper rash to making bookends out of two up-holstered bricks.

This book doesn't attempt to duplicate what's in the household-hints books. Our tips are limited to those we genuinely believe may save you dollars, not pennies, and that don't involve a lot of extra time. Not that spend-ing the time to do it yourself isn't the best as well as the most obvious way to save money when you own a house. If you always pay a plumber to fix a leaky faucet or a painter to put a new coat of paint on your bedroom walls, you are either very rich or very foolish. You most certainly are not a penny pincher.

Learning how to do a few basic repairs around the house is not that difficult, even if you've never held a hammer. Buy a good, illustrated, single-volume do-it-yourself reference and turn to it first when something needs fixing. We depend on the *Reader's Digest New Complete Do-It-Yourself Manual* ($30 list price). You can also get some terrific free advice on all sorts of do-it-yourself repairs and projects on the Internet at *Home-time* (http://www.hometime.com). Another resource you should cultivate and use is your local hardware store. We have carried leaky faucets into ours and got-ten advice that saved us a $60 plumbing bill for the price of a 35-cent washer. We're grateful and still buy there. But in the past few years, we have also come to rely on the giant Home Depot discount warehouse in our area. It has some knowledgeable salespeople, consistently low prices, and an enormous range of items in stock.

The few do-it-yourself tips in this chapter won't help you fix anything that needs major repair work. They may help, however, when something is so simple to fix that you would have been seriously embarrassed had you called in a service person. Finally, you'll find tips that suggest cheap substitutes for expensive brand-name products everyone uses around the house.

▶ SAVE 20 PERCENT ON WATER HEATING

Hot water is usually the second most expensive item on your total annual energy bill, right after heating the house. Consider doing these simple things and save at least 20 percent a year:

- Buy and install a programmable water heater timer (about $100). How often do you need hot water at 3:00 A.M.?
- Buy and install an insulation blanket (about $25) to put on your water heater, especially if it feels very warm to the touch. All water heaters lose some heat through the walls of the tank. Depending on how well yours is insulated, a blanket could save up to 10 percent on your water heating bills.
- Drain sediment and mineral deposits regularly—at least every three to four months—from the bottom of your water heater. If you haven't done this in years, though, have a plumber check it out first to reduce the risk of creating a serious leak.
- Lower your water-heater temperature from 140 degrees F to 125 degrees F. This is more than hot enough for bathing and washing clothes. Note: Check first to see if the lower temperature meets the specifications for your dishwasher. Some require the higher temperature.
- Wait until your dishwasher is full before turning it on. One less load per week can save you as much as $50 a year.
- Fix any faucet drip, of course, but fix a drip from a hot-water faucet immediately. It could easily add $25 a month to your fuel costs.

- Replace your showerhead with a low-flow head (about $20). This is simply a matter of unscrewing the old showerhead and installing a new one. Two people each showering five minutes a day will use over 18,000 gallons of hot water a year. With a low-flow head, you can cut that by as much as 8,000 gallons and pay for the new showerhead in less than three months.
- Take showers, not baths. A shower using a low-flow head produces a flow of about 3 gallons a minute, approximately 15 gallons for five minutes. It takes 30 gallons of water to fill the average tub. Assuming you use half-hot and half-cold water, the five-minute shower saves $7^1/_2$ gallons of hot water each time you substitute it for a bath. You can more than double that savings if you are spartan enough to use the next tip.
- Take a boat shower. Anyone who has lived on a small boat, where saving water is a necessity, knows the routine: Get wet quickly, turn the shower off immediately, lather up, turn the shower back on, and rinse off as quickly as possible. Yes, we know that a long hot shower is one of life's great pleasures for many people, but if you can change the habit, you'll save from $75 to $125 a year while helping to conserve a precious, dwindling resource.
- Try using a cold-water detergent and cold water for most laundry loads. We've found that only very dirty or greasy laundry needs hot water.
- Install aerators in bathroom and kitchen faucets. They cost a few dollars apiece and, by reducing the amount of hot water used, pay for themselves within a year.
- Insulate hot-water pipes. This will reduce the heat lost through the pipe walls as hot water flows from your water heater to the faucet. You will also save gallons of water by reducing the time needed to bring hot water to the faucet when you first turn the water on.

▶ **CLEAN YOUR FURNACE AND FILTERS**

If you have an oil burner, it pays to have the furnace cleaned and properly adjusted once a year. You can easily save 10 percent a year. At least once every two months during the heating season, clean the air filters on forced warm-air furnaces.

▶ **REPLACE FURNACE BURNERS**

Ask whoever services your burner whether you have a conventional or a retention head burner. Retention head burners have smaller nozzles and can save as much as 12 percent on your fuel bill.

▶ **LIGHT A CANDLE NEAR YOUR DOORS AND WINDOWS**

The easiest way to check on whether your doors and windows need better weather stripping and/or caulking is to move a lighted candle around the frames. You'll know immediately if air is passing through.

▶ **CAULK AND WEATHER-STRIP**

Caulking and weather-stripping two doors and a dozen windows should cost less than $50. Savings in annual energy costs could amount to 10 percent or more.

▶ **SEAL ALL KINDS OF AIR LEAKS**

Even in otherwise well-insulated houses, there may be drafts around electrical outlets and where plumbing and electrical wiring go through walls, floors, and doors. Check for drafts and seal with caulk and weather stripping.

▶ **INSULATE FLOORS OVER UNHEATED SPACES**

Even in newer homes, insulation during construction was sometimes skipped over in unheated spaces such as garages and crawl spaces. Any do-it-yourself reference will show you how easy insulating is to do, and you'll cut energy bills significantly. One of the best short do-it-yourself guides is *Homeowner's Guide to Insulation and Energy Savings,* free from *Owens-Corning Fiberglass* (800-438-7465; http://www.owenscorning.com).

▶ SEAL THE BASE OF THE HOUSE

If the base of a house is exposed, as in the case of mobile homes, build an insulated "skirt" around it.

▶ BUY HEATING OIL IN THE SUMMER

You can nearly always save 10 to 20 percent by having your tank filled during the summer months, instead of waiting for a regular delivery in the fall.

▶ JOIN A FUEL OIL CO-OP

You can save a few cents a gallon, and perhaps more, by joining one of the local fuel-buying cooperatives that seem to be springing up all over the country. There is no national association to call, but check your Yellow Pages under "Oils-Fuel" or check with local consumer organizations.

▶ TAKE ADVANTAGE OF UTILITY OFF-PEAK USAGE DISCOUNTS

In some areas of the country, electric utilities offer residential customers cheaper rates at certain times of the day. If yours is one of them, it is easy to run your dishwasher, washer, and dryer at off-peak times and cut your electric bills by a few dollars a month.

▶ USE CEILING FANS

Ceiling fans use less than one tenth as much electricity as a room air conditioner. If it is too hot for a ceiling fan alone to keep a room comfortable, you will still save money by turning the fan on along with the air-conditioning. Because a good ceiling fan can make you feel from five to seven degrees cooler, you don't need to set the thermostat of your air conditioner as low.

▶ USE VENTILATING FANS SPARINGLY

One of those ventilating fans in the kitchen or bathroom is capable of blowing away a houseful of warmed or cooled air in just one hour. Turn it off quickly after it's done its job.

▶ OPEN A WINDOW NEAR YOUR FIREPLACE

It may seem strange, but if you open a window near the fireplace by about half an inch, air needed by the fire will be drawn from the outside instead of from the (expensive) heated air in the house.

▶ USE GLASS FIREPLACE DOORS

Those wonderful old-fashioned open-hearth fires create a draft that draws air heated by your furnace right up the chimney. They definitely remove more heat than they give off. If you use your fireplace often, a set of glass fireplace doors ($100 and up) will stop the draft that allows warm air to escape.

▶ CLOSE YOUR FIREPLACE DAMPER

Once the fire is completely out, close the damper immediately. It can let up to 8 percent of the heat in your house exit via the chimney.

Don't have a damper? Install one immediately. That 8 percent heating loss adds up to a lot of dollars going up the chimney every year.

▶ CLOSE THE DOORS TO UNUSED ROOMS

Turn off the radiators or close the hot-air vents in rooms you don't use regularly, then close the doors to those rooms. Why heat a guest bedroom before the guests arrive?

▶ WEAR A SWEATER INSIDE

Most people discover they are just as comfortable wearing a sweater with the thermostat set at from 66 to 68 degrees F as they are without one with the thermostat set from 68 to 70. You will save about 2 percent of your heating bill for each degree you lower the thermostat.

▶ GET CREATIVE WITH YOUR THERMOSTAT

Turn it to its lowest setting when you'll be away for even a couple of days. Turn it down before a party—a crowd will generate heat. If you don't have a clock thermostat that you can preset for lower temperatures at night, or for during days when no one will be in the house, it is a good investment.

▶ USE A HUMIDIFIER

The thermostat can be set lower if there is sufficient humidity in the air.

▶ USE SHADES AND DRAPERIES

During cold weather, open them on sunny windows during the day and close them at night. During warm weather, do the opposite.

▶ UNBLOCK RADIATORS AND REGISTERS

If you have a piece of furniture blocking a hot-air register or a radiator, move it. A blocked heating unit is not operating efficiently.

▶ AIM AIR-CONDITIONER VENTS UP

Hot air rises, cold air falls. Air circulation will be more efficient and energy costs less if you aim an air conditioner's vents up. Keep the unit away from drapes, furniture, doors—anything that might interfere with air circulation. Also make sure the unit—the outside part as well as the inside—isn't near appliances that heat up or in direct sunlight.

▶ GET A FREE ENERGY AUDIT

There are a number of ways to save on energy costs involving such things as boiler efficiency, but it is best to get advice that can be applied to your specific needs. In most areas, there is an easy way to do this. Call your local utility and ask if it will send a conservation expert to your house to do a complete energy audit. Many utilities offer this service without charge; others charge a small fee. It is always a worthwhile expenditure. After the inspection, most will give you an individualized computer printout that will recommend various energy-saving measures. The printout will also tell you how much these measures are likely to cost and how much each one will save on your annual energy bill.

▶ GET PAID BY YOUR UTILITY

In some areas of the country, local utilities will pay part of the costs you incur to make your home more energy-efficient. It only takes a phone call to see if yours is one of these areas, and what the utility will pay for.

▶ GET BACK YOUR SECURITY DEPOSIT

Another quick call to your utility, if you paid a security deposit to it when you first moved into your home. After you establish a decent record of timely payments, you should get your deposit back plus interest. Ask for it.

▶ TURN OFF ELECTRIC STOVE BURNERS EARLY

Your stove is a major user of electric power, so get in the habit of turning off the burners a couple of minutes before the necessary cooking time is up. The heating element on an electric burner stays hot for about that long after it is turned off.

Do the same with either a gas or electric oven. If you don't open the door, an efficient oven will maintain its temperature for five to seven minutes after being turned off.

Have you been in the habit of leaving a pot of food on the burner or in the oven for minutes after turning them off? Now you know why you have been overcooking things.

▶ BOIL WATER IN A CLOSED POT OR KETTLE

It takes twice as long and costs twice as much if you bring water to a boil in an open pot. Don't boil any more water than you need, either. Why fill a teakettle half-full and spend seven minutes heating it up when the three quarters of a cup you want will come to a boil in three minutes?

▶ USE SMALLER PANS

Use the smallest pans possible; they require less energy.

▶ MATCH THE PAN TO THE BURNER

If you put a 6-inch pan on an 8-inch burner, about 40 percent of the heat produced will be wasted.

▶ KEEP AN INSULATED CARAFE NEXT TO YOUR COFFEEMAKER

After the coffee is made, pour it into a thermos bottle or carafe and turn the electric coffeemaker off. You can save a few dollars a year by not using the coffeemaker's "keep warm" feature.

▶ BUY A SLOW COOKER

If you often cook foods that require long cooking times, such as casseroles, stews, and soups, using an inexpensive slow cooker like a Crock-Pot will soon pay for itself.

▶ USE TOASTER OVENS AND MICROWAVES

Use your regular oven only when necessary. Full-size regular ovens use four times as much electricity to accomplish the same cooking task as microwave ovens. Toaster ovens are more efficient, too. But don't use your microwave to boil water; a stovetop burner is more efficient for this task.

▶ SELF-CLEAN OVENS WHILE THEY'RE HOT

If you have a self-cleaning oven, the best time to take advantage of this feature is immediately after you've cooked a meal. The oven will still be hot and less energy will be required.

▶ USE A PRESSURE COOKER

Pressure cookers save energy by reducing cooking time by from 25 to 50 percent.

▶ KEEP YOUR FREEZER FULL

Because food retains cold more efficiently than air, a half-empty freezer actually costs more to operate than a full one. If you don't have anything else to put in a freezer, load it up with plastic containers of water.

▶ CLEAN THE CONDENSER COILS ON YOUR REFRIGERATOR

Unfortunately, they're not very conveniently located, so it's easy to forget about them. But you'll never ignore them again after you've watched a $75-a-visit service person get your refrigerator back in peak condition simply by vacuuming the condenser coils.

At least twice a year, pull your refrigerator away from the wall, unplug it, and vacuum or brush off the coils you'll see on the back of the machine. The dust and dirt that collect there seriously reduce its operating efficiency. If allowed to build up, in fact, the grime can totally block the heat transfer between the coils and the outside air and cause a breakdown of the refrigerator.

When you push the refrigerator back in, make sure that air can circulate freely around the condenser coils. There should be a minimum of 1¼ inches of space between the wall and the refrigerator.

▶ CHECK REFRIGERATOR DOORS

The easiest way to do this is to put a dollar bill in the door when you close it. If the seal on the door doesn't hold the bill firmly in place, it is not working properly. New seals for refrigerators and freezers are not cheap and should be installed by experienced repair people. Before doing so, consider whether you might not be better off buying a new, energy-efficient model (see Chapter 5).

▶ CHECK YOUR REFRIGERATOR'S TEMPERATURE

Don't depend on the settings inside your refrigerator and freezer. Check temperatures with an accurate thermometer every month or so. They should be between 38 and 40 degrees F in the refrigerator and within one degree of 0 F, either plus or minus, in the freezer. Keeping a freezer at minus-10 degrees can increase energy use by as much as 20 percent.

▶ INSTALL A GREENPLUG

If you have an older, energy-inefficient refrigerator, you can reduce its use of electricity by as much as 20 percent by plugging it into a device called a GreenPlug®, available for about $35 at some hardware stores and from *Energy Federation Incorporated* (see tip below).

▶ COOL AND COVER FOODS BEFORE STORING

Let hot foods cool off before putting them in the refrigerator or freezer, and cover all foods, especially soups and other liquids, to avoid releasing moisture and raising the temperature.

▶ USE WAXED PAPER AND STORAGE CONTAINERS

Washing and saving old aluminum foil (recommended in all those household-hint books) seems to us to be taking penny pinching to extreme limits. Nor do we wash and reuse every plastic bag in which we have stored leftover food. But it is easy to save money by adopting two simple, environmentally friendly ways of storing and cooking food:

- Use waxed paper. Plastic wrap (at least twice as expensive) is better for certain kinds of storage, but biodegradable waxed paper is just as good or even preferable for some food wrapping (sandwiches to be eaten within a couple of hours) and for microwave cooking.
- Store leftovers in reusable glass or plastic containers. If they are sealed tightly, food will stay fresh longer and you'll cut way back on your use of expensive wraps and disposable bags.

▶ USE COLD WATER WITH YOUR GARBAGE DISPOSAL

Two reasons: Hot water costs extra money, and cold water solidifies grease so it can be ground up by the unit and efficiently washed away.

▶ USE A SPONGE

Too many people habitually use a paper towel every time they clean off a kitchen countertop. That can cost a few more dollars a year than using a sponge. Also, extend the life of a sponge by cleaning it the easy way—put it into your dishwasher.

▶ LET YOUR DISHES AIR-DRY

You can save up to 10 percent of the cost of using your dishwasher with the automatic air-dry switch available on new models. If your unit doesn't have such a switch, you can get the same saving simply by turning off the control knob after the final rinse. Prop the door open a little and the dishes will dry faster.

▶ PRESOAK HEAVILY SOILED CLOTHING

You'll avoid two washings and save energy.

▶ DRY CLOTHES IN CONSECUTIVE LOADS

Stop-and-start drying uses more energy because a lot goes into warming the dryer to the desired temperature each time you begin. Also separate drying loads into heavy and lightweight items; the dryer won't have to stay on as long for the lighter loads.

▶ CHECK FILTERS AND HOSES

It doesn't take much of a buildup of lint to reduce a dryer's efficiency and add extra dollars to your electric bill. Check hoses every couple of months and filters after every other use.

▶ FORGET FABRIC SOFTENER SHEETS

You'll save a few dollars a year if you don't use sheets in your dryer. Instead, toss in a sponge that you have soaked in a half-and-half mixture of water and liquid fabric softener.

▶ GAS BEATS ELECTRIC

A gas dryer is initially more expensive, but it is up to 50 percent less expensive to operate.

▶ REMEMBER THE OLD-FASHIONED CLOTHESLINE

A lot of people have forgotten the ultimate energy saver. As a bonus, clothes dried outside often seem fresher than they do when you use an electric or gas dryer.

▶ IRON WHILE YOU SHOWER

Hang clothes in the bathroom while you are showering. The steam will remove wrinkles, saving you both ironing time and energy costs.

▶ DO A LIGHTBULB AUDIT OF THE HOUSE

Most Americans overlight their homes. Room by room, analyze how much light is really needed. In many areas of a normal house, such as hallways, basements, and attics, replacing lightbulbs with bulbs of lower wattage is an easy way to cut electric bills.

▶ FINALLY! A USE FOR BURNED-OUT LIGHTBULBS

Many older houses are overlit and have fixtures that require two, three, or four bulbs. In areas where light can be reduced, put one burned-out bulb in a multiple light fixture. It is safer to have a bulb in a live socket, but the burned-out bulb won't use any electricity.

▶ AVOID LONG-LIFE BULBS

A long-life incandescent bulb in a hard-to-reach place can make sense, but it is less energy-efficient than a normal bulb, so shouldn't be used generally.

▶ SWITCH TO FLUORESCENT LIGHTS

State-of-the-art, screw-in compact fluorescents are ecologically friendly and can save significant amounts of money despite their high initial cost. That's because they use about 75 percent less electricity to produce the same amount of light as incandescent bulbs. They also last about ten times as long.

Compact fluorescent lights have the same threaded base as incandescent bulbs and provide soft, warm light comparable to that of an ordinary bulb. Currently none of them provides light output quite as high as a 100-

watt incandescent, however, so consider them only for replacing lower-wattage bulbs—40, 60, 75, and sometimes 100—that get a good deal of use or are in hard-to-reach fixtures.

An 18-watt compact fluorescent used in place of a 75-watt bulb will save about 600 kilowatt hours over an expected lifetime of 10,000 hours. If you pay 10 cents per kilowatt hour in your area, that's a savings of $60. The initial price of the fluorescent—about $25—is higher than the total price of the ten to fifteen incandescent bulbs (each with an expected life of 750 hours) it would replace. Nevertheless, you will still save close to 50 percent.

More and more lighting stores and home-improvement discounters such as Home Depot have begun carrying good selections of compact fluorescent lights. Or order from the *Energy Federation Incorporated* catalog (see below).

A few utilities have a rebate program for each compact fluorescent bulb you install. Check to see if yours is one of them.

▶ GET A FREE CATALOG OF ENERGY SAVERS

You'll find many of the energy, water, and lighting products recommended in this chapter in the free catalog offered by *Energy Federation* (800-876-0660; http://www.efi.org). The prices are fair and the catalog also answers many commonly asked questions about energy and resource conservation. The web site has a good selection of links to other energy conservation sites.

▶ RESEARCH ENERGY CONSERVATION ON THE INTERNET

The Department of Energy's *Energy Efficiency and Renewable Energy Network* site (http://www.eren.doe.gov) is a good place to start. Your taxes pay for it, but few people seem to realize that information on the full spectrum of renewable energy technologies and energy conservation is available free.

If you can't find answers to your questions about such matters as insulation techniques, active and passive solar energy, alcohol fuels, wind energy, and the like at this site, you probably will at one of the links it suggests.

▶ BUY A BATTERY CHARGER

A nickel-cadmium charger with six rechargeable batteries (two each of three sizes) cost $12.99 at our warehouse club last year. Packages of two nonrechargeable batteries cost between $1.99 and $2.79 at our hardware store. We expect to save at least $25 to $40 a year. If you have children who play with lots of battery-operated toys, or if you or your teenagers are heavy users of something like a portable cassette player, your savings could easily add up to $200 or more in a year.

▶ BUY ALKALINES

Try rechargeables first, but for really heavy-duty use you may need regular batteries. Although initially more expensive, alkaline batteries are far less expensive in the long run than nonalkalines because they will last at least twice as long.

▶ BUY STORE BRANDS IN BULK

Store-brand alkalines are usually much better buys than the name brands, especially when you buy them in the large "value paks." Check the "best if used by" date on any package of batteries, however. Most often you'll find packages good for at least three years from the date of purchase.

▶ TURN OFF THAT SECOND REFRIGERATOR

Except for central air-conditioning, a refrigerator is the single largest devourer of electricity in most homes—responsible for from 10 to 15 percent of most monthly bills. So it makes sense to operate one large refrigerator/freezer rather than two small ones. The next time we buy a new one, we plan to take our own advice. In the meantime, we cram everything possible into the unit in our kitchen, and turn on the old unit in the cellar no more than two or three times a year, when we need the extra room before Christmas or a big party.

▶ INSTALL A FAUCET AERATOR

They are cheap, simple to install, and can cut down on the amount of water used by a kitchen faucet by as much as 50 percent. You won't notice any significant change in water flow, either.

▶ DON'T PUT BRICKS IN YOUR TOILET TANK

This often recommended technique for saving water in older, pre-low-flush toilets usually doesn't work. Chances are, you'll find you often have to flush twice instead of once—an annoyance as well as a waste of water. Better to experiment by lowering the water level an inch or so (just bend the float rod or make a screwdriver adjustment, depending on the type of assembly in the tank). If the toilet still operates efficiently, you'll save a significant amount of water. If not, unbend the float rod a bit until it does.

▶ CHANGE TOOTHBRUSHING HABITS

Actually, change just one pointless habit shared by millions of people: allowing the water to run while brushing. Wet the brush, turn off the water, apply toothpaste, brush, then turn the water back on to rinse. Savings: in a family of four, each brushing two times a day, from 20,000 to 30,000 gallons of water a year (cost in our area: $35–$40).

▶ SWITCH TO LOW-FLUSH TOILETS

Since about 1980, most new and remodeled bathrooms have been equipped with "water conserving" toilets, which typically use about 3.5 gallons per flush instead of the 7 that was the standard for the preceding half a century. In the past few years, efficient "low flush" toilets, which use only 1.6 gallons, have been widely introduced.

Over 35 percent of residential water use in this country is directly attributable to the flushing of toilets, so the environmental benefits of toilets that use less water are compelling. As far as saving money is concerned, especially if you live in an area where water is expensive, replacing a 7-gallon water-waster with a new low-flush toilet will probably pay for itself in two to five years.

It's easy to work out your own math yourself. *Example:* Six flushes a day times 5.4 gallons (7 gallons minus 1.6 gallons) times 350 days a year you are in the house equals 11,340 wasted gallons a year. If you pay $4 per thousand gallons of water (check your water bill for your actual cost), that's $45.36 wasted each year. A new toilet will cost from $100 to $250 plus a plumber's installation charge.

▶ CHECK YOUR WATER METER

A few years ago, after receiving two quarterly water bills that seemed ridiculously high, we had our water company check the meter. The meter was fine, but they discovered a leak in the system. Now, a couple of times a year, we turn off the main valve, check the meter, wait an hour or two, and check the meter again. If there is ever any difference at all in the readings, however slight, we will call the water company right away.

▶ USE CHEAP BUT GOOD SUBSTITUTES: BAKING SODA

It is hard for many people to accept, but a lot of brand-name products are no better at certain tasks than some simple, cheap alternatives that our great-grandparents knew about. In many cases, the only active ingredient in the brand-name products is the alternative; what you pay dearly for are things like fragrances, fancy packages, and brand images.

This is not to say that because plain baking soda has a multitude of possible uses it is as effective in all of them as any brand-name product. It isn't. Until the introduction of fluoride toothpaste, a good case could be made that baking soda was as effective a dentrifice as anything else. It no longer is.

What follows, then, is not a complete catalog of all the ways you might use baking soda. But we believe baking soda is still superior to, or at least as effective as, branded products for these uses:

- *As a carpet deodorizer.* Sprinkle it on a dry carpet, brush it in a bit, leave for at least an hour, then vacuum.
- *To remove odors from refrigerators and freezers.* Keep an open box in your refrigerator as a preventative.
- *To clean and deodorize thermos bottles, coffeepots, etc.* Use it just as you would any cleaning powder.
- *As a general scouring powder.* Baking soda is an effective cleaning agent for pots and pans, stovetops, etc. It's good on porcelain because it is less abrasive than other scouring powders.
- *As a toilet-bowl cleaner.*
- *As an antacid.* If you are on a low-sodium diet or have other medical reasons to avoid sodium bicarbonate (baking soda), check with your doctor first. But sodium bicarbonate is the only active ingredient in many brand-name antacids sold for twenty or thirty times what it will cost you by the teaspoon out of a plain baking-soda box. Just add a teaspoon to a 6-ounce glass of water.
- *As a fire extinguisher.* Keep a box next to the stove to use in case of a small grease fire. Water won't work on a grease fire and will probably make it worse.

Want more? The *Arm & Hammer Company* (800-524-1328; http://www.armhammer.com) offers free brochures and a web site filled with tips about using baking soda.

▶ USE CHEAP BUT GOOD SUBSTITUTES: WHITE VINEGAR

White vinegar is just as good as or better than brand-name products for these uses:

- *To scour copper pans.* Mix half a tablespoon salt with a quarter of a cup of vinegar. Scrub on, remove with water, then wipe dry to shine.
- *To clean and shine chromium faucets.* Wipe on, wipe off with a paper towel.
- *To remove coffee oil residue.* Once a week, soak and then scrub the filter holder of your coffeemaker with vinegar diluted in an equal amount of water. You can also use a vinegar-water mix in your automatic coffeemaker, turning it on after you insert a clean filter. After all of the vinegar solution has come through, repeat the process, using plain water to rinse.
- *To remove soap residue from clothing.* Add half a cup of vinegar to your washer's last rinse cycle. This is safe for most fabrics and will also eliminate static cling.

▶ USE CHEAP BUT GOOD SUBSTITUTES: MINERAL OIL

- *Instead of baby oil.* Actually, baby oil is mineral oil plus a fragrance.
- *To remove eye makeup.* Read the ingredients on your current brand's package. Mineral oil is the only active ingredient.

▶ USE CHEAP BUT GOOD SUBSTITUTES: CORNSTARCH

- *Instead of talcum powder.* It is at least ten times as absorbent, and it is pure enough to use as a baby powder.
- *As a carpet cleaner.* Probably not as effective on hard-to-remove stains as some other products, but an effective absorbent powder for general use and safe on any

fabric. Brush it on, leave for at least an hour, then vacuum. Mix one cup of cornstarch with two table-spoons of ground cloves and two cups of baking soda to deodorize as well as clean carpets. Leave on over-night before vacuuming.

■ *For grease stains.* Shake on, let dry, brush off.

■ *After polishing furniture* with furniture oil, sprinkle on a little cornstarch and wipe off. It will absorb oil and help maintain a finger-proof surface.

■ *In a spray starch.* You can make a perfectly adequate substitute for expensive aerosol spray starches by filling a spray bottle with a well-shaken mixture of a tablespoon of cornstarch in a cup and a half of water.

▶ MAKE YOUR OWN WINDOW-CLEANING FLUID

There are a number of cheap alternatives to the expen-sive blue stuff inside that fancy brand-name spray bottle. Save the pump sprayer and the bottle, but when it is empty fill it instead with:

■ Two ounces of household ammonia mixed with one quart of water. This will be good for most jobs. If you miss the color of the expensive stuff, add a drop of blue food coloring; it won't do any harm.

■ Two ounces of household ammonia, four ounces of rubbing alcohol, and half a teaspoon of dishwater de-tergent mixed with one quart of water. This will help keep windows frost-free. (A mixture of white vinegar and warm water in equal parts is also effective, if you prefer not to use ammonia.)

■ One ounce of deodorized kerosene mixed with a quart of water. This is particularly effective on ex-tremely dirty, greasy windows.

To avoid streaking, don't wash windows when they are in direct sunlight. All cleaners can damage painted surfaces; wash them off quickly with plain water and dry. Using old newspapers is cheap but messy; we pre-fer paper towels.

▶ ON-LINE HELP IN STAIN REMOVAL

You can get a fast answer to a sudden "How do I get that stain out?" question on the Internet. Use a search site such as *Yahoo* (http://www.yahoo.com) to locate sites sponsored by companies like Du Pont which have web sites that offer stain-removal advice about their own products. Cutting across product lines are two sites that offer advice on removing a wide variety of common household stains:

- *University of Illinois Cooperative Extension Services* (http://www.ag.uiuc.edu/~robsond/solutions/consumer/stain.html)
- *Mississippi State University Cooperative Extension Service* (http://www.ces.msstate.edu/pubs/pub1400.htm)

▶ FREEZE CANDLES BEFORE USING

Not only will they burn more slowly, saving money, but candles will also burn more evenly and with minimal wax dripping if you put them in the freezer for a few hours before lighting.

▶ PLUMBING: QUICK AND EASY FIXES

- *For running toilets.* The odds are that all you need is a new flapper or tank ball. Turn off the water valve under the toilet, take the tank cover off, and unscrew the ball or (in newer assemblies) lift off the flapper. Buy a new one ($3 to $6), install (it will come with instructions, but essentially you are just reversing the procedure by which you removed the old one), and turn the water back on. If the toilet still runs, check out other possible solutions in a good do-it-yourself repair book.
- *For clogged drains.* Try a plunger first. It will usually work. You can avoid most clogged drains in kitchen sinks, usually the result of grease deposits, by pouring a half cup of baking soda and a half cup of vinegar

down the drain once a month. Wait fifteen minutes, then flush with hot water.

- *For obstructed showerheads.* Unscrew, soak in a half-and-half solution of vinegar and water, then remove sediment using a small brush. If this doesn't work, buy and install a new one.
- *For leaky faucets.* Buy an inexpensive box of assorted washers at any hardware store or discounter. The next time a faucet leaks, just turn off the valve controlling its water supply, loosen the packing nut at the top of the handle with an adjustable wrench taped to prevent scratching, and remove the handle. Then remove the entire valve assembly, unscrew the old washer at the bottom of the unit, and replace it.

▶ APPLIANCES AND ELECTRIC CORDS: QUICK AND EASY FIXES

- *For defective electric-stove burners.* Turn off the stove, pull up the burner, and unplug it from its outlet. Do the same thing with a working burner of the same size. Replace the defective burner with the working burner. Turn it on. If it works now, all you have to do is buy a replacement at an appliance store. If it doesn't, call the repair service.
- *For clothes dryers that won't heat.* It is embarrassing to call in an expert to clean lint from the filter inside the dryer or the one you'll find in the venting pipe. That's often the only problem, though.
- *For loose or damaged electric plugs.* Buy a snap-on plug for about $3. All you have to do is cut the old plug off the cord, push the cord into the new plug, and snap it shut. No involved knot-typing and handling of wires is necessary. Snap-on plugs work on the kind of flat cord used with most lamps and appliances.

▶ DOORS: QUICK AND EASY FIXES

- *For stuck door locks.* Buy a tube of graphite at the hardware store and squirt it into the keyhole. Work it in by turning the key a few times.

- *For doors that won't latch.* First check the hinges and tighten the loose ones with a screwdriver. If that alone doesn't solve the problem, put some colored chalk on the latch bolt, close the door, and see how far from the hole in the strike plate it hits. Usually the difference is so slight that you can tap the top or bottom edge of the strike plate with a small hammer, enlarging the hole enough to allow the bolt to engage.

- *For doors that won't slide.* Clean and wipe the tracks of the sliding door assembly. Then spray with a high-viscosity silicone product such as It or, in a pinch, rub the tracks down with a bar of soap.

▶ USE A MANUFACTURER'S HELP LINE

Many appliance manufacturers offer free technical assistance by telephone or at their web sites to help you resolve minor problems without calling an expensive repair person. Among them: *General Electric* (800-626-2000; http://www.ge.com); *Maytag* (800-688-9900; http://www.maytag.com); and *Whirlpool* (800-253-1301; http://www.whirlpool.com). In addition to explaining the problem, you'll need your model number, serial number, and date of purchase.

▶ RENTERS: GET INTEREST ON SECURITY DEPOSITS

It's the law in some states. Even where it isn't, tell your landlord you expect to be paid the going amount of interest on your security deposit. When you renew a lease, ask for your initial security deposit back—plus interest. If you have been an exemplary tenant, you might just get it. Demand the interest in any case.

▶ GET THE LANDLORD TO PAY FOR DO-IT-YOURSELF PROJECTS

Many people who rent would love to build in some bookcases or make other significant improvements in their living space, but don't do so because a) they need the landlord's permission, and b) they don't want to spend money on improvements that eventually will just make the apartment more valuable for the landlord.

If you show your landlord what you want to do and he thinks it makes sense, he may be willing to pay for all of your materials. After all, he's getting your labor free and he'll eventually benefit from the improvement.

▶ SHARING A RENTAL IS CHEAPER

Renting a larger apartment but sharing the cost with a roommate or roommates is nearly always much cheaper than renting on your own.

▶ WATER YOUR GARDEN AND LAWN AT NIGHT

At noon on a sunny summer day, probably half the water a sprinkler throws on your lawn evaporates before it does any good. If you water at night, you can cut back significantly on the amount used. Your grass, flowers, and shrubs won't know the difference.

▶ USE SOAKER HOSES

Soaker hoses, especially when used with timers, are the most water-efficient way to water gardens and flower beds.

▶ GET THE MOST FOR YOUR FERTILIZER DOLLAR

A 25-pound bag of fertilizer for $20 may not be a better buy than another at $25. The easiest way to judge is by nitrogen content; a higher count is worth more.

▶ MAKE YOUR OWN PESTICIDE

It won't work on every bug or pest, but most of them will avoid this environmentally friendly, homemade spray formula:

Put two heads of garlic, three onions, and four teaspoons of Tabasco (or any hot-pepper sauce) in a blender with a pint of water. Liquefy the garlic and onions. Thoroughly mix the result with a tablespoon of liquid soap and another pint of water.

▶ PLANT DECIDUOUS TREES TO THE SOUTH AND WEST

Trees and vines that lose their leaves in the winter can cut your costs of heating and cooling significantly. Plant them on the south and west sides of your house; they will provide shade in the summer but allow sunshine in during the winter.

▶ TRY A PUSH LAWN MOWER

Unless you live on a third of an acre or more, it won't take much more effort or time to use a nonpower push lawn mower instead of a smoky gas guzzler. Most people are surprised at how little effort is needed to push one of the well-made new models. You'll cut your annual mower maintenance bills by at least 300 percent (a bit of lubricating oil and an occasional blade sharpening will do it), save on gas, save at least 100 percent on the initial price of the mower, and reduce air pollution. And most of us can use the extra exercise.

▶ START A COMPOST PILE

You'll save by using your garbage disposal less often as well as by avoiding the costs of expensive commercial fertilizers.

▶ RELOCATE

The ultimate way to reduce housing costs may be to take advantage of the wide disparity in housing and living costs in different parts of the United States. Utility costs and taxes may be 75 percent less for similar houses in two different areas. A house with a market value of $250,000 in one area might be duplicated for less than $100,000 in another.

Places Rated Almanac by David Savageau and Richard Boyer (Prentice-Hall Press) is a good source of information on housing costs in 343 metropolitan areas in the United States. You'll find it in most libraries. You may also want to use the very good calculators at *Homebuyer's Fair* (http://www.homefair.com/home) that help you compare costs in different locations, tell you how much your moving expenses are likely to be, and even tell you what your new auto insurance rates will be.

▶ SOME MOVING ADVICE

Every year, one out of every five American families moves from one residence to another. Here is a catch-all of tips to consider before and while you move. You will find more helpful advice on the Internet at http://www.themovingman.com.

- *Move off-season.* The summer months are the busiest season for moving companies and therefore more expensive.
- *Have flexible moving dates.* Try to give the moving companies you contact for estimates some leeway about dates. Mondays through Thursdays will invariably be cheaper than Fridays and weekends. If you make a reservation far in advance, you will normally be able to change dates without incurring an extra cost.
- *Do your own packing.* Get some free boxes at supermarkets and liquor stores and pack your own china, silver, knickknacks, etc. In the process, toss out everything you weren't able to unload in that last-minute garage sale.
- *Don't forget your tax breaks.* The laws are complicated (IRS Publication #521 covers them), but if your move is job-related and you are moving at least fifty miles away, your moving expenses are probably tax-deductible.

3

§ Spending Less on Computers, Phones, and the Information Revolution §

We don't believe that anyone, including Bill Gates, could write a book in 1998 that told you with absolute certainty what computer equipment you will want to have in the year 2000. The experts who are predicting that the majority of homes will have some kind of computer capability by the year 2002 hedge their bets when it comes to what form that capability will take. Some believe that the personal computer as we now know it won't even exist in a few years, that it will be replaced by some kind of hybrid machine that will combine the capabilities of television, computers, telephones, and who knows what else.

We certainly don't, and you aren't reading this book to get our predictions anyway. There are at least a few tips about computers we can pass along, however, that will probably be useful no matter what changes occur in the next couple of years.

Back in 1984, the breakup of AT&T was a momentous

event in terms of revolutionizing how we all buy telephone equipment and services. By now, most of us have become accustomed to choosing from what once seemed a bewildering array of equipment, services, competing long-distance carriers, and billing options.

If you think you are bewildered now, "you ain't seen nothing yet." Your choices should multiply in the next few years. Your regional telephone company no longer has a protected monopoly, and will ultimately have to compete for your business with cable companies, companies like AT&T and MCI that had previously been limited to long-distance service, and/or anyone else who wants to enter your market. Regional companies are beginning to fight for long-distance business in many areas. Cable companies may soon offer both long-distance and local telephone service.

The acquisition by AT&T of TCI, the country's largest cable television operator, was announced shortly before this edition went to press. It may be the first of a wave of mergers that will begin to blur the distinctions we now make among telephone, computer, cable television, and cellular companies. So we freely admit that by 2000 this chapter may be far less useful than others in the book; that's how rapidly we expect things to change. But not all of our tips about telephone service will be outdated by the end of 1999. Not every local telephone market will be immediately invaded by aggressive competitors. Some people, especially in rural areas, may never have a choice of more than one local telephone service provider.

Whatever changes do come to your area, new competition should result in lower prices. Even if you live within a market affected by fierce competition, however, in order to get lower prices you are going to have to make some effort to keep up on developments in a rapidly changing telecommunications environment. In the meanwhile, we hope some of these tips help.

▶ LEARN COMPUTER BASICS, THEN KNOW YOURSELF

If you are an absolute novice, don't know a hard drive from a floppy disk, and just have a general feeling that you ought to own a computer, perhaps because you are afraid of being left behind, don't go near a computer store. You are not ready.

First, learn what a computer can do and, just as important, what it can't do. The best way to do that is to take a quick course in computer basics. Many school districts have excellent, inexpensive adult education courses. If you don't want to take a course, visit a patient friend who is seated before a computer that he or she has been using for at least a couple of years. Look. Ask. Play with the mouse. Visit a few Internet sites. Don't worry about the technical stuff.

While you are sitting there, ask your friend whether you should buy an Apple or an IBM-compatible machine. Invariably, she will tell you to get what she uses. The great advantages of IBM-compatible PCs are that a lot more software is being written for them, many more people use them, and they are cheaper. So opt for the IBM-compatible unless you have a compelling reason to do otherwise.

When you leave your friend's house, go to your library or buy a copy of the most basic book you can find. The best one we know is *PCs for Dummies* by Dan Gookin and Andy Rathbone ($16.95, IDG Books). The only thing we don't like about this book is the title, but the publisher of the wildly popular *Dummy* series could care less. Just remember you are not a dummy; you are simply new to a lot of dumb techno-babble that the old-time computer nerds love to use to keep their club exclusive.

The last thing you want to do is learn much of that stuff. But you should know some basics—the difference between hardware and software, for example, and what hard drives, memory, CD-ROMs, and modems do. Any basic book will explain all of these things. Then go back to your patient friend with even more questions. You are never going to know how to write a computer program or how a microprocessor works, but you don't know how to tune up your own automobile engine either. You know enough to proceed to the next step:

Second, decide what you want a computer to do for

you and other members of your family. Do you just want to write a few letters and be able to send and receive E-mail? Do you want to play games? Do your own taxes and improve your family budget? Load the machine up with all kinds of memory-hungry software programs?

Of course, you won't be absolutely sure how you will ultimately want to use your computer, but if you walk into a store without some sense of what kind of machine you need to accomplish what you want to do, you will encounter a salesperson eager to sell you the most expensive machine possible. You don't need a Porsche to go to the supermarket and back, and you don't need a top-of-the-line computer for 99 percent of most in-home use.

We won't make any specific recommendations, given how rapidly the technology changes, except for these few sure-to-still-be-relevant tips:

- Blazing speed in a microprocessor (how many megahertz, or MHz, it runs on) is wonderful if you are crunching huge spreadsheets of numbers or doing major-league computer graphics work, but most of us can settle for more modest speed for less money. If you plan on playing a lot of games, however, you may want to pay extra for a speedier machine.
- You don't need a huge hard drive, but you will need more hard-disk storage than you originally estimate. Buy something in the mid-range.
- Spend the extra money for more than whatever the current "minimum" random access memory (RAM) recommendation is. Recommendations about minimum memory requirements from some software programs are inaccurate. To run well, they need more memory. Whatever you buy, make sure that the RAM you buy is expandable.
- If you are buying a first computer, you will want all the hand-holding advice and technical backup possible during your first few months of use. Pay for that up front, probably at a retail store. Check out exactly what support is offered as part of your purchase price

in different stores; this is as important a part of your purchase decision as the machine itself. Yes, you can save money by buying from one of the large mail-order vendors, but don't believe a word they say about how easy it will be to get their help by telephone or modem.

▶ BUY YOUR *SECOND* COMPUTER BY MAIL

Your library has the latest copies of computer magazines full of ads from mail-order vendors. When you know what you are shopping for, and are confident enough to take a chance on their technical support systems (which are periodically reviewed in the magazines), you can nearly always get a better price on computer hardware from a mail-order source than from a retail store.

Two reliable sources: *Dell* (800-847-4029; http://www. dell.com) and *Gateway* (800-846-5357; http://www. gateway.com). Both of these Internet sites, in addition to selling computers, offer a wealth of technological information. Gateway's site is particularly user-friendly if you are a novice.

▶ BUY SECONDHAND

Here is a true penny pincher's way of looking at the purchase of a computer: Whatever I buy is going to be obsolete in a year, so why not buy a machine that has already been obsolete for a year—at a fraction of the price of the new one? Is saving 80 percent and being just one year behind all that terrible?

Not for most people. Check your Yellow Pages under "Computer Sales, Used." Or check out the classified ads for used equipment in a magazine called *Computer Shopper*. You can also contact *Data Path Technologies* (914-769-1999; http://www.datapath.com) and the *Boston Computer Exchange* (800-262-6399; http://www.bocoex. com). They will usually be able to give you a price over the phone, whether you are a buyer or a seller of equipment.

You may also want to check out one of the Internet auction sites that often have great buys on used or discontinued computer equipment. See Chapter 5 for a list of sites.

▶ DONATE YOUR OLD COMPUTER

Buying secondhand is attractive because there is always a glut of old computers on the market. Selling into that glut may be far less attractive. By all means establish a price you might get for your old computer (see above resources), but then consider donating it to a school, church, synagogue, or some other nonprofit organization. The tax deduction may be your best bet. The *National Christina Foundation* (800-274-7846) accepts used computers and will give you a written receipt of its value. *Gifts in Kind America* (703-836-2121; http://www. cwire.com/giftsinkind) will give you the names of organizations in your area that may need your equipment.

▶ BUY DURING THE EARLY SUMMER MONTHS

There has been a consistent price-cycle pattern in computer sales during the past few years. It will probably continue. Vendors introduce new systems at the big Comdex trade show in late spring. Inevitably, retailers then lower prices on existing inventory.

▶ CHECK COLLEGE CAMPUS STORE PRICES

Computer and software vendors have given special discounts to colleges for years, no doubt on the theory that the college years are a good time to establish relationships with new customers. If your college-bound son or daughter doesn't yet have a PC, you might want to wait and buy at the campus store. That store will also know what equipment and software is in general use on campus, so you can be sure what you buy will be compatible with the college's system.

▶ CHECK OUT PRICESCAN

Pricescan (http://www.pricescan.com) searches thousands of other web sites for the lowest prices on all kinds of computer hardware—systems, modems, printers, scanners, etc.

▶ IS A FAX CHEAPER THAN A LETTER?

You don't need an expensive stand-alone fax machine to send a letter by fax. Most computer modems now include fax capabilities, so you can send a letter directly from your word-processing program to any fax number. Especially if it is a local call or you send the fax during off-hours, the price of a one-minute call may be less than the price of a first-class stamp. It is also far faster.

▶ E-MAIL IS ALWAYS CHEAPER

If you have friends and family you want to keep in touch with anywhere in the country, electronic mail—a message from one person to another across the Internet—is the single best penny-pinching resource to come out of the information revolution. In order to send and receive E-mail, you will have to pay someone a monthly fee—an on-line service such as America Online, a telephone company such as MCI or AT&T, or one of the many Internet service providers—to establish access and an E-mail address. Prices and discount plans are changing too rapidly for us to make specific recommendations. Talk to friends who already use E-mail and check out their tips.

▶ DON'T RENT YOUR TELEPHONE

There are still millions of people in this country who rent their phones, more than fifteen years after the breakup of AT&T. A basic Touch-Tone phone probably costs less than one year's rental, and any well-made telephone should give you years of trouble-free service. Since on-site repairs on rented phones are not free anymore, there really is *no* advantage to renting.

If you are still renting, look at your bill. You'll find the number to call to cancel the service and get information about buying your telephone and converting it, if necessary, to a modular instrument (the only kind you want). Check that price against the prices of telephones sold by an electronics discounter (see Chapter 5 for mail-order sources).

▶ READ THE WHITE PAGES OF YOUR TELEPHONE DIRECTORY

Prices and options in telephone service vary greatly in different areas. Different people use their telephones in different ways. So it is impossible to spell out exactly the best penny-pinching strategy for you to use with your local telephone company. But you may very well discover quick and easy ways to save money simply by spending a few minutes reading the first few pages of your telephone directory.

Every detail about different charges, rate time periods, calling plans, etc. must by law be set forth in this directory. Match various plans against the usage detailed in your last few telephone bills. If a competitor to your local company has appeared in your area, factor its plans into your calculations.

▶ STOP PAYING FOR TELEPHONE "WIRE MAINTENANCE"

Pull out your last telephone bill. If you see a charge for wire maintenance (usually from $1.50 to $2 a month), call your phone company's business office and cancel this "service." Why? Because you are paying a high premium to insure yourself against an unlikely event.

The phone company is already responsible for maintenance of wires that lead up to your house. The charge on your bill also makes the company responsible for fixing the wires that lead from that point to your telephones. Since problems with inside wires are rare, you are better off taking your chances and either paying an electrician or fixing them yourself in the unlikely event that something goes wrong.

▶ BUY LONG-DISTANCE SERVICE THAT FITS YOUR USER PROFILE

Fierce competition among long-distance telephone companies has resulted in a competitive standoff in terms of most regular rates for most users. All the companies offer discount plans for different kinds of usage, however, and it is possible to cut your bills substantially using one of them.

Which plan? Which company? Those aren't the right first questions. The single best penny-pinching strategy is first to analyze how you and your family actually use long-distance service and only then to look into different discount plans. If you make just a few short calls a month, a discount plan offering a flat rate for the first hour of service may not make sense. If you make most of your calls to a single area code or to the same numbers, there are discount plans that will make these call patterns cheaper. If you access the Internet, you can sign up for a plan that packages free hours with other long-distance services. If your local telephone company has begun offering long-distance service, or special rates for regional long-distance service, you must factor these prices and plans into your decision as well.

As confusing as this may sound, one thing is certain as we write this: If you are among the long-distance customers who haven't switched to a discount plan, you are paying more than you should for long-distance service. There is definitely a discount plan that will save you money.

One common mistake is to buy a plan that offers steep discounts with a minimum fee for late-night use, based on a vow to change your habits by talking to your sister on the other coast only after 10:00 P.M. After an initial period of compliance, you will probably fall back into old routines and end up paying a fee for an unused service.

It's a good idea to look into competitive plans whenever your long-distance calling habits change—when a child goes away to college, for instance, or when a close friend moves. Don't sign a long-term contract (more than six months) with any long-distance company, no matter what promotional advantages are offered. And don't sign up with carriers because they promise rebates stretching into the far future. Reason: None of them will guarantee that their rates won't change, and the rebates—or the terms of your long-term contract—may not look so attractive in a few months. You have a legal right to switch long-distance carriers whenever you like, so keep them competing for your business.

The long-distance companies don't want you to know it, but quite a few penny pinchers switch back and forth between competing long-distance carriers, month after month or as soon as the initial contract period is over. They take big up-front cash rebates when they switch, and some have ended up with free service plus a few dollars more!

When you do decide to switch, make sure to ask your new long-distance carrier to credit you for the switching fee (currently $5 in our area) charged by your local telephone company. Also, watch your bills carefully during the following ninety days; your old carrier may conveniently neglect to drop you and still bill you some kind of monthly fee.

For up-to-date information on available discount plans, contact *AT&T* (800-222-0300; http://www.att. com); *MCI* (800-444-3333; http://www.mci.com); and *Sprint* (800-877-4646; http://www.sprint.com). Or, if you prefer a single source that gives you comprehensive listings and comparisons of various long-distance plans currently available, from these companies and others, send $5.55 with a SASE to TRAC (*Telecommunications Research & Action Center*), Box 27279, Washington, D.C. 20005. Ask for the *Tele-Tips Residential Long Distance*

Comparison Chart. TRAC also has a web site (http://www.trac.org) that provides a lot of useful information, as well as an analyzer you can use to determine your long-distance calling patterns.

There is also a very good analyzer at the *Teleworth* web site (http://www.teleworth.com). You simply enter a complete record of your last month's long-distance calls. Teleworth analyzes that data and suggests the four best plans for you. The only problem is that it doesn't take into account promotional rates offered by many companies.

▶ AVOID YOUR HOTEL'S LONG-DISTANCE LINE

If you don't yet have one, get your own long-distance charge card from AT&T, Sprint, MCI, or another carrier, and place your calls through its operator. Whether it is a great luxury hotel in a major city or a budget motel out in the sticks, long-distance calls by guests are often looked upon as a source of incremental profits. Surcharges of 100 percent or more are common.

If you are traveling abroad, things are even worse. But MCI, Sprint, and AT&T have toll-free access numbers you can reach from your hotel telephone in most countries that connect you with an operator in the United States. Not only will you save money; you'll also avoid non-English-speaking operators.

An even better alternative if you travel abroad frequently is to get an international calling card. Among the issuers that may beat the prices offered by AT&T, MCI, or Sprint calling cards: *GA Telecard* (800-685-0420; http://www.lcpi.com).

▶ BEWARE OF PAY PHONES

One of the best reasons to carry a telephone calling card is to use the access number on it when you are at a pay phone. When you dial this access number, you'll be connected to your carrier's operator and will pay its rates for calling-card or collect calls. Otherwise, if you are unlucky enough to be calling from a pay phone owned by a company that pays a commission to the owners of the facility in which the phone is placed, you risk paying up to five times as much for your call.

Remember that most calling-card calls made from pay phones carry a 30-cent charge that goes to the owner of the phone, so coins are still usually the best choice for local calls or calls to a nearby area code.

▶ GET THE BEST DEAL IN A CALLING CARD

Major long-distance companies offer discounts on calls made with calling cards issued to home subscribers ("primary users" to the carriers). If you make frequent calls with a card, you may want to factor this into your decision about a long-distance carrier. You may also want to consider an alternative calling-card company such as *VoiceNet* (800-274-0962), which offered a lower rate than any of the major carriers as this book went to press. You can get a free up-to-date calling-card comparison chart, with the latest prices from five different providers, by contacting the *Tele-Consumer Hotline,* Box 27207, Washington, D.C. 20005; http://www. teleconsumer.org/hotline/organizations.html

▶ USE A PREPAID CARD

Using a prepaid phone card may be as cheap as using a calling card, especially if you make short calls when you are away from home. You'll find prepaid cards for sale just about everywhere these days, including gas stations and supermarkets. You buy a card in denominations usually ranging from $5 to $50 and get a preset number of telephone minutes for calls anywhere in the United States. When you make a call, you dial the access number printed on it and press in an identification number. Before you dial your party, you will be told how many minutes of use you have remaining. However many minutes you use will be deducted. When all of your minutes are used up, you just toss the card away.

Avoid cards with activation fees (per-call charges in addition to the pay-phone access charge). One company with a bargain per-minute rate with no activation charge as this book went to press was *USATel Calling Card* (800-390-6891). Finally, make sure you buy a card from a reputable company. Some fly-by-night operations have gone out of business, leaving customers with useless unused minutes.

▶ CALL ON THE INTERNET (NO COMPUTER NECESSARY)

If you are a fairly heavy user of long-distance service, you may want to check out one of the many companies that now route calls from a regular telephone over the Internet instead of over traditional telephone communication networks. The sound quality of such calls may not be quite as good, but it is definitely acceptable. In the spring of 1998, some of these companies were undercutting the best prices from traditional long-distance companies by as much as 50 percent for domestic calls and even more than that for international calls. By the time you read this, however, the Federal Communications Commission may have changed rules that allowed these Internet providers to escape some of the fees the major companies have to pay. We would expect that eventually the price differential will narrow. Among the companies offering Internet telephone service, including calling cards: *IDT* (800-225-5438) and *I-Link* (800-238-9465).

▶ GET YOUR OWN 800 OR 888 NUMBER

This could make sense if someone in the family travels a great deal, you have kids away at college, or there are other reasons why you pay for hours of long-distance calls made each month to your home number. Some companies charge a small monthly fee (typically $5) plus the cost of calls. Others charge no monthly fee but charge more per call minute. Either way, using an 800 or 888 number is cheaper than calling-card rates from most distances. You don't need any new equipment and don't even have to pay a connection fee; calls come in on your present line. You also have complete control over who knows about the 800 or 888 number.

For information and current rates, call the numbers listed in the tip about buying long-distance service. Ask for details about a personal 800 or 888 number.

▶ USE THE PHONE BOOK

Telephone companies have turned their directory-assistance operations into major profit centers. In our area, it costs 48 cents to get an in-state number from an operator. How much longer does it take to look a number up yourself?

Even if you've lost Aunt Tilly's phone number and she lives two thousand miles away, a phone book is probably available. Our local library has a CD-ROM with every telephone number in the United States on it. On the Internet, we use *Switchboard* (http://www.switchboard.com).

▶ BUT CALL 800-555-1212 WHENEVER YOU LIKE

The 800/888 directory-assistance line is free—*in most areas*. If you are unsure about your area, check your local telephone company. Once you ascertain that the line is free, the next time you are about to make a regular long-distance call to a company or organization, call 800-555-1212 first. Very often, you'll find the company has an 800 or 888 number you can call toll-free. You can also access AT&T's directory of customers who lease 800 or 888 numbers from it on the Internet (http://www.tollfree.att.net/). Also check out Switchboard (previous tip).

▶ HOLD DOWN FAX OR MODEM EXPENSES

If you plan to buy a dedicated fax machine, get one with an answering machine built in. You can then use the same line for both fax and voice calls. Even when you are away, the machine will be able to recognize a fax call and accept it, as well as take voice messages.

If you have a fax or modem that you use only occasionally and want to avoid the expense of an additional line, look into the "distinctive ringing" plans that most telephone companies offer. You can get two or three different telephone numbers that share the same line for a lot less a month than the extra lines would cost you.

▶ HOLD DOWN CELLULAR-PHONE EXPENSES

Unless you absolutely have to have one, the best penny-pinching advice is to avoid using a cellular phone. The average cellular-phone user spends between $60 and $70 a month on it. During peak hours a call can cost up to 80 cents a minute. At those prices, we prefer to stop at a pay-phone booth.

If you do decide you need a cellular phone, think first about how you plan to use it. If you will use it infrequently, perhaps only in case of an emergency, look for a plan that offers a low monthly access fee, usually including a few free minutes of use, combined with high usage charges. If you will use the phone constantly, look for a plan with the lowest usage charges, especially during the hours when you will make the most calls.

Until you're shown otherwise, don't concern yourself with claims from any carrier about superior quality or service; in most areas there's not much difference. Once you have chosen a phone that has the features you want, buy the cheapest package available. The phone itself may cost you little or nothing if you sign up for certain plans. You will nearly always be given some free minutes of use during your first three months. Shop around and add up all the elements of the package.

It may pay to switch cellular-phone carriers after your initial contract period is up. If you can get a lot of free minutes, a front-end rebate (often of up to $100), a lower monthly access fee, or cheaper time rates, why not? Just make sure either that the new company will waive its activation fee or that the deal is so good it makes sense even with the fee included.

A new wireless technology—Digital PCS (Personal Communications Services)—has been introduced in most parts of the country. Digital PCS provides better reception than cellular, but it is more expensive as well. If PCS is catching on in your area, chances are good that a cellular operator is cutting prices in order to compete.

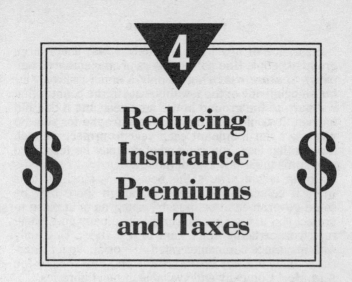

4

Reducing Insurance Premiums and Taxes

Twenty-five years before he uttered the immortal phrase "Nothing is certain but death and taxes," Benjamin Franklin started America's first insurance company. Obviously he still had no idea how inevitable a part of our lives insurance premiums would become.

That very inevitability leads some people to treat their insurance bills, along with taxes, as fixed and unalterable. They wince when they get their semiannual automobile insurance premium bill and see that the premium has gone up once again. But they decide it is easier to pay the bill than to open up that boring file filled with a few years' worth of unexamined policies, policy changes, and premium notices.

These people frequently make two basic mistakes about insurance. They pay more than they should for the insurance they have, often because they don't really need all of it. And they either don't insure or grossly underinsure themselves against some very real risks.

Insurance of any kind is simply a way for a large group of people (the policyholders of an insurance company) to *share risk*. There's only a small risk of your house being one of the few thousand in the country that will burn to the ground in the next year, but if that did happen, it would be a financial catastrophe for you. So you pay a small amount each year to protect yourself against that loss. You *want* what you pay for insurance premiums to be "a waste of money."

Cheap is not always the best penny-pinching idea when it comes to insurance. Although there may be some governmental or industry safety nets in place to protect you in case your insurance company goes bankrupt, you certainly don't want to test them. Deal only with insurance companies rated A+ or above for financial stability in *Best's Insurance Reports,* published by the A.M. Best Company and available in most libraries.

Only after you have established that the companies you are considering are financially sound should you begin comparison-shopping among them. Price now becomes a compelling factor, but so is service; talk to people who have dealt with the company when a claim was necessary. Don't avoid paying a bit more if it will give you access to a knowledgeable agent who is willing to tailor a program that is right for your individual needs.

Finally, keep in mind that too many insurance agents love customers whose eyes glaze over because all the details are confusing and the whole subject is, well, *dull.* You can't afford to feel that way about your money and your family's security.

As for taxes, Ben Franklin has yet to be proven wrong. But simply because taxes are inevitable doesn't mean you shouldn't do everything legally possible to minimize them.

This book is not an income-tax guide. But many readers of tax preparation guides who are concentrating on line-by-line instructions for their returns are likely to miss the penny-pinching strategies included in this chapter. These strategies may also require you to analyze your tax situation well before the end of a calendar year. If you wait until next April, it is often too late to activate some very easy ways to reduce this year's—or next year's—taxes.

▶ BUY THE HIGHEST POSSIBLE DEDUCTIBLES

Whether you are buying automobile, home, or medical insurance, the purpose of insurance is to protect against sudden, unforeseen expenses that you could not afford yourself. If a leaky pipe were to cause $300 worth of damage to a ceiling, for instance, spending that sum might be frustrating, even painful. But if you can afford it, you shouldn't insure yourself against it by paying for a homeowner's policy with a $100 deductible.

Such a policy would pay for $200 of the damages in this case. But the premium paid for a policy with that low a deductible will be much more expensive than one with a $500 deductible. The lower your deductibles (the amount over which your insurance company has to pay the damages), the higher your insurance premiums. The difference in premium cost between a $500 and a $100 deductible for your home or car can be 30 percent or even more.

There's another practical reason to buy the highest possible deductibles for auto and home insurance. Many insurance companies punish people who file too many claims by raising their premiums. In fact, just a couple of small claims may be too many for some companies. If you are therefore going to limit your claims to large amounts of money, it would be extra foolish to pay for low deductibles at the same time.

▶ BUT DON'T UNDERINSURE

The big risks are the ones you are worried about. If you have a car that's less than three or four years old, don't try to save on auto insurance by skipping collision coverage. If your family would need $200,000 to live decently were you to become unable to provide for them, don't try to get away with a smaller life insurance policy. If you live in a house that would cost $150,000 to replace if it burned to the ground, don't settle for anything less than a homeowner's policy that guarantees full replacement cost.

Pinching pennies doesn't mean being pound foolish; the worst way to save money is by risking future financial catastrophe.

▶ KNOW HOW MUCH LIFE INSURANCE YOU NEED

How much you need is more important than what kind you buy. So you must calculate what your family would need to replace you—financially—if you died tomorrow.

There is a bewildering number of different kinds of life insurance policies. But the first basic choice you must make is between term insurance, which pays off only if you die, and one of the many forms of permanent insurance, which also pays the amount of the policy in case you die but in addition is worth something while you are alive. As the agents say, it has both insurance and investment components.

You'll pay less for term insurance. Many parents use a combination of term and permanent insurance during the years before their children are self-sufficient, then drop the term insurance. You'll have to spend some time in your library and with life insurance agents before you decide what's best for you. Just one word of advice: Take with a grain of salt the arguments of both the "buy only term and invest the rest" crowd and the "term is a waste of money" gang. There is no answer that fits everyone, and many people are best off with a combination of both.

Back to the big question: How much will you need? Start with the worksheet in this chapter; it will be a big help if you fill it out before talking to agents. Actually, this worksheet is a simplified version of the capital needs analysis form a good agent will use.

Because it is easier to use such a worksheet if you can see how it applies in a real-life example, we've included a

How Much Life Insurance Do You Need?

To Cover:	What they'll need	Example
1. Funeral		$ 3,000
2. Other miscellaneous final expenses	+	+ $ 1,000
3. Estate taxes	+	+ 0
4. Pay off mortgage	+	+ $120,000
5. Pay off other debts	+	+ $ 1,000
6. College fund	+	+ $ 44,000
7. Other needs	+	+ $ 5,000
8. Total	=	$174,000
Living expenses:		
Current living expenses		$ 45,000
× 80%		$ 36,000
− Spouse's take-home pay	−	$ 12,000
− Social Security survivor benefit	−	$ 16,000
= Annual need	=	$ 7,200
× number of years needed		20
9. Total living expenses	=	$144,000
10. Total assets needed (add 8 + 9)		$318,000
11. Group insurance proceeds	−	$100,000
12. Income-producing assets	−	$ 10,000
13. Your insurance need (10 − 11 − 12)		$208,000

column with numbers filled in. Our example is a man of thirty, married, with an income of $50,000 a year. His wife works part-time, making $12,000 a year, and they have a two-year-old child. The man has a $100,000 group life insurance policy through his job. They have just moved into a $150,000 house, using all but $10,000 of their total joint savings for a down payment of $30,000.

The example covers this man's life insurance needs only; his wife's should be calculated separately. Note that he needs assets of $318,000 to pay off the mortgage on the house and other debts, send his child to college, and cover twenty years of living expenses for his wife and child. In this case, he and his wife decided that she and the child could both be self-supporting after the child graduates from college. Since he already has a $100,000 group policy and $10,000 in assets that could provide income, his insurance need comes to $208,000.

Not many thirty-year-olds making $50,000 a year will be able to afford that much permanent life insurance, so some combination of term and permanent is likely.

The worksheet doesn't take inflation into account; if the beneficiaries invest the insurance proceeds wisely they should be able to keep pace with inflation. There are no taxes on estates of less than $650,000 (the 1999 exemption; this amount will increase to $1,000,000 by 2006). Your family might not choose to pay off your mortgage and other debt, but doing so simplifies the necessary calculations.

Adjust up or down our estimate of 80 percent of current living expenses as the amount your family could live on. *Don't* use the Social Security Survivor Benefit number in the example. Contact the *Social Security Administration* (800-772-1213; http://www.ssa.gov) and ask for a Request for Earnings and Benefits Estimate Statement. You'll eventually get an estimate of your own current survivor's benefits. Finally, adapt or add to this basic worksheet in any way necessary to fit your individual needs.

▶ SHOP FOR TERM INSURANCE BY TELEPHONE

It's an easy way to check out rates and compare them with what your agent or bank has offered. There is no fee involved; just contact the quote services below and tell them how much coverage you want. They'll ask your age, what the general state of your health is, and other pertinent questions that may or may not qualify you for preferred rates. A few days later you'll receive a free computer printout from each of them, listing prices from several companies.

These services can also give you advice on what you need, but you will be better off figuring that out yourself beforehand. They get commissions on sales from the insurance companies they represent, and have a vested interest in selling you as large a policy as possible.

Before you buy, check the company out in *Best's* (see page 74) and make sure you understand all the terms of the contract. Companies to call:

- *Select Quote,* 800-343-1985; http://www.selectquote. com.
- *MasterQuote,* 800-337-5433; http://www.masterquote. com.
- *Quotesmith,* 800-431-1147; http://www.quotesmith. com.

▶ STOP SMOKING AND REDUCE PREMIUMS

If you were a smoker when you took out your life insurance policy, you are paying higher premiums than a nonsmoker. If you have been off cigarettes for a year, call your insurer and ask for nonsmokers' rates.

▶ SKIP LIFE INSURANCE FOR CHILDREN

Your kids won't need life insurance until they have dependents. Insurance cushions you only against financial losses, not emotional ones.

▶ GROUP RATES AREN'T ALWAYS BETTER

Many companies pay the premiums on employee life insurance policies. Obviously, this is a great deal. Many also allow you to buy additional life insurance at group rates. This *isn't* always a good deal—first, because you may not have the right to convert to an individual policy if you leave the company, and second, because "group rates" for this kind of insurance aren't necessarily less expensive than a term policy you could buy on your own. Comparison-shop before you sign up.

Exception: If you are in poor health, you should probably grab any group-rate policy you can get, since you won't have to take a medical exam to get the insurance.

▶ SAVE ON DISABILITY INSURANCE

Don't save by skimping on it. Disability insurance, which provides ongoing monthly income if you are physically unable to work due to accident or illness, is essential if you have to work to maintain your lifestyle. That includes most of the nonretired population, but too many people believe Social Security and workers' compensation laws provide adequate protection. They don't. Since one of every seven workers in the United States will suffer a period of disability of five years or longer before age sixty-five, a good disability policy is just as important as a good life insurance program.

Most people are covered by group disability insurance where they work. More and more often, they must choose from among different features within flexible benefit plans. If you aren't covered by a group plan, you will have to pay higher individual rates. In either case, the best way to save on premiums without skimping on necessary coverage is to choose a longer waiting period. A thirty-day waiting period—the time between the onset of a disability and when benefits start—is often 20 percent more expensive than a ninety-day waiting period. If you have a reasonable emergency fund, you won't absolutely need the money within the first ninety days and you'll save a significant amount in premiums.

You definitely want a policy that can't be canceled and offers some written rate-hike protection. Finally, although you can save on premiums if you buy an "any occupation" policy, pay extra for the "own occupation" policy. With this policy, the insurance company has to pay benefits if you are unable to perform your own job.

▶ HAVE FLEXIBLE BENEFITS? PAY YOUR OWN DISABILITY PREMIUM

More companies each year are offering flexible benefit plans, allowing employees to choose from a smorgasbord of health, life, and disability plans but limiting the company's total contribution to premium payments. It makes sense to have the company pay the nondisability premiums first. If there's none of their money left over, buy your own disability insurance through the company's low group rate. Why? If the company pays disability premiums, and someday you need to collect benefits, payments will be taxable to you as ordinary income. If you pay the premiums, payments will be tax-free.

▶ CHECK HMO RATINGS

Contact the *National Committee for Quality Assurance* (800-839-6487; http://www.ncqa.org) to get its free Accreditation Status List. Some badly run HMOs avoid NCQA review, and some HMOs with good reputations simply don't want to pay the fee NCQA charges for an evaluation. But just about all of the larger HMOs are now getting these evaluations. If you are making a choice, the information you will get—on everything from the qualifications of the HMO's physicians to how appropriately they respond to patient's needs—will be invaluable.

▶ SHOP FOR AUTO INSURANCE BY TELEPHONE

The next time you get the premium bill for your auto insurance, take a few minutes to do some comparison shopping. It really isn't much trouble when you do it by telephone, and the results may surprise you. If nothing else, you can satisfy yourself that the rates you are paying are competitive. Ask friends whom they use and how satisfied they have been; among the companies you might try are USAA, State Farm, GEICO, and Allstate.

Most insurance companies will quote prices by telephone. Even those that at first say they won't may change their minds when you tell them it's the only way you'll do business. Enter the information they'll need from you along with the prices from your current policy in the worksheet in this chapter. Don't volunteer any information they don't need, but be honest about mileage, moving violations, etc.

Establish all of your current deductibles and get prices based on those. If you want to explore different deductibles, make sure you get a quote from your current company as well as the competition.

It's possible other companies may offer discounts your present company doesn't. Ask.

▶ CHECK ON ALL POSSIBLE DISCOUNTS

The worksheet lists the most common discounts on automobile insurance: for air bags/automatic belts, antitheft devices, safe-driver education courses, and senior drivers. There may be others (some insurers give discounts if you have antilock brakes or if the car is driven only a certain number of miles a year, for instance), so ask. If you belong to a credit union or an auto club, check with it to see if it has any arrangement for group rates.

▶ DROP COLLISION INSURANCE ON OLDER CARS

Especially if you follow our penny-pinching advice on buying high deductibles, it doesn't make sense to pay for collision insurance on a car that is worth less than $2,500. If you have a $500 deductible, the most you could collect would be $2,000. Your collision premium for that maximum coverage could be from $100 to $200 a year—5 to 10 percent of your highest possible claim. That's far too high a price to pay for the risk involved.

▶ SHOP AROUND FOR YOUR TEENAGER'S CAR INSURANCE

Depending on where you live and how your insurance company handles the issue, adding one newly licensed

Comparing Automobile Insurance: A Worksheet

A. List cars you plan to insure:
    Car A: Year, model, vehicle i.d. number ....
        Miles driven per year ....
        Percentage used for commuting ....
    Car B: Year, model, vehicle i.d. number ....
        Miles driven per year ....
        Percentage used for commuting ....

B. List members of family who use the cars:
    Include name, age, driver's license number,
    convictions for moving violations and dates,
    accident records, percentage of use on each car

C. Comparing premiums:

	CURRENT POLICY		CO.		CO.		CO.	
	Car 1	Car 2	Car 1	Car 2	Car 1	Car 2	Car 1	Car 2
1. Bodily injury liability: $ _____ per person $ _____ per occurrence								
2. Property damage liability: $ _____ per occurrence								
3. Medical payments: $ _____ (Note terms/deductibles, etc.)								

4. No-fault personal injury protection:
$_____

5. Uninsured motorists:
$_____ / _____ bodily injury person/occurrence

6. Auto medical payments:
$_____ each person

7. Collision:
$_____ deductible
$_____ deductible
$_____ deductible

8. Comprehensive:
$_____ deductible
$_____ deductible
$_____ deductible

9. Discounts:
% of _____ for air bags/automatic belts
% of _____ for antitheft devices
% of _____ for safe-driver education
% of _____ for senior drivers
% of _____ for _____
% of _____ for _____

TOTAL COSTS (total using deductibles selected, less applicable discounts): _____

teenager to your policy could double your premium cost overnight. Before this happens, make a few telephone calls, first to your present insurer and then to some competitors, to check on different coverage. Some companies offer discounts to teenagers who have completed driver's education courses, are "good students," or qualify as occasional drivers.

A couple of years later, if your teenager heads off to a college more than 120 miles or so away from home, call your insurer and ask for a rate reduction. The teenager is no longer residing in your house full-time.

▶ SAVE ON HOMEOWNER'S INSURANCE

Homeowner's insurance is easier to buy than some other types because the industry has a standard coding system (the HO number) that identifies different types of policies.

Many policies also label themselves as "comprehensive" or "all-risk," but these are meaningless terms. The HO number tells you what you are buying.

HO-1, HO-2, HO-3, and HO-5 policies are for house owners. An HO-6 policy is for owners of condominiums or co-ops. An HO-4 policy is for renters who need coverage for the contents of their houses or apartments as well as the same kind of personal liability insurance (in case someone is injured on the premises) homeowner policies provide.

If you are a homeowner, avoid the HO-1 and HO-2 policies, which are too limited to provide adequate protection, and price out HO-3 ("open peril") and HO-5 ("comprehensive, all-risk") policies. The HO-5 is more expensive because, although it has the same coverage as the HO-3 on the structure, it offers broader coverage on contents. Many people find the extra coverage isn't worth the increase in premium payments.

Among the ways to save on homeowner's insurance:

- Install smoke alarms.
- Consider some form of antitheft system, but don't install an expensive system just to save on insurance

premiums. Depending on where you live, the savings may not be very large.

■ Get a nonsmoker's discount if you qualify.

■ Use the same company for your automobile policy, and get a combination-policy discount.

■ Shop around. For most people, automobile insurance is more expensive than homeowner's insurance, so you may want to price that out first. But look at the total costs of both from different companies. Most of the companies mentioned in the tip about auto insurance sell homeowner's as well, and you should also talk to at least one independent agent in your area.

■ Check group availability. Some employers and some membership organizations now offer group homeowner's and/or automobile policies. Even if you are eligible, though, don't automatically assume the policy is the best deal you can get. Compare it with what you can get on your own.

▶ BUY A RENTER'S INSURANCE POLICY

If you rent an apartment or house, it is foolish not to buy a renter's (HO-4) policy that covers the contents of your premises in case of fire or theft. It also protects against liability suits if someone has an accident in your home or you cause an accident outside it.

In most parts of the country, such policies are less than $200 a year. If you live in an metropolitan area with higher-than-average burglary statistics, you'll pay more. In any case, get estimates from a number of different insurers, compare exactly what is covered in each policy, and weigh the premium costs of different levels of deductibles.

▶ VALUABLE JEWELRY? GET AN IN-VAULT FLOATER

If you get a normal floater on a homeowner's or a renter's policy to protect against the loss of a specific item of jewelry, your annual premium for the coverage can easily approach 4 to 5 percent of its value. Since most women who own valuable jewelry wear it only on special occasions, a far less costly alternative is an "in-vault" floater that may cost less than half of 1 percent. You must agree to keep the jewelry in a safe-deposit box and to wear it no more than a set number of times a year—typically four times. Also, you must notify the company when you do wear it and pay a small day rate for the time it is out of the vault.

▶ BUY AN UMBRELLA POLICY

Personal umbrella liability policies pick up where homeowner's and automobile policies leave off. You need one if you have assets that amount to more than the liability coverage in those policies. An umbrella policy will provide overall protection against a variety of claims—such as being sued for a million dollars because of an automobile accident or because someone slips on your sidewalk. Most companies that sell home and auto insurance also sell umbrella policies, and a million-dollar policy is relatively inexpensive.

▶ AVOID CREDIT INSURANCE

Most credit-granting organizations (banks, auto dealers, etc.) will attempt to sell credit life and/or disability insurance to you in connection with the loans they make. It is hardly ever a good idea. If you need more life insurance, a separate term policy sold by a bank or an insurance agent will always be cheaper. What's more, if you buy credit insurance, the beneficiary is not your family, but the lender. That's not who you want to protect in case of your death or disability.

▶ ONE FAIL-SAFE WAY TO SAVE ON CAR INSURANCE

Most states now mandate a discount in car insurance premiums for anyone who has recently taken a defensive driving course. Admittedly, there's a trade-off of time here—the courses typically run six to eight hours in two evening sessions—but the savings can be major (as much as $150 a year) and are recurring (for three to five years), and you get an important dividend: You may just learn something that could help you avoid an accident.

▶ RATES TOO HIGH? CHECK YOUR CREDIT RATING

Many auto and home insurers use the credit ratings of applicants to help establish rates. If they don't like what they see, your rates could increase by 50 percent or more. Incorrect information turns up in a disturbingly high percentage of personal credit histories, so it is a good idea to check on yours from time to time. Unless you live in a state that by law allows you to get a free copy of your credit report each year, it will cost you about $10 to get your credit report from one the three major agencies: *TransUnion* (800-888-4213), *Equifax* (800-685-1111), and *Experian* (800-682-7654). Getting just one report is probably fine unless you discover errors in it. If you do, get all three and make sure they all correct the mistakes.

▶ SKIP CREDIT-CARD INSURANCE

Selling credit-card insurance is profitable for issuers, but you simply don't need it. If your cards are lost or stolen and you notify the issuers right away, you aren't liable for their misuse. Even if you never notify the issuers, your maximum liability, mandated by federal law, is $50 per card.

▶ SKIP AIR-TRAVEL INSURANCE

Don't buy it at the airport, and don't buy it from the credit-card company that makes it "so easy," after you allow it to automatically add a "small" charge for $100,000 worth of insurance whenever you use the card to buy your tickets.

That "small" charge is actually a ridiculously high insurance premium, given the statistics on airline fatalities. If your dependents need protection, they need it whether you die in an airplane crash or from a heart attack. For the same reason, and because premiums are similarly overpriced, never buy illness-specific life insurance either.

▶ SKIP CAR-RENTAL INSURANCE

You can't unless you are already covered, of course, but the majority of people are. Most personal automobile insurance policies cover you for damage to a rental car. Many credit-card companies also now offer free car-rental insurance as a way to persuade you to use their card. If the credit-card companies can afford to give it away free, think how profitable selling the insurance must be for the rental-car companies.

▶ SKIP STUDENT-ACCIDENT INSURANCE

If you have family health insurance coverage, you don't need this coverage, which is offered by many school districts. They like selling these policies because the district is less likely to be sued by a purchaser in case of an accident.

▶ REVIEW LIFE INSURANCE NEEDS AS YOU GET OLDER

When you have been paying life insurance premiums regularly for a number of years, it is easy to lose sight of just why you bought the insurance in the first place. Most people do so to protect their families in case of loss of income. As you get older, put kids through college, and build a good retirement fund and substantial other assets, you may not need life insurance at all.

Certainly, once you have retired, your family doesn't need protection from loss of your income. In fact, your spouse's expenses would be reduced if you die. Paying larger and larger premiums for renewable term insurance makes no sense at all for many older people.

▶ CHECK WITH YOUR STATE INSURANCE DEPARTMENT ON THE INTERNET

Insurance departments in every state provide basic consumer information about all kinds of insurance as well as easy ways to get a fast complaint about any insurer to the proper state authorities. Check in with the *National Association of Insurance Commissioners* (http://www.naic.org) for links to your state's insurance department web site.

▶ FIGHT FOR LOWER PROPERTY TAXES

Maybe you think your property is being assessed at too high a rate. Maybe you didn't think so until you got a computer-generated letter in the mail from a property-tax consultant telling you how much she can save you by challenging the assessment authority on your behalf.

Don't hire anyone to do this for you if he asks for an up-front fee. He should be willing to work for a percentage of your first year's tax reduction. Local real-estate agents may be able to recommend consultants who are reputable and have a good record of success in your area.

Another way to reduce property taxes is to take all the exemptions you are entitled to. Depending on where you live, senior citizens, the disabled, veterans, owners of historic homes, and those in a few other special categories may be eligible for exemptions. Your local tax office can tell you what exemptions are available in your area.

▶ PREPARE YOUR OWN TAX RETURNS

Unless you have extraordinarily complicated tax problems, two tax software programs now make it relatively easy for you to do your own tax returns and feel confident that they will be both correct and save you as much money as possible. Prices vary from year to year, but both *TurboTax* (from Intuit, the makers of Quicken personal finance software) and *Kiplinger's TaxCut* should be available in discount stores for around $30 in February and March. Both also offer companion state tax programs at extra cost.

If you have a fairly simple return (salary, some straightforward investment income, and a few basic itemized deductions) check out *TurboTax Online* (http://www.turbotax.com). You can fill out the federal tax forms on-line, with help every step of the way, at no cost. If you decide to print the return or to have TurboTax file it for you electronically, you will be billed $9.95.

▶ BEGIN DECEMBER WITH A TAX-STRATEGY SESSION

Too many people put off thinking about income taxes until March or April, when the forms are due. By that time it is too late to take advantage of a few simple techniques that can transfer income and/or expenses from one year to another.

Suppose you are reading this in late 1999, and know roughly what your final income will be for that year. If you expect your income, tax rate, and/or tax bracket to be lower in 2000, you have got a good reason to a) defer as much potential 1999 income as possible to 2000, and b) move as many deductions as possible from 2000 to 1999.

If it looks like your 2000 taxes will be higher than 1999's, on the other hand, you will probably want to a) move as much potential 2000 income into 1999 as possible, and b) defer deductions from 1999 to 2000.

The next two tips show you how.

▶ PAY LOWER TAXES THIS YEAR

It is December 1999 and you think your potential taxes will be lower for calendar year 2000 than for calendar year 1999. Consider doing the following:

- Look ahead at the charitable contributions you would normally make in 2000. Write those checks, and mail them, on the last day of 1999.
- Prepay real-estate taxes. If a property-tax bill is due in January, pay it instead in December.
- Prepay state and local income taxes. Even if they're not due until April, if you pay in December you can deduct them on your 1999 federal return. Pay all outstanding estimated state taxes in December.
- Prepay your mortgage payment. Make your January payment on December 31 instead, and deduct that month's mortgage interest from your 1999 return.
- Look over medical expenses for the year. If your total medical expenses (including insurance premiums, doctors, dentists, hospitals, drugs, eyeglasses, contact lenses, hearing aids, and medically necessary travel) amount to 7.5 percent of your adjusted gross income (AGI), you can deduct expenses that exceed that threshold. This would make December 1999 a great time for any kind of elective medical or dental care you know you'll need sooner or later.
- Defer bonuses. This is a bit tricky, and you should get the advice of a tax expert, but if you have been getting a regular bonus at the end of December and can change that on a permanent basis to January, you should be able to defer your tax liability as well.
- Buy CDs and treasury bills that mature next year. You are not credited with the interest on either until they mature. Actually, if you are trying to reduce interest income for the year, doing this in December doesn't help much. If, however, back in July you had bought a six-month CD maturing in January 2000, you could have deferred quite a bit of interest income. Tax planning is really a year-round activity.
- If self-employed, bill clients in early January instead of late December.

▶ PAY LOWER TAXES NEXT YEAR

It is December 1999 and you think your potential taxes will be higher for calendar year 2000 than for calendar year 1999. Consider doing the following:

- If you normally get a bonus in January, ask if you can instead get it on the last workday of 1999.
- If you normally make charitable contributions at the end of the year, write the checks instead on January 2.
- Delay payment of medical and dental bills until 2000.
- Cash in CDs that would mature in 2000, or ask your bank to credit the interest on them by the end of 1999.
- Cash in savings bonds before the end of the year. Especially if your income in 1999 was considerably lower than you think it will be for the next few years, you have a good reason to cash in savings bonds that may have accumulated years of accrued interest income.

▶ DON'T BUY SHARES IN A STOCK MUTUAL FUND IN EARLY DECEMBER

Unless you have other good reasons to do so (dollar cost averaging being one of them), you are probably better off waiting until the very end of December or January 2 of the new year to buy shares in a stock mutual fund. The reason: These funds usually make their capital-gain as well as major income distributions for the year in mid-December. You incur a tax liability for that year on whatever amounts are distributed to you (even if you take the distributions in the form of more shares in the fund).

This is no reason to avoid a stock mutual fund you want to invest in for the long term, but toward the end of the year you should at least call the fund's customer-service department to check on when a distribution will be made.

▶ MAKE TAX-ADVANTAGED DONATIONS

You probably think only multimillionaire philanthropists can take advantage of the tax laws when making donations. But a lot of middle-class people give sizable sums of cash to a church, synagogue, alma mater, or charity.

The question is: Why cash? Suppose you own 100 shares of a stock or mutual fund you bought for $5 a share years ago. Now the price is $10. If you sell the shares for $1,000, you will have to pay a capital-gains tax on a $500 gain. If you give the 100 shares to a charity, neither you nor the charity will owe a penny in taxes and you can deduct the full $1,000 contribution.

Still like the stock or fund? Buy 100 new shares with the $1,000 cash you would otherwise have given the charity. Advantage: Your basis is now $10 a share instead of $5. If the share is someday worth $20, you will pay tax on only a $1,000 capital gain instead of a $1,500 one.

Given transaction costs, this works better with no-load mutual fund shares than with shares of an individual stock.

▶ TAKE ADVANTAGE OF THE CHILD-CARE TAX CREDIT

Only 5 percent of U.S. households now conform to the traditional ideal of a working father and a mother who stays at home full-time taking care of minor children. So there are a lot of people who can take advantage of the child- and dependent-care credit on their federal tax returns. Surprisingly, many don't.

Any good income-tax guide will explain the rules. Basically, if your work causes you to incur expenses for care of a dependent, you may be eligible. Potential savings: up to $4,800 a year if you have more than one qualifying dependent.

▶ TAKE COLLEGE-EDUCATION TAX CREDITS

Hope Scholarship and Lifetime Learning Credits can be deducted by qualifying taxpayers from whatever income tax is owed in the year they are taken.

For each of the first two years of college or other postsecondary education, the Hope Scholarship Credit allows a qualifying family to claim a maximum tax credit of $1,500 per year per student for tuition and related expenses (including registration fees but not meals or housing).

The Lifetime Learning Credit allows qualifying taxpayers a 20 percent tax credit that can be applied to the first $5,000 of qualified expenses through 2002 and the first $10,000 of qualified expenses thereafter. This 20 percent credit applies to junior and senior college students, graduate students, or working Americans pursuing job-skill training. The credits can be spread out however the taxpayer chooses to do so.

To qualify for these education tax credits, single taxpayers must have adjusted gross incomes below $40,000 to get the full credit (it's phased out entirely at $50,000). Joint filers must have AGIs below $80,000 (phased out entirely at $100,000). The income qualifications are the same no matter how many children are in college at the same time.

The expenses must be those of the taxpayer, spouse, or dependents under the age of twenty-four. Half-time students qualify for both Hope Scholarship and Lifetime Learning Credits.

In any given tax year, a taxpayer may elect for each eligible student *either* the Hope Credit, the Lifetime Learning Credit, or the exclusion from gross income for certain distributions from an education IRA. Also, in any year you choose to claim a Hope or Lifetime Learning Credit, you cannot cash in Series EE savings bonds and still claim the tax break on the bonds' interest earnings.

▶ TAKE DEDUCTIONS FOR STUDENT-LOAN INTEREST

A deduction from adjusted gross income is allowed to qualifying taxpayers on interest payments on any qualified education loan during the first sixty months of the loan. The maximum deduction is $1,500 in 1999, $2,000 in 2000, and $2,500 thereafter. To qualify, single taxpayers must have AGIs of less than $40,000 to get the full deduction (it's phased out entirely at $55,000) and joint filers must have AGIs of less than $60,000 (phased out entirely at $75,000).

▶ SHIFT INCOME TO YOUR KIDS

A dependent child under fourteen can receive up to $600 unearned income (dividends and interest) and pay no income tax on it. On the next $600 in income, the tax is 15 percent. After that, the child is taxed at your rate.

You can give a child up to $10,000 a year ($20,000 with your spouse) without paying any gift tax. So it is easy to shift income-producing assets to your child and save on taxes overall. If your rate is 28 percent, you would pay $280 in taxes on $1,000 in dividends or interest. Your child would pay only $60 (0 percent of $600 plus 15 percent of $400). Savings: $220 a year.

After the child turns fourteen, all income, earned or unearned, of less than $22,100 is taxed at 15 percent.

▶ TRANSFER CAPITAL GAINS TO YOUR KIDS

Suppose you want to sell a stock or a mutual fund you bought years ago, your basis price (what you bought it for) is $2,500, and it is now worth $12,500 (a very pleasant "suppose" indeed). If you pay a capital-gains tax of 20 percent, you would pay $2,000 in taxes on your $10,000 gain. Since you and your spouse can give up to $20,000 a year to a child without paying a gift tax, you could instead make a gift of the stock to a child over fourteen, who would pay only $1,500 in taxes on the sale.

One reason you might want to do this is because the stock represents money you had put away for college expenses anyway so making the gift and having your child pay a tuition bill is a simple way of picking up an extra $500. Unfortunately, there's a catch-22 to transferring assets if your child will be applying for financial aid to attend college; see Chapter 11.

▶ PUT KIDS ON THE PAYROLL

A child's *earned* income (distinct from unearned income; see previous two tips) is taxed at that child's tax rate. If you own a business, you can pay a child a salary for work performed, thus shifting some family income into a lower tax bracket. What's more, the child can take the full standard deduction against earned income, so a lot of the salary won't be taxed. There are other considerations, of course, and what you pay the child must bear some relationship to the value of the services performed.

▶ CONSIDER FILING SEPARATE TAX RETURNS

If you are a two-income family and either you or your spouse has high medical or business expenses, you may be able to reduce your tax bill by filing separate returns. If one of you had $3,750 in medical expenses and your joint adjusted gross income was $50,000, for instance, you couldn't deduct any portion of your medical expenses because they are not more than 7.5 percent of your AGI. If you filed separately, and your AGI was $25,000, you could deduct $1,875.

▶ BIG TAX REFUND EVERY YEAR? BIG MISTAKE

Some people seem to feel a tax refund check is a kind of gift from Uncle Sam. In fact, the gift has been from them to the IRS. By overwithholding taxes from your salary check, you are losing the interest income you could have earned on that money all year long.

If you usually get a refund check, review the number of deductions you have been claiming and consider adding to it.

▶ GET HELP ON THE INTERNET

- The IRS web site (http://www.irs.ustreas.gov) is, surprisingly, both easy to navigate and useful. You can get free downloads of any IRS form you are likely to need as well as advice on how to fill it out. For anyone who ever waited for hours to connect by telephone to the IRS information service, this is a giant leap forward.

- A good place to start a search for any kind of tax help is http://www.taxsites.com, which groups hundreds of different tax web sites into categories (state taxes, help and tips, etc.).

5

Shopping Smart for Appliances, Furniture, Housewares, and Gifts

§ §

When they buy cars, most people are very aware of the miles-per-gallon numbers and realize that an 18-mile-a-gallon gas guzzler is going to cost a lot more over the long run than a car that gets 30 miles to the gallon. Yet as conscious as many people have become about the costs of energy, not many estimate the long-term costs before they buy a new appliance. In some areas of the country, the cost of the electricity to run a refrigerator during its working life will be five times the amount paid for it. Given a worst-case energy scenario and a refrigerator that lasts for twenty years, even that estimate could prove to be extremely conservative.

What this means is that the initial price of an appliance is only one factor—in many cases, the least important factor—in deciding how much that appliance will actually cost over its lifetime.

The same basic point (that initial cost is only one factor shoppers must evaluate) is also true when you make purchase decisions about furniture and housewares you hope to use for years to come. You will usually save money by paying more for quality goods and taking good care of them.

That said, there is no reason to pay more than is necessary for those quality goods. Tips in this chapter suggest both strategies and specific sources for value-conscious shoppers. One simple thing to keep in mind if you tend to be a bit shy or just don't like to negotiate: If you ask for a lower price, the answer may be no. But you haven't lost a thing. *If you never ask for a lower price, you will never get one.*

▶ IS IT A STORE OR A BAZAAR?

The sign on the television set says: "Retail price $899. Our price $599." But the $599 is crossed out and "Special sale! $549!" is written next to it. You are in a chain discount-appliance store. What's your next step?

Quietly ask the salesclerk, out of hearing range of other customers, for the store's *best* price on the set. Often, without any further conversation, he'll call up the item on his computer terminal and come back with an even lower price than the supposed "special." At that point, you can either accept that price or make an even lower offer. Depending on all sorts of factors you can never know—including inventory levels, the chain's cash-flow situation, and deals offered to the chain by that manufacturer—your offer may be accepted (although probably only after an act involving the clerk and a "manager") or rejected.

Many people are surprised by how many American retailers really do operate these days as open bazaars where quoted prices are only a starting point. Therefore, it is foolish not to attempt to negotiate a price on most high-ticket items. If you have decided on a specific brand and model, first call three or four stores to get their "best price." If one store's price is higher than another's, let it know. You'll get a sense of how much maneuvering room there is on the price of that model.

Caution: The oldest trick of the bazaar operator is to

quote you an extremely low price, whether by telephone or on the selling floor, then return from the stockroom apologizing for suddenly being out of that model but ready to give you a terrific deal on an even better one. Tell the clerk you won't deal with a "bait and switch" operation and walk away. Slowly, of course. There just might be one left of the model you want after all.

▶ HAGGLE WITH OWNERS AND MANAGERS

In many stores, it is useless to ask clerks for discounts off ticketed prices; they aren't authorized to make special deals. But the owner or store manager definitely can. If you figure the store is working on a 40 percent markup and you ask for a 25 percent discount, an owner can quickly decide that a 15 percent profit is better than no sale at all. Remember to do your haggling quietly, out of hearing of other customers.

▶ LIKE A FLOOR MODEL? DO YOUR HOMEWORK

When you identify the manufacturer and model number of a store's floor model, call the manufacturer's toll-free number (dial 800-555-1212 for toll-free directory assistance) or check out its web site to see what the cost would be if you bought direct. Armed with this information, you should be able to get the store to match that price—and avoid the shipping charges you would have incurred if you had bought direct.

▶ ESTABLISH YOUR TARGET PRICE ON THE INTERNET

The nonprofit *Center for the Study of Services* has a web site (http://www.checkbook.org) where you can find a "target price"—the lowest price the center finds in its continuous survey of retailers nationally—on over five thousand brand-name products, from televisions and audio equipment to dishwashers and watches.

You can also comparison-shop a wide range of products at the *Compare.Net* site (http://www.compare.net). All you do is check off options you want in a product and you will get a comprehensive listing of all the available products and models that meet your criteria. The site also has a section of "smart tips" for getting a good buy.

▶ "THROW IN" SOME ACCESSORIES

Even if you can't get a reduced price on a big-ticket appliance, you may be able to get the store to "throw in" with your purchase some kind of accessory to it that you would otherwise have to buy.

▶ "WILL IT BE ON SALE SOON?"

This is often a much better question to ask a store clerk or owner than "Will you reduce the price for me?" Once you are told that the item will probably be on sale, say, next month, simply ask if you could save another trip and get the sale price right now.

▶ SHOP AT THE END OF THE MONTH

Stores that have not met their monthly sales quotas may be more anxious to sell at reduced prices.

▶ SKIP EXTENDED WARRANTIES

See Chapter 4 for a discussion of the purpose of insurance, which is what an extended (beyond the time limit offered by the manufacturer) warranty on an appliance or an electronic product really is. In the case of the extended warranties offered (and usually aggressively sold) by retailers, the cost of the premium (the price of the warranty) is far higher than it should be, given the risk it protects you against.

The salesperson you deal with probably gets a very healthy commission on sales of extended warranties. And the stores can afford the commissions, because many of them make as much on the sale of the warranty as they do on the sale of the product itself; they may make even more.

A better idea: When you buy a new appliance, put half the money an extended warranty would have cost into a repair fund. Unless you have bought an inferior product or are very unlucky, you should cover necessary repairs and save a lot of money.

And check your credit card. You can automatically extend the manufacturer's warranty on an appliance or electronic product, usually for an extra year, if you use the right credit card to buy it (American Express and some Visa and MasterCards; check to see if yours is one of them). Unless you can get a cash discount, this is an extra reason to use your card. See Chapter 8 for more on penny-pinching credit cards.

▶ OFFER TO PAY CASH

If you offer to save a small store the commission it pays when you use a credit card to make your purchases, it may be more willing to negotiate.

▶ ASK ABOUT CORPORATE DISCOUNTS

If you own your own company, many stores offer corporate discounts. For instance, if you are incorporated, even the august Tiffany & Company will give you a 10 percent discount. Actually, if you have even a part-time business on the side, all you may need in some places is a business card, and perhaps a separate bank account.

▶ CHECK IT OUT FIRST IN *CONSUMER REPORTS*

Consumer Reports is published by the nonprofit Consumers Union, which independently tests different products and services and rates them in terms of safety, relative quality, and price competitiveness. This is the best single source of advice on buying just about anything from a VCR to a new convertible. The writing is clear and straightforward, if humorless and for our tastes too often a bit self-righteous. We wouldn't buy a major appliance without knowing how *CR* rates different brands and models, but we skip its monthly report on readers' movie preferences and often disagree with taste panels that rate various foods and beverages. You may also sometimes be unable to find a model of a product highly rated by *CR* because that model is no longer available.

If you are at a point in your life—perhaps just moving into a first house—where you are making a lot of decisions on major purchases, a subscription to *Consumer Reports* could be an especially wise investment. Or do what we do: Make a few notes about some upcoming purchasing decisions, then visit your local library to check them out with *CR*. You can also access *Consumer Reports* on the Internet at http://www.ConsumerReports. com. For most full reports, you will have to subscribe (currently $24 a year), but there is a lot of useful buying advice that is free as well.

▶ CALL AHEAD

When you are shopping for an unusual item or a specific model, telephone ahead to see if the store has it. It's a simple idea, but it can save a lot of time and cut down on travel expenses.

▶ BUY IN OFF-SEASONS

Sales of air conditioners peak in the summer months. The best time to buy them is in September, when stores want to unload excess inventory, and in January and February, when just about all big-ticket appliances— including ranges, refrigerators, washers, and dryers— are discounted most heavily.

The same principle applies in just about every product category. Lawn furniture, outdoor grills, garden tools, and golf and tennis equipment are much better buys in August and September than in May and June, the beginning of the season when people are planning outdoor living activities. Those are the months to buy utensils for indoor cooking and appliances like humidifiers and portable heaters.

Beware of calendars that purport to tell you exactly the best month to buy everything. They are no longer dependable. In fact, because "everybody knows" the best time to buy china and silver is in February, manufacturers and retailers target that month for widely promoted "sales" in which prices may not be as low as they are later in the year.

▶ SAVE RECEIPTS, WARRANTIES, AND MANUALS

Get a receipt for everything you buy, and save every receipt for a major purchase—appliances, furniture, cars, and household repairs and improvements. To be supersafe, put these in a safe-deposit box; you'll have proof of ownership for the insurance company if the purchase is destroyed in a fire or other catastrophe.

▶ USE THE ENERGYGUIDE LABELS ON APPLIANCES

Federal laws mandate the display of EnergyGuide labels on most home appliances. The efficiency ratings claimed on these labels are based on standardized tests and they are generally reliable. The ratings are expressed in one of two ways. Energy Efficiency Ratings (EERs) measure the efficiency of one product in relation to similar products. With EERs, the higher the rating, the more efficient the product. For instance, a central air conditioner rated 10 would use 50 percent more energy than one rated 15.

The second, more common, way appliance labels measure energy use is in terms of dollars. The dollar figures on an energy label represent the estimated annual cost of operating that specific appliance. The lower the dollar amount, the more efficient the product.

The problem is, most people don't do much more than glance at the big dollar number in the middle of the label under the arrow. Let's say that on refrigerator Model A, the number is $80 (the annual cost of energy to run this model in an average home). On Model B, it is $110. You prefer Model B and decide that the extra $30 a year isn't too great a price to pay for the features you like.

You are making a hasty decision. Before you shop for any major appliance, make sure you check your latest utility bills to see how much you are paying per kilowatt hour for electricity. We, for instance, live in an area with particularly high energy costs. The $80 and $110 annual costs given on the two refrigerators in question are probably based on a national average cost of 8.25 cents per kilowatt hour. But our cost per kilowatt hour is 14.44 cents.

If you divide $80 by 8.25 cents, you know that Model A is expected to consume 975.61 kilowatt hours in an average home. Model B is expected to consume 1,333.33 kilowatt hours in that same average home. But our costs would be $141 annually for Model A (975.61 × 14.44 cents) and $192 (1,333.33 × 14.44 cents) for Model B. That makes the difference between the two models not $30, but $51 a year.

That annual difference of $51 adds up to $1,020 in twenty years, the life span of an average refrigerator. So we have a major incentive to buy the most energy-efficient refrigerator we can find, even if its initial cost is hundreds of dollars more.

Actually, of course, the initial cost of energy-efficient refrigerators is nearly always less, not more, than less efficient models, which are equipped with devices such as automatic icemakers and through-door dispensers.

▶ BUY A GAS RANGE WITH AN ELECTRONIC IGNITION SYSTEM

If you cook with gas, avoid ranges that use pilot lights. An automatic ignition system will cut down your gas use by at least one third.

▶ CHECK UTILITY REBATES FOR EFFICIENT APPLIANCES

Many utilities now offer rebates to customers who buy energy-efficient air conditioners, refrigerators, freezers, heat pumps, water heaters, and other appliances. Before you buy a new major appliance, call the conservation office of your utility company to see what rebates are offered.

▶ CHECK OUT SECONDHAND STORES

There are some things we wouldn't consider buying secondhand, but there are many more where the idea doesn't bother us at all. We must have a lot of company, because there has been a definite growth trend in specialized secondhand retailers in the past few years. One franchise company, *Grow-Biz International* (800-433-2540; http://www.growbiz.com), has more than 1,400 outlets nationwide, each specializing in one of five areas: sporting goods, computers, products for children, musical instruments, and compact discs.

You can find other secondhand shops near you listed on the Internet at both http://www.narts.org and http://www.sonic.net/~rtnc/resale

▶ BUY FROM MAIL-ORDER AND INTERNET DISCOUNTERS

It's a lot easier to find deep discounts on appliances, furniture, and other items if you are looking for them and comparison-shopping in a large metropolitan area, where strong competition holds prices down. If you live in a less populated area, your best sources of bargains may be discount catalogs that you can order from by mail, telephone, or the Internet.

You can save on just about anything by mail, and often the prices are better than at any retail store in the country—large metropolitan area or not. The next few tips list specialized mail-order and Internet sources for various kinds of merchandise that we, and our network of sources, have found particularly noteworthy for price, dependability, and service.

In addition to these specialized sources, there are a number of general shopping sites on the Internet that offer a wide variety of merchandise at discount prices. Among the best:

- *Shopping.com* (http://www.shopping.com) sells just about everything you might expect to find in a department store, except apparel.
- *Macy's* (http://www.macys.com) has over 250,000 items available for on-line purchase and a virtual community bridal registry for gifts, dresses, and wedding planning.

▶ AUDIO/APPLIANCES/VIDEO/ELECTRONICS BY MAIL

All of the discount operations listed below will give price quotes by phone but require manufacturers' model numbers. None of them sell "gray market" merchandise (products intended for sale in other countries; their manufacturers may not warrant them if sold to U.S. customers). Make sure you know exact shipping charges and return policies before ordering, and use a credit card if you do.

- *LVT Price Quote Hotline* (516-234-8884) Major appliances, vacuum cleaners, video, and electronics. Free catalog.
- *Dial-a-Brand* (800-237-3220) Large and small appliances, video, air conditioners.
- *Crutchfield* (800-955-9009; http://www.crutchfield.com) Home and car audio, home theater, video. The free catalog is especially informative.

▶ CAMERAS AND PHOTOGRAPHIC SUPPLIES BY MAIL

- *Porter's Camera Store* (800-553-2001; http://www.porters.com) A free catalog any camera enthusiast should receive regularly, with a wide range of heavily discounted merchandise.
- *Access Discount Camera* (888-293-4422; http://www.accesscamera.com) This is an outstanding web site, offering a wide selection of discounted cameras and equipment.

- *Mystic Color Lab* (800-367-6061; http://www.mysticcolorlab.com) A good film-processing service at terrific prices. Contact for price quotes and free film mailers.

▶ **FURNITURE BY MAIL**

- *Quality Furniture Market of Lenoir* (704-728-2946) Deeply discounted prices quoted by phone or mail on furniture and bedding from hundreds of different manufacturers.
- *Blackwelder's Industries* (800-438-0201; http://www.homefurnish.com/blackwelders) Various catalogs available for nominal costs, refundable with purchase, on high-quality furniture, clocks, pianos, rugs, carpeting, and home accessories. The on-line catalog is particularly impressive.
- *Cherry Hill Furniture* (800-852-0933; http://www.cherryhillfurn.com) Home and office furniture, rugs, and carpeting. Free brochure and price quotes by phone.
- *Ephraim Marsh* (704-782-0814) Made-to-order traditional furniture. The catalog ($5, refundable) is worth having just for its descriptions of quality points in each group of furniture. Will use your fabric.

▶ **BETTER THAN MAIL OR INTERNET: GO TO NORTH CAROLINA**

It is no accident that all of the furniture discounters mentioned above are located in North Carolina. The state produces at least 60 percent of the furniture sold in the United States and hundreds of deep-discount retail furniture operations are now located in and around the cities of High Point and Hickory. If you are planning to buy enough high-ticket items, making a special trip to the area is a good idea. A few North Carolina furniture manufacturers, who want to pacify their retail customers in the other forty-nine states, have put pressure on the North Carolina retail mail-order operations to stop discounting their products out of state. But if you shop right there, you'll find furniture from all manufacturers at consistently lower prices than anywhere else in the country.

Although they are deep discounters, many of the furniture retailers in the area operate handsome, spacious showrooms and offer professional interior-design assistance.

Before you go, contact the Convention and Visitors Bureaus in Hickory (800-849-5093; http://www.hickory metro.com) and High Point (800-720-5255; http://www. highpoint.org). Each will send you big packets of maps, brochures, and special deals on motel accommodations.

▶ LIGHTING BY MAIL

■ *Golden Valley Lighting* (800-735-3377; http://www. gvlight.com) sells table and floor lamps as well as lighting fixtures from most major manufacturers at discounts that range from 25 to 50 percent off retail prices. Make sure you have the exact model number and other necessary specifications when you call for a price quote. A catalog ($5, refundable, but free for Internet users) is also available.

▶ COOKWARE BY MAIL

■ *Broadway Panhandler* (212-966-3434) sells cookware for both home and professional use at discounts up to 40 percent. Check out the lowest prices you can find elsewhere for names like Calaphon, Sabatier, and Braun, then call here with exact model numbers.

■ *Peerless Restaurant Supplies* (800-255-3663; http:// www.prls.com) is a distributor to the restaurant industry but its 224-page catalog ($10), with over six thousand items in stock, is a good bet for serious home cooks as well.

■ *The Internet Kitchen* (888-730-0199; http://www. your-kitchen.com) has a good web site and offers competitive prices on a limited variety of quality cookware, cutlery, etc.

▶ WALLPAPER BY MAIL

The companies listed below offer big discounts off the retail prices of virtually all wallpapers. Call with the name of the sample book and page number of the wallpaper you want to buy, and you will normally get an immediate price quote, usually 40 to 50 percent less than the suggested retail price and often 20 percent less than retail-store discounters offer. Delivery is usually quick and efficient as well.

We have felt a bit guilty about using our local store's sample books to choose wallpaper and then giving our order to a lower-overhead competitor. So we were glad to hear from Trudy Myers, a reader from Nanty Glo, Pennsylvania. She wrote to tell us that when she quotes the best price she gets from a mail-order supplier, her local wallpaper store will match it. We'll try the same strategy next time; as Trudy points out, all the store can say is no.

- *Peerless,* 800-999-0898.
- *Wallpaper Outlet,* 800-488-9255.

▶ CHINA, CRYSTAL, AND FLATWARE BY MAIL

Once we know patterns, these are the places we check first when buying wedding presents. We have learned that prices vary greatly. One source may have much deeper discounts on one china pattern than another, but the reverse can be true on the next pattern. Check as many as you can before buying.

- *Barrons* (800-538-6340) sells only by mail and will quote discounts of from 25 to 50 percent off the list prices of tableware and gifts. Free catalog.
- *Thurber's* (800-848-7237; http://www.thurbers.com) had some of the best prices during our most recent shop-by-phone experience.
- *Ross-Simon* (800-556-7376; http://www.ross-simon. com) is a major retailer of jewelry, gifts, and tableware. The web site is particularly good.

- *Fortunoff* (800-283-2234; http://www.fortunoff.com) is also a major retailer of jewelry and gifts. Good catalogs and will quote prices by phone.

▶ STUFF FOR BABIES BY MAIL

- *One Step Ahead* (800-274-8440) guarantees to match any other catalog's prices on the products it sells—feeding and safety equipment, travel accessories, furniture, toys, clothing, etc.
- *The Right Start Catalog* (800-548-8531) has good prices on a wide range of merchandise and a friendly, helpful staff.

These two specialized catalogs are hardly the only good sources of discount baby products. Among general merchandisers, *JCPenney* (800-222-6161; http://www.jcpenney.com) has especially good catalogs and prices devoted to children's products. Finally, check out a book called *Baby Bargains* by Denise and Alan Fields. It is filled with money-saving tips, sources, and name-brand reviews. You'll find it at most libraries or at discount bookstores for about $11.

▶ SHEETS AND TOWELS BY MAIL

- *Fieldcrest Cannon Factory Outlet Store* (800-841-3336 or 800-236-1912) sells sheets, towels, blankets, bath rugs, and comforters at savings of 40 to 60 percent. Friends who can afford the best buy Fieldcrest Charisma sheets and towels this way, saving 60 percent on the most expensive mass-produced linens made in the United States. The telephone representatives are especially helpful.

▶ CONSIDER SECONDS IN SHEETS AND TOWELS

Now that everyone knows about January white sales and many, if not most, people wait for them, buying in January no longer guarantees you the best bargains in sheets and towels. In fact, manufacturers and department stores now target January as a key sales month even for new merchandise. "On sale" and "Marked down" don't necessarily mean a thing.

The real bargains in sheets and towels are often found in stores and factory outlets selling discontinued patterns and/or "seconds" of brand-name merchandise. Most often, particularly with sheets and towels, it is very difficult to tell why a second is a second—a skipped stitch that won't affect wearability, or perhaps a slight variation in color that will be completely unnoticeable after one or two washings. Yet 50 to 75 percent discounts off list prices are common.

▶ STOP BUYING GIFTS ON A DEADLINE

Most people make the same mistake over and over again, year after year, when they buy gifts. A week before Aunt Betty's birthday, they begin to think about what to get her. Then they rush out and buy something often not quite the right color or model. They also make a panicked whirlwind tour of stores two weeks before Christmas to buy for everyone on their list.

These are the kind of gift shoppers that swell retailer profits, but they are wasting their own time and money.

The alternative is simple and guaranteed effective. Except for unpredictable events like weddings, you know exactly who you will buy gifts for annually. Get a small, pocket-size notebook and make a list—every birthday and anniversary as well as everyone on your Christmas list. Update the list once a year to add graduations, bar mitzvahs, and other predictable special occasions.

Take this notebook with you whenever you think there is even a remote chance you will be shopping. Every time you enter a store of any kind, take ten seconds to review the list. Aunt Betty lives in Vermont and loves sweaters of all kinds. You are on vacation in Mexico in April and see two different sweaters in her size that would cost at least twice as much at home. Too bad her birthday was a month ago, right?

Wrong. Buy both. For the next two years, you won't have to spend frustrating hours shopping specifically for her. And you've bought two years' worth of birthday presents for the price of one.

Obviously, there are limits to your attic space. Ten years from now, Aunt Betty might be two sizes larger. Styles may change. But the principle is an important one. The right gift, at the right price, simply doesn't appear as if by magic just because someone's birthday is a week away. The same sweater will nearly *always* cost much more on December 1 than it will in April. Different categories of merchandise are invariably cheaper during certain times of the year.

Remember to make notations of what you have bought in your notebook, or you are likely to forget what's up in the attic. Check items off as they are given. For safety's sake, because your notebook will become increasingly invaluable as a record of what you have given and what you've got stored, photocopy its pages from time to time and keep the copy in a safe place.

The only hard part of this is getting in the notebook habit. Once you have, you'll save hours of frustration and a lot of money—easily 30 percent or more.

▶ BEWARE THE $50 ROLEX

Of course you know you'll never find a real Rolex or Cartier watch for the price of the illegal counterfeit you may encounter for sale at a flea market or on the street. Some people are tempted, though—it may look so "real."

The sad fact is that, when compared directly with the original, the counterfeit invariably looks shoddy. Save yourself the embarrassment of being discovered.

▶ SHOP OUTLET STORES

Among the many companies that sell seconds and irregulars, first-quality goods, or both through factory outlets are Bose (audio equipment), Corning Revere (Corningware, Pyrex, Corelle, and Revereware brand cookware and dinnerware), Dansk (Scandinavian-design cookware, flatware, gifts), Emerson Radio (Emerson and Scott electronic equipment), Hamilton Watches, Lenox (china), Oneida Silver (stainless and silver-plated flatware), Royal Doulton (china), Samsonite (luggage), and Wamsutta/Springmaid (sheets, towels, linens).

Outlet stores are unquestionably sources of great bargains, but see Chapter 8 for shopping strategies to use.

▶ TRY AN ON-LINE AUCTION

Be very careful when buying anything from an on-line auction site. Your primary concern is the reputation and reliability of the seller. Some on-line auction sites have bulletin boards available on which previous buyers rate sellers. Especially if the seller hasn't established credibility on the site, make sure you pay with a credit card. Don't buy anything from someone who simply has an E-mail address. Get a telephone number and call before buying.

Warnings aside, on-line auctions can be a very good way to get great deals on a variety of products, from computers to appliances of all kinds. Among the auction sites you should check out: http://www.ebay.com; http://www.onsale.com; http://www.bid.com; and http://www.firstauction.com.

▶ SHOPPING ABROAD: AVOIDING THE VAT

Most European countries, Japan, Israel, and Canada add a hidden tax (usually called a value-added tax) onto the cost of merchandise sold domestically. To encourage tourism, however, most also allow foreigners to escape some or all of this tax (which in Europe can be as high as 20 percent of the displayed retail purchase price), especially on expensive items.

In some stores, such as Harrods in London, the clerks are so accustomed to selling to foreigners that all you have to do is tell them you are an American and they'll make sure all of your tax-avoiding paperwork is done. You may have to work a bit harder elsewhere.

It doesn't make sense to ask about the VAT on low-cost items, and most countries spare their merchants the bother by setting a minimum purchase amount for a VAT refund (ranging from less than $100 in England to about $500 in Italy). Most countries also limit VAT refunds to purchases of merchandise, not services.

Here's what to do:

Before you buy a high-ticket item, ask if the store participates in the local VAT-reduction program, if your purchase qualifies, and how much your VAT refund will come to. Usually, the minimum amount necessary for a refund is not on a per-item basis but on a per-store basis—purchases listed on one form. This makes shopping in as few places as possible preferable.

Buy with a credit card if at all possible (it isn't everywhere) to get the best exchange rate on both the purchase and the refund.

When you leave the country, you show the customs official all the VAT refund forms you have received from stores. You either get a refund from customs then and there, or you mail validated forms back to the appropriate stores. They will either credit your account (if you paid by credit card) or eventually send you a refund check.

Many countries permit stores to deduct the VAT from the purchase price if you don't take possession of the item but instead have it mailed to your home address. If such shipments are limited each day to merchandise worth less than $50, you don't have to pay a customs duty tax on them. Otherwise, you will have to pay U.S. duty and clearance expenses.

There can be enough of a hassle involved in all of this to discourage even a dedicated penny pincher if only a few dollars are involved, but it is more than worthwhile if you buy an expensive piece of jewelry or an antique vase.

▶ BUY 364 DAYS EARLY

Don't you feel foolish standing in a long line at the hardware store on December 24, waiting to pay for Christmas tree lights you know will cost 50 percent less at the same place (with shorter lines) two days later?

Christmas tree lights and ornaments, Christmas cards, holiday gift wrapping—all go on sale after December 25 for at least 50 percent off nearly everywhere. Even if you overestimate next year's needs, sooner or later everything you buy will be used.

The price of chocolates goes down right after Easter. Look for sales in wine and liquor stores right after New Year's Eve. And why not send a dozen roses to your valentine on February 15 (typically at a discount of at least 75 percent off February 14 prices) with a note declaring your ardor 364 days *ahead* of time. Now, *that's* romantic (just don't try it as a *substitute* for a gift the day before).

▶ SHOP CHARITY THRIFT SHOPS

Many churches, synagogues, hospitals, and charitable organizations operate thrift shops either year-round or on an occasional basis. Unless you are an inveterate shopper, forget 98 percent of them. The ones you are interested in are located in the most affluent sections of your metropolitan area. What gets donated to them is sometimes anything but thrift-shop junk. Especially if you are looking for crystal, china, cutlery, and high-quality cookware, try a couple of these first.

▶ CHOOSE THE MAILING LISTS YOU WANT TO BE ON

Why settle for what they want to send you? When you shop for the first time in a store you like, don't leave until you've asked to be put on its mailing list. Most retailers now have a mail-order capability, and many send advance notice to special customers when they are having a sale.

When you shop in a factory-outlet mall, ask to be put on its mailing list, too. You'll learn about mallwide sales in advance.

§ Minimizing Car Expenses §

You should find some useful money-saving tips in this chapter no matter what kind of car you now own. But the first step in minimizing automobile expenses is to calculate what owning and operating a specific make and model will cost on an annual basis *before* you buy it.

One of the keys to this process is estimating the price you will be able to get for a car when you sell it or trade it in. Some new cars will still be worth 50 percent of their purchase price four years later. Others will lose 75 percent of their value. If you buy an $18,000 car and trade it in for $9,000 four years later, it has cost you $2,250 a year plus fuel, maintenance, insurance, etc. If you buy a $16,000 car and trade it in for $4,000 four years later, your cost is $3,000 a year.

Nobody knows for sure how much any car will be worth years from now, but the annual (December) auto issue of *Kiplinger's Personal Finance Magazine* uses historical data on different manufacturers and models to estimate the two- and four-year resale value of the next year's cars. It's good information to have. Note especially how rapidly all new cars depreciate in value during their first two years. Typically, a car that is worth 55 percent of its initial price after two years is worth from 40 to 45 percent after four years. There is no more compelling argument for either buying a good used car or hanging on to the car you own for a lot longer than two years.

Whether you are buying a new or used car, you should also study the annual (April) auto issue of *Consumer Reports,* which is full of information about safety, repair records, prices, fuel economy, comfort and convenience, and handling on the road. Most libraries have both magazines.

Another expense to consider before you buy is what your insurance premiums will be. Similarly priced cars do not necessarily cost the same to insure. The difference, based on the car model's past and estimated future claims for theft and accidents, can be significant. Before you buy, talk to your insurance agent.

Working with an insurance agent, the magazines mentioned above, and prices negotiated with three different dealers in our area, we estimated annual costs on three similarly priced makes and models. The results are shown in the "Annual Cost Worksheet" in this chapter. The most expensive car in terms of initial price turned out to be the least expensive over a four-year period.

When you next buy a car, use the same worksheet to establish estimated annual costs for each make and model you are considering. In fact, why not get your figures together now and estimate what your present car is costing you.

Once you actually analyze how much you spend to own and operate a car on an annual basis, you may come to some surprising conclusions. We have city friends who figure they saved at least $3,000 a year by getting rid of their car and renting one when they went away on weekends or on a vacation trip. Many people decide that the convenience of a second car is not worth the price.

▶ SAVE MORE THAN 50 PERCENT ON OIL CHANGES AND LUBRICATION

Today's cars need less normal maintenance than the gas guzzlers of the 1960s and '70s, and this kind of maintenance is easier to perform than it ever was. The complicated stuff in modern cars—electronics—usually gets replaced, not repaired. But you'd never know that when you look at the bloated bills most new car dealers hand you after a normal periodic warranty checkup.

If something is wrong or you even suspect something might be wrong with your car, by all means take it to a good mechanic or back to the dealer. Otherwise, use one of the franchised quick-lube-and-oil-change outlets. Their employees are trained to check all the essentials—belts, tires, brakes, etc.—lubricate what's necessary, and change the oil and oil filter.

Some manufacturers insist you must use factory-authorized parts to keep your warranty in force. No problem. Stop by the dealer's service center, buy a factory-authorized oil filter, and give it to the quick-lube outlet when you drive in, which will deduct the price of an oil filter from a bill that is nearly always at least 50 percent less than the same service would have cost at a car dealer or a full-service garage.

▶ CHANGE MOTOR OIL MORE FREQUENTLY

Most cars spend the better part of their lives being driven for relatively short distances in urban areas, with lots of stops and starts for traffic lights and traffic jams. These are exactly the conditions that age an engine prematurely, so it is important not to pinch pennies by stretching out the intervals between oil changes. Unless your car is driven under ideal conditions—long trips at a constant 55 miles per hour in temperate weather—

Annual Cost Worksheet for a New Car
(Sell/trade-in after 4 years and 60,000 miles)

		Car 1	Car 2	Car 3
A.	Estimated purchase price (including taxes)	$17,100	$16,500	$17,400
B.	Estimated resale value	6,000	4,800	7,830
C.	Subtract B from A	11,100	11,700	9,570
D.	Annual cost (C divided by 4 years)	2,775	2,925	2,393
E.	Estimated annual insurance costs	1,200	1,150	920
F.	Estimated cost of gas @ $1.20* a gallon, 15,000 miles a year (Divide 15,000 by estimated miles per gallon; multiply by $1.20)	857 (21 mpg)	720 (25 mpg)	643 (28 mpg)
G.	Estimated average yearly maintenance	200	240	130
H.	Estimated average yearly repairs/new parts	350	300	150
	TOTAL ANNUAL COST	$ 5,382	$ 5,335	$ 4,236

*Adjust to current conditions

don't go much more than three thousand miles or three months between oil and filter changes.

▶ GAS-SAVING TIPS

- *Don't pay for worthless higher-octane-rated gas.* It is a waste of money ever to buy gasoline with a higher octane rating than is specified in your owner's manual (for most cars other than high-performance V-6s and V-8s, unleaded 87 octane). Some people think their car's engine needs a "super" gas treat now and then, that higher octane is somehow better for the engine. It isn't, despite the claims of the oil-company ads. One note of caution: Modern engines do need high-detergent fuels with special additives. Stations selling no-name brands may offer cheaper gas with the octane rating you require, but poor-quality fuel can reduce efficiency and cause engine problems. Best to stick with the brands from the major oil companies.

- *Pay cash and pump it yourself.* Why pay cents a gallon extra to use a credit card at those stations that offer a discount for cash sales? And why pay cents extra to have someone else pump gas for you unless you are also getting some other useful service free? It's usually quicker, and requires hardly any more effort on your part, to use the self-service lane.

- *Buy gas early in the morning.* Especially in the hot summer months, you'll get more for your money—as much as 5 percent more—if you buy gas before the sun's heat has expanded the gas in the service station's fuel tank.

- *Don't top off your fuel tank.* Again, especially in hot weather, don't pump more gas in your tank after the automatic cutoff for a full tank. Heat may make the gas expand and overflow. You can probably get away with this simple trick, though: Turn off the meter and then pump the remaining gas out of the hose. Hold the hose vertically while you do so. You'll get a few cents of free gas.

- *Use your car's air conditioner.* Most new cars (utility

vehicles less so) have become highly efficient in terms of aerodynamic design. Especially at higher speeds over long distances, you will waste more fuel in hot weather by opening windows and creating drag than you will by turning on the air conditioner. There are still good reasons to turn the air conditioner off and open the windows, of course. When you are driving short distances at low speeds, leave the air conditioner off. Always turn it off when you are caught in a traffic jam and your car is hardly moving at all. Any engine idling with the air conditioner on in hot weather is working too hard for its own good.

■ *Check tire pressures regularly*. With the days of full-service-with-a-smile long gone at gas stations, most people put off checking tire pressures for months at a time. Yet you will lose about 2 percent fuel economy for every pound of pressure under the recommended pounds per square inch. Buy your own gauge (less than $5) and check tire pressures according to the manufacturer's recommendations at least once a month. You'll also save by prolonging the life of your tires.

■ *Check wheel alignment* whenever the car gets routine service. Even if the wheels are only slightly out of line, they can affect gas mileage as well as shorten the life of tires.

■ *Use steel-belted radials*. They are safer, last twice as long as bias-ply tires, and will give you at least a couple of extra miles per gallon.

■ *Remove your roof rack*. If you're not using it regularly, take it off to reduce both drag and the car's total weight. Clean out the trunk, too. Extra weight reduces gas mileage.

■ *Check your air filter*. A dirty filter will lower gas mileage.

■ *Don't idle a cold engine*. Letting a car idle for two or three minutes to warm up a cold engine was once a recommended procedure. That's no longer true. Modern cars need only a few seconds of idling time; any longer and you are just wasting gas. In fact, you reduce engine wear when you move the car after a fifteen-second warm-up, hold the speedometer down to under thirty for a couple of miles, then increase your speed as you see the engine temperature begin to rise.

- *Wait to use heaters and air conditioners.* In cold weather, save gas by waiting until the engine begins to warm up before turning on the heater. In hot weather, save gas by waiting until after you start the car to turn on the air conditioner.

▶ CHANGE A FEW DRIVING HABITS

If you can break a few bad driving habits, you can add at least 10 percent to your car's fuel efficiency.

- *Minimize braking.* Anticipate speed changes. When you see a red light ahead, take your foot off the accelerator and coast to it.
- *Accelerate smoothly.* Unless you are trying to fight your way onto a crowded freeway, there's no reason to jam your foot down on the pedal. Once you have reached your desired speed, keep a steady pressure on the accelerator, just enough to maintain speed.
- *55 saves money.* The average car will use 17 percent less fuel when driven at 55 mph rather than 65 mph.
- *Turn off the engine.* It takes less gas to restart the car than it takes to let it idle for more than a minute.

▶ TRADE IN YOUR CAR JUST ONE YEAR LATER

The quality of all makes of cars has improved dramatically in the past fifteen years. If you have been in the habit of trading in a car every three or four years, stretch that to four or five—or even seven to ten.

After a car is three years old, the annual cost of owning it drops dramatically. You'll probably spend more on repairs and replacement parts, but the years of big depreciation (the amount by which the car's value decreases simply because of age) are over, and insurance costs are lower. If you take proper care of your car and it remains rust-free, there is no reason not to get well over a hundred thousand miles of dependable service from it.

▶ BEFORE BUYING ANY CAR, CHECK ITS SAFETY RECORD

■ *The National Highway Traffic Safety Administration* (800-424-9393; http://www.nhtsa.dot.gov) operates an Auto Safety Hotline that you can contact to check on any safety recalls of the make, model, and year of a used car you are considering. You can also get information about how any new car model stacks up in the government's car-crash tests.

▶ GET AN INSURANCE REBATE FOR KIDS' CAR SEATS

Some insurance companies offer special deals, others offer rebates. So check yours before you buy a child safety seat. For ratings and good advice on how to use and install it, visit the National Highway Traffic Safety Administration web site (see above tip).

▶ MAXIMIZE GAS MILEAGE ON ANY CAR YOU BUY

All new-car specification sheets tell you how many miles per gallon the car supposedly will deliver in both city and highway driving conditions. All make clear you'll get better mileage with a manual transmission than with an automatic. No matter what make, model, or type of transmission you buy, if you want to get the best possible gas mileage, you should also know:

■ A car with a sunroof, even when it is closed, will get slightly worse gas mileage than the same car without one. An open sunroof can cost you a mile or more per gallon.
■ A light-colored car reflects the sun, keeping the car

cooler in hot weather. The less your air conditioner
has to work, the better your fuel efficiency.

- Cruise control is a worthwhile option. It will help you
get better mileage when you are driving on a relatively uncrowded, flat highway.
- In most of today's cars, overdrive is standard equipment. If it isn't in the car you choose, buy it as an
option. At higher speeds, it can cut your gas con-
sumption by 20 percent. In a manual-shift car, a fifth
gear is essentially the overdrive gear.

▶ SKIP FOUR-WHEEL DRIVE

Four-wheel-drive vehicles have become extremely popular, but unless you really need it, it is an expensive
option. It not only adds to the purchase price, it also
guarantees that you will spend more for gas and insurance.

▶ BEFORE BUYING, KNOW WHAT
YOU WANT

Buying a car can be a confusing process, and dealers
love a customer who will accept their explanations. Start
shopping after your research is done, not while you are
doing it.

Don't start negotiating for any car before you have
narrowed your choices to two or three models. One
good way to do this is to first spend some time in your
library with *Consumer Reports* and other publications.
You can also visit the web site of any car manufacturer;
most now have sophisticated graphic displays of interi-
ors and exteriors as well as complete specs for every
model. Most web addresses are obvious—www.buick
and www.ford—but search the automotive section of
Yahoo (http://www.yahoo.com) if the obvious doesn't
get you where you want to go.

Finally, there are a number of Internet sites that have
made comparison car shopping far easier than ever before. Our favorite—in fact one of the best web sites of
any kind we have ever used—is Microsoft's *Carpoint*

(http://www.carpoint.com). Tell Carpoint what make and model you are interested in—new or used—and you get an overview of the car, photographs, complete specifications, reviews, safety information, and comparisons with similar cars. You can pull up a screen that compares any two cars on a spec-by-spec basis. You also get both the manufacturer's suggested retail price (MSRP) and the dealer's invoice price on the car and on any options you choose to add to it. *Edmund's,* the publisher of a number of consumer automotive buying guides, has a web site that is similar to Carpoint (http://www.edmunds.com). If you are trying to decide what to buy, new or used, visit both sites.

▶ KNOW THE DEALER'S COST BEFOREHAND

This is absolutely essential information to have before you begin negotiating the purchase price on any car. As mentioned in the previous tip, both Carpoint and Edmund's give you this information; Carpoint has the edge in presentation, but double-checking with Edmund's is a good idea. The annual automobile issues of *Consumer Reports* and *Kiplinger's Personal Finance Magazine* give you the dealer cost of the car but not the options you may want. *Consumer Reports New Car Price Service* (800-205-2445) gives you very thorough pricing information but charges $12 per report. The report will also include current information on any factory-to-customer or factory-to-dealer rebates, a depreciation rating, and tips on how to deal with the dealer.

To make it even more complicated, most dealers actually pay less than their invoice price for the car. They get what is called a "holdback" from the manufacturer, usually 2 to 3 percent of the MSRP. Even if the dealer were to sell you a car with an MSRP of $20,000 for the dealer's invoice price of $17,000—"the price the showroom paid for it"—he would make $600 if his holdback was 3 percent. That's unlikely to happen unless demand for that car model is especially slow. But knowing the invoice price and the range of manufacturer's dealer allowances gives you a lot of room to negotiate.

Tell the salesperson you deal with that you want to negotiate the price based on the dealer's invoice, not on MSRP, normally about 15 percent higher. That way, your conversation will be about how much profit he'll make on the car, not on what a great deal he is giving you.

Don't expect to buy a car at invoice price; the dealer must make a profit of some kind beyond his holdback. If you want a car that is wildly popular at the time and in short supply, you may have to pay close to the MSRP. Normally, though, you should be able to negotiate a deal at 2 to 6 percent above dealer's invoice.

▶ CHECK THE "DAYS' SUPPLY" NUMBERS

Will the dealer be willing to negotiate a favorable deal for you on the make and model you want? You can get a very good idea beforehand of how strong your bargaining position will be by checking the "days' supply" statistics published once a month in *Automotive News,* which is available in some libraries. The statistics are also published in the financial pages of some newspapers. If the number of cars sitting on dealers' lots is equivalent to a hundred days' supply at the current rate of sale, you are far more likely to get a terrific deal than if there is only a twenty days' supply. The higher the days' supply, the more likely the dealer will be under pressure to move cars.

▶ CHECK ON MANUFACTURERS' INCENTIVES

Automotive News has another useful feature, a weekly column called "Incentive Watch" that lists all the rebate and financing deals currently offered by domestic and foreign manufacturers. It provides details—the amount of the rebates and expiration dates—not only for consumer deals, but also for the incentives available to dealers to sell certain makes and models. Deduct the dealer's rebate from the car's invoice price to know the true current wholesale price of the car.

▶ WHILE NEGOTIATING, DON'T TELL THE DEALER HOW YOU'LL PAY

No matter how many times salespeople ask (and ask they all will), don't talk about how you'll pay until you have reached a definite, final agreement on price. And if asked about a trade-in during the negotiating process, tell them you won't be trading in your old car. You can always change your mind after you have established the price of the new one.

Why the secrecy? You don't spend your life negotiating car deals; they do. It is in your interest to keep the discussion as simple as possible. Once financing and trade-ins become part of the picture, the deal will get so complicated you'll never know just how much your new car actually cost. Also, if the dealer knows you intend to pay cash or have arranged financing elsewhere, the price may go up. Dealers make money on financing.

▶ ASK FOR MANUFACTURERS' REBATES UP FRONT

If the manufacturer is advertising rebates, tell the dealer you want the rebate deducted from the final negotiated price of the car, not in a check mailed later on from the manufacturer. You'll save on sales tax this way.

▶ FIRM BUT PLEASANT WORKS BEST

It's easy to forget a lot of good advice on how to buy a car once you are negotiating with a skillful salesperson. You'll be subjected to sales techniques and psychological tricks that have worked in millions of negotiations. If you've done your homework, though, you'll know a lot about how strong your bargaining position is. Smile, stay with it, and be prepared to walk away. There are always other dealers.

▶ GET A PRENEGOTIATED PRICE

Some people simply hate haggling or feel they don't have the time for it. If you are one of them, you can use one of the many services that either negotiate on your behalf or have agreements with dealers to offer their customers discounted prices. In either case, once you submit a form with full details of make, model, and options, you will be given a final discounted price without ever having to deal with a salesperson. Among those offering the service:

Price/Costco and *Sam's Club* (see Chapter 1 on joining a wholesale club) now refer members to dealers who have agreed to sell vehicles at a fixed amount over their invoice cost.

Auto brokers—independent sales organizations that work for dealers, not for you—are another way to get discounted prices on a new car. You'll see their ads in classified sections of newspapers, and calls to a couple of them are an easy way to establish a price that you may or may not be able to get on your own.

Auto-by-Tel (http://www.autobytel.com) is an Internet site that sends your request to one of its 2,700 accredited dealers. A local dealer then contacts you.

Carpoint (see "Before Buying") offers a service similar to Auto-by-Tel's. Since these services are free, why not get a price this way? But do it after you have shopped around, because the price you get from an Auto-by-Tel or Carpoint dealer may be contingent on a fast response.

CarBargains (800-475-7283; http://www.consumer. checkbook.org/consumer/carbarg) is run by the Center for the Study of Services, a nonprofit consumer group in Washington, D.C. You tell CarBargains the make, model, and options you want. It then negotiates on your behalf with dealers in your area and submits bids from at least five of them, along with complete information on dealer invoice costs. CarBargains charges a hefty fee—$165—for this service, but it could very well be worth it. The other services may have conflict-of-interest problems, since they rely on their dealer networks for some of their income. In effect, by getting competing bids, CarBargains does just what you would do if you were shopping yourself. Perhaps better; dealers can't tell CarBargains to "shop around and we'll beat any price." They either bid or lose any chance of making the sale.

▶ SET YOUR PRICE ON PRICELINE

Just getting started as this edition went to press, the *Priceline* automobile service on the Web (http://www.priceline.com) allows you to set the total price you are willing to pay for a new car with the optional equipment you want. Priceline says that it then contacts all the dealers in your area, without revealing your name, to see if any of them are willing to agree in writing to accept your price. If Priceline finds a willing dealer, that dealer transmits a signed contract to priceline.com. You are then notified and pick up your car at the dealership with a certified check.

Obviously, you are not going to find a willing dealer if your price bid is too low. In fact, Priceline will almost certainly monitor bids to make certain you are a serious buyer.

Will this work? The concept is enormously appealing, but we wonder how dealers will react and if the process can really be as trouble-free as Priceline would have you believe. By the time this edition is published, we expect the Priceline automobile service to be either an enormous success or yet another failed Internet venture.

▶ SHOP AT THE END OF THE MONTH

Dealers all have monthly sales quotas to fill. If you catch one who is desperate to fill such a quota, you may get a much better price than you would have gotten at the beginning of the month.

▶ SAME CAR, DIFFERENT LABEL?

As automobile manufacturers struggle to cut costs and remain competitive, there are more and more cases of the same basic car being priced differently by two or more divisions of the same company or by two companies that have cooperated on its design and production.

A Chevrolet Prizm, for instance, is usually hundreds of dollars cheaper than a comparable equipped Toyota Corolla, but they are built in the same factory and their differences are purely cosmetic. Chryslers, Dodges, and Plymouths use the same main components. So do most Fords and Mercurys. Many GM cars are built on the same platforms and share the same engines, even though there may be thousands of dollars' difference in prices for similar cars.

One of the best sources of information about car clones, twins, and "kissing cousins" is *Consumer Reports*. Check its report on the car you are thinking of buying, and it will usually mention any similar models with another name.

▶ BUY FROM A NO-HAGGLE DEALER? MAYBE

GM's Saturn started the trend, selling cars through its dealers only at one posted price. The success of the Saturn led some dealers of other makes of cars to establish no-haggle, nonnegotiable prices. Typically, these dealers post their discounted set prices next to the manufacturer's sticker price on car windows.

It is a pleasant way to shop for a car. Most no-haggle dealers post fairly low prices and many of them also offer other attractive customer-friendly services (free cab rides to work when your car is being serviced, for instance). But a tough, informed buyer can nearly always negotiate a better price for the same car (except a Saturn) at a competing traditional dealer. Even if you can't, you can always go back.

In fact, Saturn dealers *do* haggle with most buyers—if

not on the price of the new car, then on the amount they will pay for the trade-in. The end result—a lower overall price—is the same.

▶ CHECK LOAN RATES BEFORE YOU SHOP

If you must borrow money to buy a car, talk to your bank (and check loan rates in other banks) before you negotiate with the dealer. Particularly in these days of dealers' either/or choices between rebates and low manufacturer financing, it is difficult to evaluate different deals. Are you better off taking a $1,000 rebate and financing with your bank? Or should you skip the rebate and pay the lower interest rate offered by the manufacturer? You'll have to work the numbers out yourself (or ask a friendly accountant to do it), but generally if the car costs less than $20,000 a rebate is usually the better deal. A rebate, after all, lowers the total price so that you have to borrow less and thus pay interest on a lower initial amount. The more you have to borrow, the more likely it is that the low financing is a better choice. (See Chapter 9 for more on auto loans.)

▶ AVOID DEALERS' LOANS

A low interest rate offered as a special deal by the manufacturer is different from a normal dealer loan on an automobile. It is rarely a good idea to borrow from the dealer. See Chapter 9 for details.

▶ NEVER SHOP FOR A MONTHLY PAYMENT AMOUNT

The worst possible mistake you can make when negotiating with a car dealer is to reveal how much you can pay for a car on a monthly basis. If he knows that's your primary concern, he'll tailor a loan to fit that amount, adding more monthly payments, higher interest rates, and a far higher total price.

▶ SKIP THE DEALER'S RUSTPROOFING OPTION

It is not only useless, it may actually be damaging. All new cars today are rustproofed at the factory and all manufacturers provide a long-term anticorrosion warranty. The compounds and drilling involved in additional rustproofing can disturb what was done at the factory. Dealer rustproofing has survived for only one reason: It is highly profitable for dealers.

▶ SKIP THE DEALER'S EXTENDED WARRANTY

See Chapter 5 on extended warranties. Same scam. Instead, buy a car with a good frequency-of-repair history (see *Consumer Reports,* April issue) and a good manufacturer's warranty. If you want to keep track of the results of this advice, put the money you would have spent on a dealer's extended warranty into a special savings account, to be used *only* for repairs that would have been covered by the warranty. Nine out of ten people will have money left over in the account.

▶ IN FACT, SKIP ALL THE DEALER'S "EXTRAS"

You've negotiated a terrific deal, so good that you wonder how the dealer can afford to take so little profit. There are smiles and handshakes all around. Now the dealer is writing out the order.

Be careful. Rustproofing and extended warranties are only two of the extra services dealers can add on, and often these add-ons are the source of most of their profit. The easiest way to handle this is to remember that you have bought a car, period. Nothing else. Maybe there are exceptions to the rule at some dealers, but we've never encountered any. If you want a dealer extra, you can find it somewhere else better and cheaper.

Among the extras you may be offered, or even told you have to buy as part of a dealer "pak":

- *Fabric protection.* Buy your own can of Scotchgard.
- *Paint sealants.* Unnecessary.
- *Glaze protection.* An extra coat of wax. Buy it at a car wash for much less.
- *A car alarm.* Many cars now come with factory-installed security devices. If so, the dealer's add-on alarm is a complete waste of money. If your car doesn't come with an alarm and you really want one, it will be cheaper to have it installed by one of the many car-alarm retailers.
- *Any kind of insurance.* See Chapter 4, but you absolutely don't want to buy accident, health, disability, or credit life insurance from your dealer.
- *Preparation charges.* The factory price of the car includes dealer preparation charges. Don't pay any extra charges. Inspect the car when you receive it, and don't accept it if it isn't clean inside and out.
- *Processing fees.* There may even be a preprinted "processing fee" of $50 or $100 in the dealer's sales agreement. Processing what? This is simply a way for the dealer to get back $50 or $100 of the money you have saved by hanging tough in your negotiations about price. Hang tough again. Cross it out. If the dealer objects, tell him you're willing to buy the car elsewhere rather than get taken by as obvious a scam as this. By now he should be taking you very seriously.

▶ NEED AN ODD CAR PART? CONTACT CAR TREK

There is nothing wrong with your ten-year-old car except for one part that must be replaced. Unfortunately, finding that part in any one geographical area can be time-consuming, difficult, or even impossible. *Car Trek* (800-728-3240; http://www.car-trek.com) puts people who need hard-to-find parts together with suppliers who stock them.

▶ LEASING IS *STILL* NOT FOR PENNY PINCHERS

We have had some spirited correspondence with readers who have taken issue with our previous editions' blanket dismissal of car leasing. Overall, we still believe that buying is nearly always more cost-effective in the long run *if you intend to keep the car for more than three years*. Any penny pincher who buys a new car should definitely plan to keep it longer than that.

However, if you insist on driving a new car every two or three years, we agree that leasing has recently become a more attractive option, mainly because car manufacturers are subsidizing leases in order to encourage drivers to switch cars more often. The best leasing deals tend to be those that are widely advertised by the *manufacturers*. The catch is that these deals are prepackaged with locked-in features. Change any of those, and you won't get the advertised price.

Whatever our opinions, leasing now accounts for more than a third of all new-car sales, and the percentage is going up.

When you lease a car instead of buying it, you pay a monthly fee for the term of the lease. At the end of that time, you normally have an option to buy the car. Most leases include down payments and/or security deposits. Some monthly fees include insurance and maintenance, and some don't. People who lease like the lower down payments and lower monthly payments, but at the end of the lease period they don't own anything.

Car leases are complicated, and it is often difficult to choose the best alternatives from among different leases or in a lease-versus-buy decision. New gimmicks and add-ons are constantly being introduced, so, before you start shopping, read the latest advice on leasing, starting with the annual automobile issues of *Consumer Reports* and *Kiplinger's Personal Finance Magazine*. Get a copy of *Keys to Vehicle Leasing,* a free booklet cooperatively published by the Federal Reserve, the Federal Trade Commission, and a number of consumer groups. Call the Fed at 202-452-3244 or download at http:// www.ftc.com. You can also go to *Leasesource Online* (http://www.leasesource.com) for a good worksheet that will help you sort out leasing pros and cons.

Here are some basic tips:

- Don't lease for more than three years. After that, the warranty will probably be up and fees lessors charge for "excess wear and tear" may get especially stiff. In any case, know exactly how the dealer defines "excess wear and tear."
- Don't accept an "open ended" lease. That means you will be responsible if the actual value at the end of the lease is lower than the target set in your lease contract. You want a "closed end" lease guaranteeing that value.
- Bargain with dealers about lease rates the same way you would bargain with them about a purchase price. The best way to do this is to negotiate—starting from the dealer's invoice price—the price of the car as if you were going to buy it. Once this is established, ask the dealer to work out a lease deal based on that price.
- Make sure you aren't responsible for future payments if the car is stolen or in a major accident before the term of your lease is up, but don't pay an exorbitant extra fee for this.
- If you plan on driving more than the preset number of miles per year allowed on the lease (usually fifteen thousand), negotiate how much those miles will cost you before you sign the lease.
- Don't lease unless you are sure you'll want the car for the full term of the lease. Termination costs are often excessive.
- Is the security deposit refundable when the lease ends? It should be. Is there a lease-termination fee even if you don't return the car until the lease agreement ends? If so, how much?

▶ **BEFORE BUYING OR SELLING A USED CAR, CALL 900-988-0828**

At $1.75 a minute, charged to your phone bill, this call to *Consumer Reports Used Car Price Service* is not a bargain—the typical call lasts five minutes. But you will get the latest market value for any used car up to seven years old—adjusted for your geographical area, mileage, condition, and the major options it has (air-conditioning, automatic transmission, etc.).

You can also find out how *Consumer Reports* rates the model in terms of its frequency-of-repair record. Check this out in the April issue of the magazine.

▶ USE THE NADA BLUE BOOK

Every month, the National Automobile Dealers Association (NADA) publishes its *Official Used Car Guide* in eight regional editions. Available at most libraries, the NADA guide is generally referred to as "the blue book," although it isn't blue. While we think the *Consumer Reports* used-car valuation (previous tip) may be worth the extra money, you should also know what the current blue book says about any used car you are seriously considering.

The most important information in the blue book is the current average trade-in price of the car when it is in good condition. You will also find "average retail" prices, "average loan" values (what a bank would lend you on the car), current values of various optional equipment, and mileage tables that tell you whether to add or subtract from the average price.

Your goal when negotiating price is to pay as little as possible over the NADA trade-in price—certainly nothing like the "retail" price also listed in the guide. How much more? That depends on the usual supply-and-demand factors as well as on whom you are buying it from; you might get a better deal from an owner selling direct than from a dealer.

▶ VISIT EDMUND'S ON THE INTERNET

Most of the web sites mentioned in previous tips in this chapter cover used as well as new cars. The best overall site for used car pricing information, however, is Edmund's (http://www.edmunds.com). In addition to giving trade-in and market prices for used cars, this site has a helpful menu of advice and tips for anyone who is selling or buying a used car.

▶ A QUICK USED-CAR INSPECTION CHECKLIST

Bill McFaul, a penny-pinching Scot reader from Manhasset, New York, says that over the past twenty years he has bought literally dozens of used cars for himself, friends, and family—usually direct from their owners. He has developed a checklist of quick ways to decide *not* to make a bid. If a car passes these tests and you think you can get it at a good price, Bill recommends you then make an offer, contingent on a mechanic's inspection.

■ Inspect the brake and gas pedals. Maybe the odometer says the car has only fifty thousand miles on it. A car with abraded, torn-up pedals may have a lot more (it is illegal to tamper with an odometer, but it has been known to happen). Or those fifty thousand miles have been in tough, stop-and-go traffic. Pass.

■ Check the tires—not for wear, although you certainly should factor in the price of new tires if they need replacing, but to see if the four tires match. Owners who maintain their cars well usually replace all four tires, or at least a pair of tires, at the same time. If one tire is a different size or make from the others, it is a good sign the owners skimped on other things, too. Pass.

■ Press down hard with both hands on both front fenders. The car should come back up just once and stop. If it shakes at all, the shocks are shot.

■ Look at the front of the car. There is "good mileage" on any used car—mileage resulting from long trips in light traffic at interstate speeds—and "bad mileage"—mileage resulting from a lot of stop-and-start short trips in heavy traffic. Naturally, the owner will tell you that all of the miles on this seventy-thousand-mile beauty are good. If they are, the front of the hood will be pitted by all the insects and small debris that are an inevitable consequence of driving at high speeds on open highways. If the hood is relatively clean, it has probably seen much more city driving. Pass.

■ Never buy a car at night. There is a reason those used-car lots have Christmas tree lights all over. Dents show up as highlights.

■ People who maintain their cars well usually maintain good files on when and why the car has been serviced. Look them over. If they are "lost," be suspicious.

■ Be wary if the car has been warmed up before your test drive. It might not act well from a cold start. When you drive it, put it in first gear ("low" for automatics) and accelerate to 30 mph. Then take your foot off the pedal, allow the car to decelerate, and check the rearview mirror for smoke and fumes. Finally, with your hands off the wheel, put on the brakes. The car should stop straight ahead.

▶ SELL YOUR OLD CAR YOURSELF? MAYBE

Although you will nearly always get more by selling your old car yourself than by trading it in, think twice before doing it, because it can be a frustrating experience. It may also take longer (adding to insurance and upkeep costs) and require more advertising (more costs) than you initially plan on. Especially if you live in an area with a high sales tax, factor that into your decision. If you buy a new car for $20,000, sales tax at 6 percent is $1,200. If, as a part of that deal, you trade in a car for $10,000, your sales tax is reduced by $600 (you pay only 6 percent of the $10,000 difference). That means you will have to get $10,600 for the car elsewhere to match the dealer's $10,000 offer.

▶ BUT ESTABLISH THE TRUE TRADE-IN PRICE BEFOREHAND

Whatever *Consumer Reports, Edmund's,* or the NADA blue book tell you about prices, car salespeople will give you a dozen reasons why they don't pertain to your car. The acid test comes when you actually try to sell it.

It will take a couple of hours, but shop the car around to at least three dealers in your area who buy used cars. Simply tell them you are definitely selling the car, you are getting prices at four or five different places, and you will be back the same day to sell it to whoever gives you the best price.

The highest price you establish this way is what you should tell your new-car salesperson you'll accept as a trade-in price. In fact, tell him who gave you that price. Chances are, he'll factor in the sales-tax differential (see previous tip), but make sure he doesn't also use this as an opportunity to go back and renegotiate the deal you've already made on the new car.

▶ BUY A "PRE-OWNED" CAR

It is just a euphemism for a used car, of course, but the term "pre-owned" is now often used by dealers specifically to denote cars they have put through rigorous tests and sell with full manufacturer's warranty protection, always one year or twelve thousand miles and sometimes longer. This has become a big business, particularly for dealers selling more expensive or luxury cars. The reason: In 1999 alone, nearly 3 million cars, most them two years old, will come "off lease."

We have a friend who figured out years ago what a bargain these cars were. There is nothing new about the critical numbers: Depending on the make and model, most cars depreciate in value from 40 to 50 percent in their first two years. After that, depreciation slows down considerably.

So our friend buys a two-year-old luxury car every four years. He says he pays extra for a very clean, obviously well cared for car, and always has a mechanic inspect it first. When he sells the car four years later (when it is six years old) he gets about 50 percent of what he originally paid for it. He figures his annual costs of driving a Mercedes for the past twenty years have been about the same as if he had traded in a new Ford every two years.

Let the non–penny pinchers of the world spend thousands of dollars extra in car expenses annually because they insist on driving a brand-new car every two years. A two-year-old car with a superior frequency-of-repair record and twenty-four to thirty thousand miles on it can be one of the best deals around.

▶ CHECK INDEPENDENT LEASING COMPANIES

More and more independent car-leasing companies are selling used cars direct to the public, cutting out the dealer middlemen. Most of their cars are just coming off a two-year lease and will come with manufacturer's warranty protection.

▶ SHOP THE SUPERSTORES? MAYBE

CARmax (owned by the nationwide electronics superstore chain Circuit City), *Car Choice, Auto Nation USA,* and *Driver's Mart* are the first names in the newest way to buy a used car—at a nonnegotiable price from a huge "superstore" of used cars. Like "no haggle" new-car dealers, these new superstore chains offer a consumer-friendly atmosphere. They also offer a much wider selection than traditional used-car dealers. As far as we have been able to tell, their prices are seldom as low as what a determined negotiator could find elsewhere. If you hate to negotiate, however, you won't do badly at these places.

▶ REBATES ON NEW MODELS MAY MEAN USED-CAR BARGAINS

When a manufacturer is offering large rebates on a new model, you can count on lower prices for the same model used car. Rebates effectively create demand for the new model and just as predictably reduce demand for the same model used car, thereby lowering prices.

▶ CARPOOL

If your drive to and from work each day adds up to fifteen miles, you'll put over thirty-five hundred miles a year on your car. Just cutting that in half—by finding one person to carpool with—will save you hundreds of dollars. If your car pool allows you to use a special rush-hour lane reserved for buses and cars with more than a certain number of people in them, you'll also save time.

Many companies have van pools. Look into joining one of them.

▶ USE PUBLIC TRANSPORTATION

Taking a bus or train is invariably cheaper than driving your own car, and by not subjecting your car to everyday bumper-to-bumper traffic jams to and from work, you'll extend its life by years.

▶ BUY A BICYCLE

Other than walking, there's no better, healthier way to minimize transportation expenses. Count up all those two-mile trips by car to the 7-Eleven and consider how much you could save in a year by substituting a bike equipped with a basket.

Because this book is about penny pinching, we don't always mention environmental benefits of certain strategies. But we do care about them. Carpooling and riding buses, trains, and bicycles are—like many other penny-pinching ideas—earth-friendly activities.

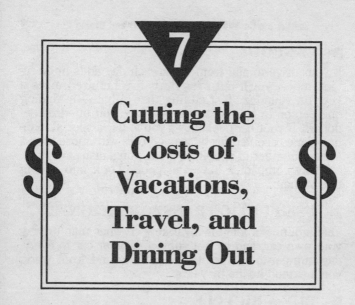

Cutting the Costs of Vacations, Travel, and Dining Out

Like fresh fish and bagels, the products of the travel industry are perishable—but even more so. A bagel maker may be able to sell his stale product for a reduced price a day later, but there is no way to sell either an empty seat after the airliner takes off or a vacant hotel room the morning after.

Car-rental companies, airlines, hotels, resorts, and cruise ships all have high fixed overhead costs. Their expensive buildings, cars, airplanes, and ships—along with the people it takes to operate them—must be paid for whether 50 percent or 100 percent of the rooms and seats are occupied. For them to make a profit, the number of unoccupied rooms and seats must be held to a minimum, even if that means reducing prices drastically.

The result is a bewildering system of ever-changing fare structures, hidden discounts, concealed wholesaler rates, and promotional deals. The tips in this chapter will help you cut through the confusion to get the best deals possible for your travel dollar. A few of them cover similar ground. If you join *Best Fares* on the Internet, for instance, you may get benefits that make a separate half-price coupon directory superfluous. Some of them make sense only if you travel a lot. If you would use only one or two coupons from a half-price coupon director, don't buy one.

If you are young (usually twenty-six or younger, especially if you are a student) or old (fifty or over, or even better, sixty-two or over), you have opportunities for discount travel denied those in the age groups in between. The travel industry is keenly aware that people over fifty are responsible for more than 80 percent of the total dollars spent on nonbusiness travel. Also, students and retired people are often flexible about scheduling, so they can fill airplane seats and hotel rooms that would otherwise remain vacant. At the end of this chapter, there are some specific tips for these two groups.

Whichever tips you decide are right for you, here are three guidelines that are always operative:

- Comparison shopping is essential.
- Discounts are the norm, not the exception, throughout the history industry. Look for them. Ask for them. Bashfulness is not a virtue among penny-pinching travelers.
- Especially if you don't have access to the Internet, establishing a relationship with a savvy travel agent who is willing to work hard to save you money can be an enormous time-saver. The best way to do this is to make sure your agent gets commissions on your easy reservations as well as your more difficult ones. And the more work you can do yourself before you put your agent to work, the better your relationship will be. Clients who habitually change their minds and cancel reservations will not get first-rate service.

How do you know if you are working with a good travel agency? A penny pincher's agent won't always settle for the airline fares displayed on her computer screen. She will also have access to a software program that continues to track fare changes after your reservations are made. On many routes, unless you are buying coach excursion tickets, she will check at least one "consolidator" (see tip below) for a possible lower rate. She will also participate in a discount program for hotel reservations; if the only rates you can get from her are "rack" rates (see tip below), find another agent. A resourceful agent can save you enough to justify full agency commissions.

If you do the work yourself—and that is becoming easier every year, thanks to the Internet—you can choose to use an agency that rebates part of the commission.

Because rates and special offers change constantly, this book restricts itself to general tips and strategies for saving money on travel. If you travel a great deal, a subscription to a newsletter is a good way to keep up with trends and special deals. The most informative travel newsletter we have seen is the monthly *Consumer Reports Travel Letter* (800-234-1970; $39 a year). Check your library, too; ours subscribes for us.

You may also want to consider *Best Fares Discount Travel Magazine* (800-880-1234). This monthly magazine concentrates on special promotional deals and travel bargains. When you subscribe, you also get free membership in a discount travel club, a 50-percent-off hotel directory, a 20-percent-off restaurant discount plan, and free membership in major rental-car preferred-customer programs. You also get free access to the *Best Fares* web site (http://www.bestfares.com), which among other things tracks airline fare wars and late-breaking special deals. At $59.90 a year, *Best Fares* isn't cheap, but if you travel a fair amount, it could more than pay for itself.

▶ EXPLORE THE INTERNET

No travel agent, however dedicated, could possibly take the time to answer all the questions we have when we are planning a trip. We still rely on the travel guides that we can take out for a month at a time at no cost from our library—*Fodor's, Lonely Planet, Mobil Guides, Michelin,* and others. But now we also surf the Web and get an extraordinary amount of free information.

Just about every destination and tourist office in the world now has a web site. *Travel Weekly,* the major trade magazine of the travel industry, has a very useful one (http://www.traveler.net) that is often the first place we go to when we are even remotely thinking about a trip or a vacation. This site indexes and gives you immediate access to thousands of other travel-related Internet sites. Pick any destination, and you are likely to find descriptions of web sites that will tell you about the weather, local attractions, and upcoming special events. You will also find commercial sites that describe local hotels, restaurants, and packaged tours. Whether you are going to Peoria or Sri Lanka, you will often find destination-specific advice and intelligence here.

If we don't find the link we are looking for at the *Travel Weekly* site, we usually go to *Yahoo* (http://www. yahoo.com), one of the major Internet search resources. Its travel indexes seem to us particularly useful.

We also use area-specific travel forums on our on-line service and have gotten great answers to some specific questions. In one case, we went to a United Kingdom forum and asked about inexpensive lodging near the Manchester, England, airport. Within a day, we had responses from four different people who lived in or knew the area well—all just being helpful, not trying to sell us anything. One of the things we most enjoy about traveling is meeting and getting to know local people. With a computer and a modem, we can do that even before we leave home.

▶ BOOK ON-LINE? MAYBE

The Internet offers a lot more than free travel information, of course. Every major airline, cruise line, car-rental agency, and hotel chain now has a web site, and you can make reservations on-line at most of them. Should you? Only if you have shopped around and are certain you can't get a better deal elsewhere.

One compelling reason to visit commercial travel sites on the Web is that sometimes they offer discounts, rebates, and special deals that are not available except to on-line customers.

You may also find some attractive offers at one of the big-multipurpose booking sites. *Travelocity* (http://www.travelocity.com) and *Expedia* (http://www.expedia.msn.com) both offer airline, hotel, and car-rental booking as well as a great deal of other travel information. We use both of them to research different airline routes and rates, although to date we have made airline reservations on-line only once. In that case, after researching a rather complicated itinerary from City A to City B to City C to City A, we stumbled on a rate that looked too good to be true. We made our reservations on Expedia, got our tickets in the mail five days later, and were delighted with the entire experience.

We haven't made any other kinds of reservations on-line because we consider the prices we get there a starting point. Talking with a car-rental agent or a hotel reservation clerk may not save us anything, but at least we can explore different discount possibilities with some give-and-take. So far, you can't do that on-line (see below for some exceptions). As for airline reservations, we want to give our travel agent any commissions we can, so that when we want her help in the future she will be there for us.

▶ OUT OF *WHOSE* SEASON?

The luxury Caribbean resort that charges $700 a day in March may reduce that price by as much as 50 percent six weeks later. By May, airlines flying to the Caribbean usually lower rates as well. Not much else has changed. The temperature may be two or three degrees hotter, but the prevailing island breezes make the difference barely perceptible. The tennis courts and golf course will be less crowded, and the duty-free stores often mark things down off-season.

You can also get terrific off-season bargains in most ski resorts. No snow, but you might not mind when you consider you can get summer mountain scenery, golf, tennis, lake swimming, hotel rooms, condo rentals, and restaurant meals at huge discounts from peak winter rates.

Is it really worth a 40 or 50 percent premium to go in season? Your answer may well be yes, if the choice is the Maine coast in January or July. But many choices aren't that dramatic. And sophisticated travelers, even those who aren't purposely penny-pinching, avoid places like Paris in August, when the Parisians flee their city and busloads of tourists take it over.

▶ SHOP THE AIRLINES' SALES

You can probably skip all of the tips that follow about saving money on airline tickets if you take advantage of periodic airline fare wars, sales on coach excursion tickets that all the major airlines announce with full-page ads from time to time. The odds of your doing any better on prices—usually 30 to 50 percent under the normal coach fares—are slim. But you must be able to make a quick decision. Typically, the sales last just a week or ten days and only a limited number of tickets are available.

If you see an ad from one airline offering sharp fare reductions, the odds are high that an immediate call to any airline serving the same route will get you a ticket at the same price.

▶ LEARN ABOUT AIRLINE FARE WARS IMMEDIATELY

Your odds of getting a ticket that is on sale for a brief period of time improve if you have an E-mail address. Visit *Travelers Net* (http://www.travelersnet.com) on the Web and sign up for a free subscription to a service that notifies you about airline fare wars as soon as they are announced by the airlines. Being among the first to know may get you a cheap ticket that might not be available just a few hours later.

▶ BUY AIRLINE TICKETS FROM A CONSOLIDATOR

When airlines can't sell all the seats on a flight, despite their promotions and special discounts, they may sell them to a ticket broker—a "consolidator"—at a wholesale price. The consolidator is then able to offer tickets for anywhere from 15 to 50 percent below normal prices. Some consolidators sell only to travel agents; others sell direct to the public as well. Some consolidators specialize in international flights, but many also sell tickets for heavily traveled domestic routes. Tickets are nearly always sold on a nonrefundable basis.

Purchase a consolidator ticket through a reputable travel agent, or, if you deal with a consolidator directly, use a credit card. We consider that an absolute rule, even if one is offered a better price for paying cash. This is the only way you can make sure you won't be stuck if something goes wrong. Also, get your tickets as soon as possible after ordering so that you'll have time to correct any mistakes.

The downside of a consolidator ticket: You may not fly at the most convenient time or by the most direct route. You may be told you can't get an advance seat assignment. You can't switch airlines at the last minute. You may not get frequent-flier credit for the miles flown (ask before you order). And don't take it for granted you are getting a discount; airlines often offer promotional fares that are better than what a consolidator can offer. In many such cases, however, that promotional fare may be loaded down with restrictions that you can't live with (travel only between Tuesday and Thursday and stay over one Saturday if the moon is full).

When you deal with a consolidator, make sure you

are buying a discounted ticket and not a ticket on a charter flight. Some consolidators aren't too scrupulous about differentiating between the two. Too many charter flights pack customers into planes the way canneries pack sardines. They are also subject to extra delays if anything goes wrong. Unless you are part of an affinity group that is chartering the flight or have booked through a travel agent you trust, we suggest you avoid charter flights.

As usual, the number one rule for an airline traveler who wants to save money is to shop all the alternatives before buying. Consolidators to call for more information: *Travac* (800-872-8800) and *Cheap Tickets* (800-377-1000; http://www.cheaptickets.com) A web site sponsored by *Travel Information Services* (http://www.tiss.com) allows you to search for international tickets from several consolidators, using your desired itinerary and travel dates. Also check out http://www.usaca.com for a membership list of the *United States Air Consolidators Association,* a group that insists its members meet certain standards of financial responsibility.

Finally, if you are a very frequent traveler, check out *Jax Fax* (http://www.jaxfax.com), a monthly catalog with hundreds of classified ads placed by consolidators offering discounted airline tickets. You will have to subscribe ($30 a year) to get complete listings, but the web site will give you an idea of what Jax Fax delivers.

▶ CHECK ON NESTED FARES

The bizarre structure of airline fares sometimes makes it advantageous to throw tickets away. A regularly priced round-trip coach ticket that called for you to leave City A on Tuesday and return from City B on Thursday might cost $800. But *two* round-trip discount fares between the same two cities that called for a minimum stay of seven days, including one Saturday night, might cost only $300 each. You would save $200 by throwing away one of the tickets from each round trip. Especially if you are flying without a Saturday stay-over, ask your travel agent to look into this alternative. You definitely won't get this kind of fare information, or information that will allow you to use the next three tips, by buying tickets directly from an airline.

A word of caution: Airlines consider this strategy a violation of their contract with ticket holders and some of them may begin to go after offenders, perhaps by taking away their accumulated frequent-flier mileage. If you have mileage to protect, ask a travel agent about that airline's current policies.

▶ FLY VIA AN INTERMEDIATE CITY

Very often, a ticket for a direct flight between City A and City C is more expensive than two tickets, one that takes you from City A to City B, the other going from City B to City C. You may have to travel quite a few extra miles (in some cases, you may even have to go in a direction opposite that of your eventual destination) and it will take some extra time. You may fly two different airlines. But savings can be considerable.

How can you know when such a deal is possible? All the major airlines utilize "hub" airports. If you know that a cheap flight from City A to that hub is available, then check out flights from the hub to your destination—perhaps on a no-frills airline. Major hubs include Atlanta (Delta), Chicago (United, American), Dallas (American), Minneapolis (Northwest), St. Louis (TWA), Pittsburgh (USAir), and Newark (Continental), but all major airlines have a few hubs each.

▶ BE FLEXIBLE ABOUT AIRPORTS AND MORE

We wanted to fly from New York City to Toledo. How did we actually get there? By flying from Newark, New Jersey (thirty minutes farther away from us than our closest airport, La Guardia in New York City), to Detroit (less than an hour from Toledo). We saved hundreds of dollars by investigating the alternatives and being flexible.

This example is not at all unusual. Especially if you are flying a route in which there is little competition between airlines, go to your atlas and investigate possible alternatives. Also check into potential savings if you fly off-peak hours and/or off-peak days.

▶ INVESTIGATE DOUBLE-CODED FLIGHTS

U.S. and foreign airlines have code-sharing arrangements that allow two different carriers to use the same airplane and crew for a flight, although by law each must set its own price for that flight. Surprisingly, those prices are often quite different. Most often, the foreign carrier will offer a lower price. A good travel agent will know about and check into double codes.

▶ FORGET THE "HIDDEN CITY" STRATEGY

Just about all of the airlines have effectively made this fare-busting strategy almost impossible, although you may still hear about it. You can no longer buy a ticket from City A to City C with a stopover at City B and get off at the stopover. Airlines are now billing such travelers or their travel agents for the difference in fares or taking away accumulated frequent-flier mileage.

▶ SIGN UP FOR INTERNET BARGAINS

All of the major and most smaller airlines have their own web sites, including both U.S. and international carriers. Many of them offer promotional fares, often special last-minute weekend deals, only at these sites. Some, including American Airlines (http://www.aa.com), US Airways (http://www.usairways.com), and TWA (http://www.twa.com), allow you to sign up for notification of these deals. Give them your E-mail address and you will be notified automatically. Go to http://www.yahoo.com for other airline Web addresses.

You can get one-stop bulletins about all of the airlines'

last-minute Internet deals by checking into *Webflyer* (http://www.webflyer.com) which searches all of the airline sites and posts their deals in one place. It is a convenient source of information, but you may still want to check with individual airlines to make sure you're not missing anything.

▶ USE A FREQUENT-FLIER CREDIT CARD

See Chapter 9.

▶ GET BUMPED

Airlines routinely overbook flights to account for no-shows, and it isn't at all unusual for them to have to ask at the departure gate for volunteers who are willing to be bumped off a flight and take the next available one instead. To encourage volunteers, the most common award is a dollars-off certificate for any future flight, often of $100 or more. If you are in no hurry to get to your destination, check in early at the gate and ask to be put at the head of the volunteers list (after you are reassured about the availability of an acceptable later flight).

▶ BEWARE THE COUPON BROKERS

When you see ads in newspaper travel sections offering 60 to 70 percent off on business and first-class airline tickets, chances are good a coupon broker placed them. These brokers buy free-travel award coupons from frequent fliers and resell them. The problem is, all of the airline frequent-flier programs specifically prohibit trading in such coupons. If you get caught—a possibility, since the airlines are making some serious efforts to catch offenders—your ticket won't be honored.

▶ FLY AS A COURIER

If you can travel alone on a flexible schedule, the cheapest way to fly to many destinations in Europe, Asia, and

South America is as a courier. Couriers have to make do with carry-on luggage, since their check-in baggage is supplied to them by a courier company. In return for a very low price on a round-trip ticket, couriers escort that baggage—usually business documents—from one airport to another. The day we called *Now Voyager,* a New York City–based courier booking agency (212-431-1616; $50 annual reservation fee), we could have gotten a round-trip ticket from New York to London or Paris for $299 or a round-trip ticket from Los Angeles to Sydney for $399.

The *International Association of Air Travel Couriers* has a web site (http://www.courier.com) that answers frequently asked questions. If you decide to join IAATC ($45 annual fee), you can access the association's posting of currently available courier trips.

▶ SET YOUR OWN TICKET PRICE ON PRICELINE

The same Web service (http://www.priceline.com) described in Chapter 6 that allows you to buy a car at a price you determine also allows you to name the price you are willing to pay for an airline ticket, supposedly for up to six months in advance of departure. *Priceline* then finds a major airline willing to release seats at that price. Within twenty-four hours, you learn whether you have bought seats at the requested price or not.

Priceline is most likely to save you money on last-minute travel; we think it unlikely that airlines will settle for bargain fares unless they are fairly sure the seats would otherwise go unoccupied. You won't earn frequent-flier miles and tickets are nonrefundable and nonchangeable. But Priceline is a good bet for leisure travelers who are flexible about specific times of departure and airlines. To have a chance to buy a ticket a substantial discount, you will have to do a bit of research and be knowledgeable about what routes and times are most likely to have empty seats that the airlines will want to fill.

▶ USE CORPORATE DISCOUNT RATES FOR PERSONAL TRAVEL

If corporate discounts are available when you are traveling for your company, there is usually no reason why you can't ask for them when traveling for personal reasons.

▶ ENROLL THE WHOLE FAMILY IN FREQUENT-FLIER PROGRAMS

It is foolish not to join an airline's frequent-flier program, even though all of them now have expiration dates for miles earned. In an age of airline mergers and rapidly changing personal plans, who knows? It takes no effort at all to join most of the programs right at the airport. Maintain a file of what you've earned in each of the programs, and it may very well affect your choice of airline sometime in the future.

▶ USE FREQUENT-FLIER MILEAGE WISELY

The temptation is to use frequent-flier mileage for a free ticket as soon as you have enough saved up. That's not always the best strategy.

Always check first to see what special deals are possible. If the airlines are engaged in one of their periodic promotional price wars, you might be better off buying a ticket, collecting more frequent-flier mileage on that cheaper-than-usual flight, and using the mileage later when prices are back to normal. Keep expiration dates in mind, of course.

▶ LAST-MINUTE FLIGHT? CHECK FREQUENT FLIER AVAILABILITY

Cashing in frequent-flier mileage, even many months in advance, has become more difficult than it once was. Every airline has cut back on the number of seats it allots to holders of frequent-flier mileage, except those who achieve elite status by flying on it more than a hundred thousand miles a year. In recent months, however, many airlines have begun to open up a few seats for frequent-flier mileage holders days or hours before a flight leaves. If you have to fly on short notice, check into this possibility first, since other discount possibilities may be limited.

▶ BUY TRIP-CANCELLATION INSURANCE

We are not great believers in most forms of specialized insurance. But if you have paid a large sum months in advance for a tour or cruise, and something—a medical or business emergency or even the failure of the tour operator—prevents you from going, you'll be glad you bought trip-cancellation insurance. Read all the fine print to make sure you are fully covered and buy from a travel agent, not from the tour operator. If he goes out of business suddenly, his insurance will be worthless.

▶ CUT ENERGY BILLS WHILE YOU'RE AWAY

Most people remember to turn the thermostat down when they're going to be away from an empty house for any length of time. But why pay to keep hot water available if nobody is there to use it? Turn off your electric hot-water heater at the circuit breaker or turn down your gas heater to its lowest setting.

If you're going to be away long enough, also clean out the refrigerator and freezer and turn them off. When you do, leave the doors open a bit to prevent mold, and leave an open box of baking soda inside.

Finally, unplug electronic devices that use electricity even when turned off—including TVs, VCRs, cable boxes, computers, and stereo equipment.

▶ CARRY A 100-WATT LIGHTBULB

Even luxury hotels often discourage inveterate readers by putting 40-watt bulbs in night-table lamps, and few hotel housekeepers in our experience have been able to supply brighter substitutes. After a midnight search a few years ago that finally resulted in the purchase of the world's most expensive single bulb, we've packed our own whenever we are headed for a hotel. We also bring along an extension cord.

A reader from Boston has another solution. She brings a flashlight and extra batteries. "It's like reading after lights-out at camp," she reports.

▶ WHAT YOU MUST KNOW ABOUT HOTEL RATES

There is no such thing as a single rate for a hotel room anywhere in the world. Instead, there are a least a half-dozen rates on a room in even a moderately priced motel, and as many as twenty different rates on a room in a luxury hotel. What's more, these rates not only change daily; they may be lower at 7:00 P.M. than they were at 3:00 P.M.

Confusing? Not even reservation desks can keep track of all the rates. The bottom line for you is simple: Unless you are desperate for a room in a hotel in a city jammed with convention guests, you should NEVER (well, hardly ever) pay the "rack" rate for a room. At a minimum, when you are first quoted a room rate, ask if that is the corporate rate. Oh, you are there on business? Of course you qualify, nearly always for at least a 10 percent discount. But that's just the beginning. Keep reading.

▶ USE A HOTEL BROKER

This is the no-hassle way to get decent discounts on middle- and high-priced hotel rooms in many major cities and resorts, both here and abroad. You may not get the best deal possible, but you will know you have a reservation. Also, many hotel brokers offer discounts on hotels that don't participate in travel-club or discount-book deals. When you call one of these brokers, you simply tell him where and when you are going; he will give you rates for different hotels and will make a reservation for you. You will pay the hotel directly.

Among those that deal with only one city or state: *Capital Reservations* (Washington, D.C.: 800-847-4832; http://www.hotelsdc.com); *San Francisco Reservations* (800-677-1550; http://www.hotelres.com); *Hot Rooms* (Chicago: 800-468-3500; http://www.hotrooms.com); *Florida Reservations* (800-495-2352; http://www.fl-room-reservations.com). There are also reservation offices that cover many different cities, sometimes including major cities abroad. Try *Hotel Reservations Network* (800-964-6835; http://www.80096hotel.com) and *Central Reservation Service* (800-548-3311; http://www.reservation-services.com).

▶ BOOK HOTEL ROOMS AT THE LAST MINUTE

It's risky if there's a big convention in town or it is "in season" for a particular city. But normally—and especially if there are stories in newspaper financial pages about low occupancy rates—you can negotiate a good rate when you call a few hotels on your arrival date. Simply ask for the lowest rate for the type of accommodations you want, and tell them you'll call back to confirm if you like what is offered.

This is a particularly effective strategy with smaller hotels. Before you leave, narrow your choices by checking guidebooks (*Frommer's, Fodor's,* etc.) that list and rate them.

▶ JOIN A "HALF PRICE" HOTEL PROGRAM

If you spend more than a few nights a year in hotels, the annual price of membership in a club that offers room discounts can be a good investment. Although most seem to promise 50 percent discounts off rack rate, that is always subject to availability and the occupancy level the hotel expects. Except during peak periods, though, the odds are good you'll get at least some kind of discount by joining one of these clubs.

When you enroll, you will be given a membership card and a directory of available hotels. Most directories include a variety of price ranges and also offer discounts on restaurants, car rentals, and tourist attractions. Using the directory, you call a hotel, tell it you are a member of the club, and ask for a discounted price for the night you want. You can then make your reservation using your usual credit card; when you check in you will probably be asked for a membership card in the half-price club.

Among the largest half-price programs:

- *Entertainment Publications* (800-445-4137) has a worldwide hotel and dining directory that it sells for a $62.95 annual fee. It also publishes a number of smaller regional United States and international directories, which you can ask about when you call. The worldwide directory includes more than 5,500 hotels and motels.
- *Encore* (800-444-9800) has a worldwide directory of over 4,000 hotels; $49.95 annual fee.
- *ITC-50* (800-987-6216) charges $49 for its worldwide directory of more than 3,900 hotels.

▶ GET MARRIED ABROAD

One way to save money on your wedding and your honeymoon is to combine them by inviting guests to join you at a wonderful destination—a Caribbean island, for example, or maybe a village on the coast of Greece. Guests pay their own travel and hotel expenses, which will probably result in quite a small wedding. But if you book a reception and a number of rooms at once, you can count on discounted prices for all. You can hire an experienced coordinator here in the States to take care of all the details. *Weddings on the Move* (800-444-6967) charges from $1,000 to $2,500 and can also suggest places, help you find a block of airline seats, and do just about anything else you may require.

▶ SPEND WEEKEND VACATIONS IN BIG CITIES

Deluxe and first-class hotels in major cities are highly dependent on business travelers, who tend to arrive on Monday morning and leave on Friday. That means a lot of expensive hotel rooms are difficult to fill on Friday, Saturday, and Sunday nights. Nearly all but the upper tier of big-city luxury hotels now offer some kind of promotional packages that can cut room rates by more than 50 percent and often include free breakfasts and other extras. Call the 800 line of any of the nationwide chains (*Hilton, Hyatt, Marriott, Ritz-Carlton, Westin,* etc.) for information about a city you are interested in, as well as chainwide promotions. The travel section of your newspaper and the travel magazines (*Travel and Leisure, Travel, Sunset,* etc.) will also feature ads about special weekend packages.

Except in resort areas and New York City, the same phenomenon makes car rentals from a big-city location a lot cheaper over the weekend.

▶ JOIN A TRAVEL CLUB

There are dozens of travel clubs offering a bewildering variety of discounts on various aspects of travel. Some target specialized audiences—golfers, singles, gamblers, etc. Others are general clubs that offer a smorgasbord of services and discounts for an annual fee. *Consumer Reports Travel Letter* usually does an annual summary article about travel clubs; see if you can find it at your library. Among the general clubs that offer hotel, airfare, rental car, dining, cruise, tour, and travel-agency discounts: *Allstate Travel Club* ($49 annual fee; 800-992-3841) and the *Travel Club* ($49.95 annual fee; 800-292-9882).

▶ ADD A VACATION TO THE END OF A BUSINESS TRIP

A very easy way to buy no-cost airline tickets is to switch from a direct route home on a business-class ticket to an alternate route with a stopover in a city you would like to visit. Instead of flying back to New York from San Francisco on a direct flight, you might find your ticket would buy you a San Francisco–Miami–New York or a San Francisco–Denver–New York route at an even lower price. Check your travel agent or call airlines direct.

▶ THROW AWAY PARTS OF PACKAGE DEALS

The big travel packagers buy at the best wholesale prices—charter airlines, hotels, restaurants, ground transportation, admission charges, etc.—and still make a profit even though they pass on some of the savings to you. Many people won't consider buying a package tour because they don't want to spend two weeks on a bus among a lot of strangers with whom they might be incompatible. If you investigate certain packages carefully, however, you may discover you can throw away such elements as prepaid sight-seeing buses and meals and still save money on what's left—usually airfare and accommodations.

▶ TRY A DISCOUNT CRUISE-ONLY AGENCY

The *Cruise Line* (800-777-0707) is a travel agency that buys cruise accommodations in bulk at wholesale prices, then sells them at a discount. It is definitely one of the calls you should make when comparison-shopping.

▶ DON'T RESERVE USING A HOTEL-CHAIN 800 NUMBER

The central reservations office of any big hotel or motel chain will frequently quote a higher rate than will the desk clerk at the specific place you want to stay. You can also often negotiate a reduced price with the desk clerk, but can't with the central office. The best idea is to first get rates from the central office (a free 800 call), then call the desk clerk to make your actual reservations.

▶ DELAY CAR RENTALS . . .

If you arrive at the airport late in the day and, except for the drive to your hotel, don't need a car until the next day, why not wait and rent it then? The cost of a shuttle bus or train is bound to be less than the cost of renting the car for a day, and you'll save garage expenses as well.

You may also save a significant amount by checking the Yellow Pages in your hotel-room phone book and calling a local car-rental company. There are lots of these companies around the country. Not burdened with the overhead expenses of the national chains, many of them offer better deals than you can get even with a corporate or other discount.

Finally, on the other end of the trip, why pay an extra day's rental charges if all you are going to do that day is drive the car to the airport? Drop it off the day before at a downtown location.

▶ BUT RESERVE ADVERTISED SPECIALS QUICKLY

When you see an ad for a special limited-time offer from a car-rental company, call and make your reservation at the special rate as quickly as you can. The companies change their rates frequently, and the special price may not be available in a day or two. Make sure you get a confirmation number.

▶ RENT YOUR CAR FROM AN OFF-AIRPORT LOCATION

It's admittedly not quite as convenient, but you can nearly always save 20 to 30 percent by renting from an office outside the airport and taking a free shuttle bus to it.

▶ RENTING A CAR ABROAD? DO IT HERE

Reserve ahead with a U.S. travel agent. You'll get a better rate than if you wait and rent directly from a European agent. Ask about the airport surcharges in some countries; you may save up to 10 percent by picking the car up at a downtown office instead. Also make sure whatever rate you are given includes the value-added tax; it can be as high as 25 percent. If you need the car for three weeks or more, you will probably save money by taking a French lease. You buy the car at a location in France and sell it back to the leasing company at that or another location in France. Your sale price is prearranged and the lease includes full collision insurance coverage. For information, call the 800 numbers of the large American car-rental companies, all of whom have operations abroad. Also call *Auto Europe* (800-223-5555).

▶ DON'T TAKE THE FIRST CAR-RENTAL PRICE

However and wherever you rent a car, ask for a discount when quoted a price. Just about anyone can ask for a corporate discount. Maybe you have frequent-flier miles you can use, or an AARP card (see later tip in this chapter). If you manage to get the "advertised special" price, you probably won't get any additional discount, but it does no harm to ask.

▶ CHECK OUT BREEZENET

Breezenet (http://www.bnm.com) offers discount coupons for on-line reservations from a number of major and smaller rental-car companies, at sixty different airport locations.

▶ TRY FOR NO-FEE TRAVELER'S CHECKS

There is absolutely no reason—other than a desire for excess profits—why issuers of traveler's checks must charge a fee for the service. After all, you are giving them ready cash. They, in return, are giving you checks that will not be cashed until sometime in the future. The income issuers make by investing your money during that "float" period is more than enough to earn them a handsome profit on an average transaction.

Depending on competitive pressures at the time of purchase, however, your bank may insist that a fee is necessary. If you keep a reasonable balance in your accounts, ask it to waive the fee.

▶ LIMIT YOUR USE OF TRAVELER'S CHECKS ABROAD

When you use a traveler's check to pay a hotel, a restaurant, a car-rental agency, or just about anybody else when traveling abroad, you will nearly always be given an unfavorable exchange rate (which is why you'll usually get a delighted smile and a yes when you ask if your traveler's check will be accepted). Instead, use a credit card for all major expenses; the rate of exchange is usually much better.

Cash your traveler's checks only at a bank or an office of the company that issues the checks, and pay only minor expenses with cash in the local currency.

▶ USE ATM MACHINES INSTEAD OF TRAVELER'S CHECKS ABROAD

You'll find automated teller machines just about everywhere in the world now. The two largest networks are Cirrus, owned by MasterCard, and Plus, owned by Visa. Both will give you the wholesale exchange rate when you use your bank ATM card to withdraw cash in the local currency. That's a much better deal (a 5 to 10 percent difference) than the exchange rate you'll get with a traveler's check. Even if you have to pay a $2 or $3 fee per withdrawal (a typical charge), you'll save on a withdrawal of at least $100. Use your bank ATM card, which immediately debits your bank account, rather than a credit card; you'll pay much steeper fees and interest charges when you use a credit card for a cash advance.

Check your PIN number with your bank before you go. It has to be four digits abroad, and you'll have to memorize numbers, not letters. To make sure that your card will be accepted in the places you plan to visit, before you leave check out ATM locations on the Internet—Cirrus at http://www.mastercard.com and Plus at http://www.visa.com.

As much as we dislike them, for safety's sake we still believe it is best to carry a few traveler's checks when abroad. If you can avoid using them, cash them in for their full, 100 percent dollar value when you return home.

▶ KEEP CURRENCY VALUATIONS IN MIND

Maybe you have your heart set on April in Paris, but if you can think of dozens of countries you would like to visit, before making final plans about a vacation trip abroad why not check first on what your dollar will buy in the local currencies. The beaches and historic Mediterranean cities of Turkey and Greece, for instance, are both beautiful, but your dollar will go a lot farther in Turkey. News headlines about currency devaluations can indicate sudden travel bargains as well.

▶ TAKE ADVANTAGE OF THE EURO

As of January 1, 1999, eleven European nations (France, Germany, Italy, Belgium, the Netherlands, Luxembourg, Spain, Portugal, Ireland, Austria, and Finland) agreed to adopt the euro as a common currency. Actual euro currency will not be available until 2002. However, it is likely that euros will be usable in electronic credit card transactions at many hotels and airlines beginning in 1999. The immediate benefit to penny-pinching travelers will be to make comparison shopping easier. Also, prices for travel packages that are quoted in euros are very likely to be cheaper than those that are not. Look for them.

▶ CHECK ON INSURANCE COVERAGE BEFORE TRAVELING ABROAD

It could prove to be an expensive mistake if you aren't sure your automobile or health insurance will cover you in the country you are visiting. Call your agent and/or talk to your benefits administrator. If you plan to drive while in a foreign country, call the American Automobile Association (AAA) to see if you'll need an international driver's license. You might also ask—even if you aren't a member—about supplemental insurance.

▶ SWAP HOUSES—*VERY* CAREFULLY

We've never swapped houses ourselves, but we have friends who have traded their condo in Hawaii for private houses or apartments in London, the south of France, and on two Caribbean islands. So far, they say, things have worked out well.

Most people use one of the services that publish directories of homes for exchange. When you subscribe to one of these services, you pay a fee to list your home in the directory, describing it and specifying where you are willing to go and when you can travel. Then, when the directory is published, subscribers who are interested in a swap call you directly. If you see a house you think you might like, you can also call its owner directly.

Don't expect overnight results. If you think you might want to swap houses in the summer, start the fall before so you can get a listing in a January directory. Your chances of a swap are obviously better if you are offering an East Side Manhattan apartment or a waterfront house in Malibu rather than a North Dakota farmhouse. In any case, you should be flexible about timing and accommodations.

If you are lucky enough to make contact with a promising potential swap, you will exchange references and ask and be asked a lot of questions. Before you trust someone to take over your home, make sure you are satisfied with his credentials. Having a trusted friend regularly stop in to "help" while you are away is a good idea.

The major directory services are *Intervac International 1* (800-756-4663; http://www.intervac.com) and *HomeLink International* (http://www.homelink.org). Prices for listings are in the $80–$100 range.

▶ GET 20 PERCENT OFF RESTAURANT BILLS

The typical restaurant two-for-one deal in an Entertainment Publications discount book (see page 160) gives you the lower priced of two entrées free.

Cocktails, wine, appetizers, desserts, and coffee aren't included. Since the price of those items may exceed the price of the two entrées, it is easy to end up with a discount of less than 20 percent off the total restaurant bill. You also have to present a special card or coupon to get the discount.

Dining à la Carte (800-257-8317; $49.95 annual membership) gives you a 20 percent cash rebate on your total bill (including tax and tip) in some forty-five hundred participating restaurants (but only one visit a month to any single restaurant). You don't have to carry a special card. Instead, you simply register all of the credit cards you might possibly use in a restaurant with Dining à la Carte and use them as you normally would. Every month, you will get a cash rebate of 20 percent of whatever charges from participating restaurants appear on any of those cards.

▶ EAT YOUR BIG MEAL AT LUNCH

The menus may be exactly the same, but the price of lunch at most of the world's restaurants is invariably cheaper—often by 30 to 40 percent—than the price of dinner.

▶ GET DINNER FOR THE PRICE OF A DRINK

We have a young friend who has systematically investigated the different free cocktail-hour appetizers at some of San Francisco's best-known and, in some cases, most expensive hotels and restaurants. His favorite place charges an outrageously high price for drinks. But one glass of wine, he points out, can be sipped for the forty-five minutes it takes to eat what he considers quite a satisfying free six- or seven-course dinner. He strongly suggests you overtip if you like the place well enough to go back.

▶ EAT DINNER EARLY

In many restaurants, the difference between ordering the same dinner at 6:55 P.M. and 7:05 P.M. isn't just ten minutes. The earlier meal may be as much as 50 percent less expensive. Ask about "early bird" and pretheater specials when you call for reservations.

▶ GET PRICES ON SPECIALS

"Hello, my name is Dave. Let me tell you about our specials tonight." Too often, Dave skips one ingredient: the price. Knowing that most people are reluctant to ask their friendly waiter the price of specials, many restaurants overprice them. Ask before you order.

▶ TAKE HOME A FREE LUNCH

Until a few years ago, we were uncomfortable about asking for what is unfortunately called a "doggie bag." Then, as guests of a business associate during a wonderful dinner in New York City at Lutèce, perhaps America's finest French restaurant, we watched a celebrity multimillionaire at the next table beam as his doggie bag was graciously handed to him. We haven't given it a second thought since.

▶ ORDER THE ALL-INCLUSIVE DINNER

If you are going to have an appetizer, side dishes, and dessert as well as an entrée, you are nearly always better off ordering from the side of the menu offering complete meals. Ordering à la carte can easily increase the cost of a meal by 30 to 50 percent.

▶ SKIP THE ENTRÉE

If you are a light eater or aren't very hungry, order two appetizers and ask that one of them be served as your main course. Appetizers are usually priced at less than a third of the cost of a main course.

▶ SHARE COURSES

In many restaurants, one salad order is more than large enough for two. In Italian restaurants, we usually share a pasta course. And we invariably share one dessert.

▶ NO PENNY PINCHER EVER USED A HOTEL MINIBAR

The only time we open a hotel minibar is to get ice (free) for the bottle of water or the wine we have brought into the room ourselves. Those silly little bottles and candy bars are usually at least 500 percent more expensive than they are at the nearest market.

▶ BEFORE YOU GO TO NEW YORK . . .

Given ticket prices of $100 or more for a new musical, going to the theater in New York City has become prohibitively expensive for people who aren't on expense accounts. But there are ways to find bargains:

- *The Hit Show Club* (212-581-4211; 630 Ninth Avenue, New York, NY 10036) prints and distributes "two-fer" coupons that you can redeem at the box office, usually for a third off the regular price of many Broadway and some off-Broadway shows. Send a SASE at least six weeks prior to your trip to get current discount tickets before you leave. You can stay on the club's mailing list from then on, if you like. If you call the above number, you will get a recorded message telling you what shows are currently offering discounts.

- *TKTS booths,* operated by the Theater Development Fund, are located at Duffy Square (47th and Broadway) and 2 World Trade Center in Manhattan. If you want to take a chance, you can go to one of these booths the day of the performance you want to attend and get half-price or three-quarter-price tickets (plus a small service charge). How good are your chances? Terrible for the hottest new shows, quite good for just about anything else, including many long-running hits. Call 212-768-1818 for information.

- *The Theatre Development Fund* (212-221-0013; 1501 Broadway, Suite 2110, New York, NY 10036) sends members periodic, usually monthly, offerings of discounted tickets, usually in the range of $14 to $16, for a wide variety of shows and events. Members can also purchase TDF "vouchers" for about $15, which are good for additional discounts (sometimes even free admission) to a variety of performing-arts events. To join TDF, send a legal-size SASE with your request for an individual application. After you fill that out, return it with a $15 check. You can get more information at http://www.tdf.org.

▶ BEFORE YOU GO TO WASHINGTON, D.C. . . .

Call your congressman's or senator's local office and get free passes to the White House and Senate and House galleries. The White House tour is more extensive than the one tourists stand in line to pay for.

▶ UNDER TWENTY-SIX? GET A CIEE CARD

The *Council on International Educational Exchange* is a nonprofit organization whose primary goal is to develop student exchanges and foster international understanding. For young travelers, especially those planning to travel, work, or study abroad, the CIEE is also a great penny-pinching resource.

The CIEE issues three International Identity Cards ($20 each) that will pay for themselves many times over on a trip abroad: *Student* (proof needed that you are twelve or over and a junior high, high school, college, university, or vocational school student); *Youth* (proof needed that you are between twelve and twenty-six); and *Teacher* (proof needed that you are a full-time faculty member at an accredited institution).

The cards make you eligible for discounts on transportation (local mass transit as well as airlines and railroads), accommodations, tourist attractions, cultural events, etc. They also include sickness, accident, life, and emergency medical insurance coverage, as well as access to a twenty-four-hour toll-free Traveler's Assistance Service. The easiest way to get a card is to visit a Council Travel office or download an application from the Council Travel web site (see next tip).

▶ CHECK OUT FARES FROM COUNCIL TRAVEL

Council Travel (800-226-8624; http://www.counciltravel .com) is the travel division of the CIEE and has forty offices nationwide. It is a good place for any budget-minded traveler to check for discounted airfares, railroad passes, and low-cost accommodations and car rentals. Some, but not all, of its discounts are available to anyone, not just students. Even students, however, shouldn't take for granted that Council Travel rates are the lowest available. They are nearly always competitive, but you should compare them with those of other consolidators and charter operators as well as with special airline promotional fares.

▶ STAY IN YOUTH HOSTELS

Whatever your age, hostels, which offer dormitory-like rooms, are the lowest-cost way to spend a night unless you are a camper. Prices range from as low as $10 to $40, and accommodations range from primitive barracks to authentic castles. Many serve meals and have recreational facilities. To stay at one of the more than five thousand hostels in seventy-one countries that are part of *Hostelling International,* first purchase an HI membership card (under eighteen, $10; eighteen to fifty-four, $25; over fifty-four, $15; family membership, $35). Cards are available at any Council Travel office (see above), or you can download an application form and get complete information at http://www.hiayh.org.

▶ OVER FIFTY? JOIN THE AARP

See Chapter 11 for other reasons, but quick-and-easy travel discounts alone make the $8 annual membership fee of the American Association of Retired Persons (800-424-3410; http://www.aarp.com) a must for anyone over fifty). Nearly all hotel and motel chains offer at least a 10 percent discount to AARP cardholders. Some offer discounts as high as 50 percent. Car-rental and some restaurant chains also give AARP members discounts, as do individually owned motels, bed-and-breakfasts, and resorts.

Once you have an AARP card, get in the habit of always asking about a possible AARP discount when you make any kind of travel purchase. You will often be pleasantly surprised. But negotiate for the best deal possible first, and only then ask for your AARP discount.

▶ OVER SIXTY-TWO? BUY AIRLINE SENIOR COUPON BOOKS

Most of the major domestic airlines sell books of discount coupons to travelers over sixty-two. Typically, the books have four coupons, good for two round-trip coach flights anywhere the airline flies in the U.S. (plus a few places in the Caribbean and Canada). As of this writing, a book of coupons from American, Delta, United, or Northwest cost $596; America West, TWA, and Continental offered even better deals. A round-trip fare of

$298 may not make sense on some flights, but it could represent a significant discount on others. Most airlines allow standby travel with senior coupons as well as frequent-flier credits. You must use all of the coupons within one year and there may be other restrictions as well, including advance reservations. If you qualify for a senior coupon book, first consider where you want to go and which airline offers the best service to that destination from your home airport.

Even if you don't buy discount coupons, most airlines give seniors over sixty-two a 10 percent discount on most tickets.

▶ OVER SIXTY-TWO? GET A GOLDEN AGE PASSPORT

The next time you visit a federal park, monument, forest, or recreational area that charges an entrance fee, don't pay it. Instead, show proof of age and citizenship and, for $10, get a *lifetime* pass. Whenever you visit a national park thereafter, just show the pass; you and anyone else in your vehicle will be admitted free of charge.

▶ OVER FIFTY-FIVE? CHECK OUT ELDERHOSTEL

Elderhostel (to get a catalog, call 617-426-7788 or visit http://www.elderhostel.org) is a nonprofit program that sponsors weeklong educational vacations at hundreds of different locations (often college campuses) in the U.S., Canada, and Europe. Prices, including rooms (often in dormitories), meals, classes, and other activities, average about $450 per person. If you go as a couple, only one of you must be over fifty-five.

(See Chapter 5 for tips on shopping for travelers.)

8

Saving on Quality Clothing

We have made an effort throughout this book to offer money-saving tips that don't involve a lot of extra time or effort. But when it comes to shopping for clothing, there are not too many time-efficient ways to get the very best bargains. Most of those are found by people who don't mind spending hours checking on sales or surfing the Internet, love to read and compare catalogs, and can spend a full day at an outlet mall and then happily repeat the experience a week later.

If you hate to shop, you can still manage to save money with some of the tips in this chapter. Tips you will probably want to avoid are labeled FSO—For Shopaholics Only.

The transformation of the retail landscape in the past few years has changed the way all of us shop for clothes. Many of the great department stores and traditional specialty stores that dominated the apparel scene for generations have disappeared. The survivors have had to adopt aggressive new selling strategies to hold on to old customers and attract new ones. The competition is fiercer than ever for your clothing dollar—among department stores, specialty stores, off-price retailers, designer and factory outlet stores, mass merchandisers, mail-order sellers, and even wholesale clubs. The opportunities for bargain hunters have never been greater, but neither has the potential for confusion.

Fewer and fewer stores can be relied on completely for quality or for knowledgeable service. Those that can usually cater to people who can afford the best at any cost. When you shop anywhere else, including many traditional department and specialty stores that now stock merchandise they might once have shunned, it is important to know how to recognize quality and a proper fit.

Nowhere in this chapter will you find advice on saving money by buying inexpensively produced clothing. Our philosophy is simple: Cheap isn't cheap if you wear it once; expensive isn't expensive if you wear it forever. The goal is to buy "expensive" for as little as possible.

▶ WHO DESIGNS DESIGNER LABELS?

Usually not the designer who has lent his or her name to the clothing label. In most cases, the rights to the name have been sold to a manufacturer who then pays a royalty, a percentage of the manufacturer's cost, to the designer.

With a few honorable and usually high-priced exceptions, a designer label is not a guarantee of quality. Three checklists in this chapter will help you avoid shoddy merchandise and spot a well-made garment. Use them no matter what the label is.

▶ DESIGNER VERSUS BRAND NAME VERSUS PRIVATE LABELS

If you suspect the industry may be out to confuse you on purpose, you aren't far wrong. What's in a label? Not much. Is Christian Dior, who died quite a few years ago, a designer label or a brand name? Certainly, in cases like this, you can at least be positive that Monsieur Dior himself had nothing to do with the hemline. Famous models and movie stars lend their names to labels, too, although this is usually seen mainly in mass merchandisers like Kmart.

Private labels are one way department stores have fought back against their dependence on designer-label clothing. If you know you may be able to buy a famous designer label cheaper at an off-price or designer outlet store, why buy at a department store? Realizing that too many people have come to this conclusion, many department stores have devoted a lot of their resources to establishing their own private labels.

Because department stores and specialty chains have so much at stake in their private labels, you will often find very good buys in quality clothing at certain stores. Stores as different as the Limited, Neiman Marcus, and the Gap have developed private-label lines that offer a consistent fit and a sense of fashion that reflects each store's image.

You should also know, however, that some private-label apparel is bought from a manufacturer who may be selling exactly the same apparel to another department or specialty store in the same area. Only the labels will be different. And the prices. It is entirely possible that the same suit will cost $600 at a department store and $350 at a second-floor walk-up discount specialty store across town.

What to do? Use the kind of quality checklists you'll find in this chapter and shop around.

▶ SAVE 50 PERCENT! BUT IS IT ON SALE?

Not always. More and more often, whether you are shopping in a department store, an off-price store, a factory or designer outlet, a mass merchandiser, or a mail-order catalog, a "sale" is not a sale but a cynical marketing gimmick. "Originally $100, now $49.95" is meaningless if the garment was never bought by anyone for $100, and, in fact, gives the retailer a handsome markup at the $49.95 price.

Some states have laws against this kind of deception, but there are few efforts to prosecute any but the most blatant abuses. When you see a price tag stating "Suggested retail price $100, our price $39.95," your first thought should be: "Suggested by whom?"

Unfortunately, there are fewer and fewer retailers who don't resort at least occasionally to such tactics. If you want to save money as well as buy quality clothing, you simply have to know how to examine every prospective purchase.

▶ ARE THERE STILL BARGAINS IN TRADITIONAL DEPARTMENT STORES?

With all the different kinds of retailers now competing for your clothing dollar, are there still bargains available in traditional department stores? Absolutely, but usually only at certain times of the year.

Department stores sell seasonally. Because they anticipate what you will want to wear next season, you can't walk into a department store in the Northeast on a 98-degree day in August and expect to find a good selection of bathing suits or summer dresses. That's when winter coats and wool dresses are featured.

To make room for next winter's clothing, summer clothes are now routinely put on sale in traditional department stores at just about the time you may want to wear them, in June. And winter clothing, on sale everywhere in January, has in recent years been put on sale by nervous retailers well before Christmas.

▶ GET DEPARTMENT STORE CREDIT CARDS

It is far more convenient to use one Visa or MasterCard for all of your purchases, and virtually every store now takes them. The only reason to go to the bother of open-

A Quick Quality Checklist for All Clothing

■ Stitching. Small stiches usually mean longer-lasting apparel. Stitches should be neat, straight, and even, although in a very well-made garment slightly uneven stitches suggest hand-sewing, always an indication of quality.

■ Seams should be flat. The seam formed where two pieces of fabric meet should be straight. Even slight puckering should be avoided.

■ Puckering at darts (the short, stitched folds that make a garment fit more closely) also indicates lower quality.

■ Patterns (stripes, plaids, checks) should "shake hands" at the seams; if two pieces aren't matched exactly, it is a sure sign of a poorly made garment.

■ Armholes and shoulders of jackets should fit smoothly, without any wrinkles.

■ Linings are not supposed to be attached all the way around.

■ Pockets should be large enough to use comfortably and should have reinforced stitching.

■ Few cheap garments use 100 percent natural fiber fabrics, so an all-cotton men's shirt, for example, is probably well constructed. This isn't to suggest that a lot of quality clothing isn't made of synthetic fibers.

■ Check the grain of the fabric. It is important that every garment be cut "on-grain," meaning that lengthwise yarns hang perpendicular to the floor and crosswise yarns at a perfect 90-degree angle. This is much easier to spot in a plaid or a stripe; if these are cut "off-grain," horizontal and vertical lines won't match. But no garment will hang well if cut slightly off-grain. They are getting hard to find, but a knowledgeable salesperson or a good tailor can point out examples of how important the grain of the fabric is.

■ Look for flaws and variations in the fabric, but remember that some are normal and desirable in certain natural fabrics.

■ Buttonholes should be evenly spaced and neatly and securely stitched.

ing credit-card accounts with individual stores is so that you get advance notice of "private" cardholder sales. If the sale involves using only the store credit card to get the savings you want, do so. Otherwise, keep all of these cards in a safe place and never use them at all.

▶ SHOP OFF-PRICE STORES

They won't always have your size or the color you want. Some of the clothing will be marked "irregular" or "imperfect." Buttons may be missing, and a thread may be loose. Service is either bad or nonexistent. But you can't think of yourself as a penny pincher unless you at least look into off-price stores from time to time. Quality is uneven, but you can definitely find quality clothing, often with designer labels, at very attractive prices—up to 80 percent off.

Off-price stores are where manufacturers dump slow sellers returned by traditional stores (this has nothing to do with quality), irregulars (defects are sometimes hard to find and usually nothing that affects wearability), and overstock. When credit crunches hit and a manufacturer needs cash quick, first-run merchandise may also turn up in off-price stores.

You've got to be careful when you find a bargain in an off-price store. Irregulars (minor flaws) and seconds (more serious ones) are supposed to be marked, but that doesn't always happen. Sizes aren't dependable either; the garments may have been incorrectly sized originally and that's the only reason they're in the off-price store. Try everything on.

Finally, make sure you know what the return policies of the store are.

These are among the leading off-price chains that we have found likely to offer at least some quality clothing at very attractive discounts (phone numbers for "location nearest you" information):

■ *Marshalls* (800-MARSHAL). Men's, women's, children's clothing. Among labels you'll find from time to time: Calvin Klein, Perry Ellis, Armani, Anne Klein.

A Quick Quality and Fit Checklist for Women

■ When you try on a coat or jacket, bend your arms; the sleeves should still come to your wrists.

■ Do the shoulder pads stay in place? Take the jacket off and put it back on a couple of times. It's a telltale sign of a poorly constructed garment if you have to keep adjusting the shoulder pads.

■ Jacket lapels that seem to be pressed flat or are stiff should be avoided. Lapels should be soft and rounded and should spring back into shape after you crumple or squeeze them.

■ When trying on a coat, wear the bulkiest jacket or sweater you intend to wear under it. The armholes should still feel comfortably roomy.

■ Sit down when you try on a skirt. It should have enough room in it to avoid creases across the front from sitting.

■ Pleats in a skirt should hang smoothly, without parting at the hip area.

■ The waistbands of all types of skirts should fit snugly, but without any indication that they will roll.

■ No matter how they are finished (hand-rolled, blindstitched, etc.), hems on a well-made garment will fall smoothly, without any signs of unevenness, puckering, or rippling. Hems are easy to alter, though, so if everything else is okay, consider buying the garment.

■ Hemline stitches should always be invisible from the outside.

■ Zippers should be dyed to match the fabric and completely covered.

■ Buttons should be functional. A button stuck on for decoration is a sign of cheap design. If buttons are supposed to match the color of the garment, they should match exactly.

■ No matter what you buy, make certain you can move easily while you have it on. "It looks great, so I don't mind being uncomfortable" is never a successful long-term strategy.

Two Marshalls stores, twenty miles away from each other, may have quite different mixes of clothing.

- *T.J. Maxx* (800-926-6299). T.J. Maxx bought Marshalls in late 1995, but is keeping both names. Together, with more than 1,150 stores nationwide, they have enormous buying clout. T.J. Maxx sells men's and women's clothing, including Donna Karan, Anne Klein, Esprit, and Armani labels. Clothing here tends to be a bit younger and perhaps more stylish than in Marshalls.
- *Loehmann's* (718-409-2000). More than eighty stores nationwide, and, with Filene's Basement, the originator of the off-price concept. Women's clothing only. You'll never find all sizes, colors, etc., but legendary buys are still possible here. More likely for sizes 4 and 6.
- *Burlington Coat Factory* (800-444-COAT). More than 230 stores nationwide. "We're more than great coats" is the slogan, and these stores do sell men's and women's clothing of all kinds. We haven't bought anything but coats yet, though.
- *Filene's Basement* (800-666-4045). More than fifty stores, still confined to the Northeast and Midwest. Men's and women's clothing. Recent find: men's dress shirts with a Brooks Brothers label for $15.

► SHOP DEPARTMENT-STORE CLEARANCE CENTERS

Some top-line department stores, including Nordstrom, Saks Fifth Avenue, and Neiman Marcus, ship unsold clothing from main stores to their own clearance centers. You won't find current-season clothing at these locations, but the quality is usually dependable and markdowns of up to 75 percent are possible.

► SHOP OFF-PRICE STORES AND EVERYWHERE ELSE [FSO]

Now let's discuss the tactics used by shopaholics. They don't "look into off-price stores from time to time"—

they haunt them. They make special trips to factory and designer outlet centers—and repeat the trip a couple of weeks later.

If you have guessed that we don't shop this way, you are right. But there's no question that those who do find the greatest bargains. And a true shopaholic loves the game, which involves such tactics as these:

- Visiting the store just before the announced sale day. Sometimes salespeople will bend the rules and allow early sale shopping. If not, the shopaholic locates every potential buy beforehand and is the first in line the morning of the sale.
- Being constantly on the lookout for clothing that isn't marked "as is," but has some easily correctable flaw (a missing button, a broken stitch, etc.). Shopaholics immediately ask for a much lower price. They also look for and, more often than you would imagine, find mismarked items early in a sale, before the manager is aware of the mistake made by some harried clerk. This is sheer shopaholic bliss.
- Getting to know clerks and managers at different stores and calling from time to time about big-ticket items. "Any change in the price of that suede coat you've never had on sale?"
- Getting on every mailing list possible and tracking prices in different catalogs.

▶ SHOP DESIGNER OUTLETS

Off-price stores are still a hit-or-miss proposition. You've got to be lucky, your timing has to be right, or you have to be a relentless repeat shopper to find quality merchandise. That's less true of the designer outlets, usually located off a main highway in one of the 350 designer outlet malls now operating in the United States. *Donna Karan, Polo/Ralph Lauren, Calvin Klein, Liz Claiborne, Armani,* and *Prada* are among the leading designers who operate outlet stores, selling their clothing at discounts of up to 75 percent.Originally, designer outlet stores were supposed to sell manufacturers' over-

A Quick Quality and Fit Checklist for Men

■ Make certain there is felt backing stitched under the collar of any suit or sport jacket.

■ Zippers should be sewn in absolutely straight and should lie flat.

■ Every well-made shirt has two rows of stitching under the arm-holes.

■ Extra fabric often indicates quality, since the manufacturer isn't cutting close to save a few cents. There should be a minimum of ⅜″ of fabric on both sides of the center seam in a pair of pants. Even if you don't need the extra length, be suspicious if a jacket doesn't have an inch or two of extra fabric under the cuff to allow for lengthening.

■ The edges of fabric inside a jacket should be stitched. If you see a piece of fabric that looks like it could unravel, avoid the jacket.

■ Buttonholes should be strongly reinforced with thread and jacket buttonholes should have a slight "keyhole" effect on the lapel side. Buttons should button easily; if the hole is too small, it is a sign of a hastily made garment.

■ Check to make sure the sleeve lining is neatly stitched to the jacket lining and the coat itself at the armpit. If it looks uneven or badly stitched, avoid the jacket.

■ Squeeze the lapels for a couple of seconds. If they don't spring back to their original shape immediately, avoid the jacket.

■ The waistbands of pants should be reinforced with a stiffening fabric inside the lining. All well-made pants also have a second button inside the fly on the left, just below the waist button, to ensure a better fit and relieve pressure on the waist button.

■ Don't even bother to go into the fitting room if a jacket doesn't lie flat on your shoulders; this is nearly always extremely difficult to alter. So is the length of the jacket.

supply and end-of-season leftovers that hadn't been shipped to department and full-price specialty stores. They have become so popular, however, that many also now feature a wide assortment of newer apparel. Some of it is exactly the same as what is sold in the designers' primary stores. But, especially if the designer operates a large number of outlet stores, you are also likely to find lower-quality clothing made specifically for sale only in those outlets. Many designer outlets also sell seconds and irregulars, not always clearly marked.

Unlike the off-price stores, most designer outlets are well furnished and are pleasant places to shop. But designer outlets are no longer a guaranteed source of real bargains. Very often, the prices are no lower than what you will find in a department store or specialty store sale. So it is a good idea before visiting the malls to know what the designer-label clothing is selling for in those traditional retailers.

▶ SHOP OUTLET STORES

A step down in chic from designer outlets, outlet stores are nevertheless a good place to bargain-hunt for clothing and footwear. The first factory outlets were actually attached to the factories and sold seconds, damaged goods, and irregulars. Because these factories were usually in the old textile and leather centers on the East Coast, the factory outlet phenomenon was limited to that part of the country until the early 1980s.

By then, factory outlets had become so profitable that manufacturers opened new stores and started producing perfectly sound, first-line merchandise for them. There are now outlet stores nationwide, most of them grouped into outlet centers. There are also quite a few retail operations that try to pass themselves off as factory outlets, but are usually just discounters of second-rate merchandise.

Long-standing agreements between manufacturers and regular retail customers, although under some pressure these days, make it unlikely that you will find the very newest lines or fashions in outlet stores. But a lot of good-quality merchandise is sold in them. As with designer outlets, it helps to know beforehand the normal retail sale price of an item you might buy in an outlet store; too often, there is little difference or the outlet item is actually more expensive. The outlets of some manufacturers are more dependable than others, and you will get a sense of this as you spend time in them.

▶ SHOP THE INTERNET

Just about every major retailer in the country has a web site. To promote shopping on-line, which is potentially far more profitable for the retailer than printing and mailing catalogs or paying rent on a mall location, many of them offer special deals that are available only at their web sites. Rather than list hundreds of possible locations, go to a search site called *HotBot* (http://www. hotbot.com) and access "Shopping and Services" from the home menu. After a couple of more menu choices you might find a selection of a dozen designer-label sites or a hundred places to buy men's sportswear.

▶ ARMY-NAVY STORES STILL HAVE BARGAINS

Sure, the variety is limited, but check out prices on basics like jeans and T-shirts at an army-navy store. If you have an Old Navy store in your area, it will probably offer basics at as low a price as you'll find anywhere.

▶ ASK FOR "ALTERATION DISCOUNTS"

Our Bantam editor reports that a short (5′0″) friend almost always has to have pants, skirts, and dresses altered. Often, when she points this out to the salesperson who has been helping her, she gets an "alteration discount" of up to 10 percent.

▶ COMPARISON-SHOP IN THE BOYS' DEPARTMENT

Our editor's friend and other small women have an opportunity to save much more than 10 percent on sweats, windbreakers, knit shirts, and other clothing items. Comparison-shop for items like these in any store's boys' department. Invariably, the prices are far less than in the women's department for the same or even better-quality items.

Questions to Ask Before You Buy Anything

- Would I like this just as much if the label read "Sears" instead of "Famous Designer"?

- Do I really believe I'll be able to wear this next year . . . five years from now?

- Is this garment well made enough to last that long?

- How much will dry cleaning cost?

- Am I prepared to wash and iron this every time I wear it?

- Does it really fit, or am I tempted to buy it because it fits pretty well and is a size smaller than I usually buy?

- How does this fit into my wardrobe? What can I wear it with that I own now?

- What else will I have to buy to make full use of this garment? Will I need special accessories? Do I really want to spend that much more?

- Where will I be able to wear this—given my actual (as opposed to my fantasy) lifestyle?

- Does it go with the coat I intend to wear it with? If it is a coat—does it coordinate with everything else I own?

- Can I use this year-round if I add or subtract a layer? If it is a one-season garment, where and when can I wear it? Do I go there/do that in summer/winter?

- Am I at least fairly confident I've shopped enough elsewhere to be sure this is a good value?

Actually, certain unisex items like knit shirts are almost always less expensive in the men's department, so women of any size should do some comparison shopping there.

▶ THE TWO-PANTS STRATEGY FOR MEN

Years ago, sales of two-pants suits were limited to low-quality bargain stores. No more. If you wear a suit to work every day, and are reasonably sure you'll wear the same size for a few years to come, consider taking advantage of the increasing number of stores and mail-order retailers that sell perfectly matched jackets and pants separately. It will cost you more in the short run to buy two pairs of pants, but jackets are far more expensive and pants invariably wear out long before jackets.

A suit with a three-year life span might have a six-year life span this way. The trick is to make certain that you alternate wearing the different pants from the very beginning and dry-clean all three pieces at the same time. That way, both pairs of pants will match the jacket after five years as well as they did when you bought them.

▶ BUY CLOTHES WITH YOUR PASTA

We wouldn't join a warehouse club (see Chapter 1) for its clothing section alone, but we do check the section out whenever we make one of our periodic trips to buy groceries in bulk. There's no telling what kind of clothes will be there, but on a couple of occasions in the past year we have found a terrific buy.

▶ BUY AND SELL AT CONSIGNMENT SHOPS

A number of readers of prior editions wrote to tell us how well they do buying and selling clothes at consignment shops. The best consignment shops buy only good-quality used clothing that is still in style and in excellent condition.

When an article of clothing is sold in the shop, the original owner typically gets 40 to 50 percent of the sale price.

Although some women use consignment shops only to sell clothing they no longer want, many sellers are also regular buyers. You can find top designer-label clothing in many consignment shops, often at a small fraction of original prices. And once you become a regular customer, some shops will call to tell you when something special turns up in your size.

▶ SHOP IN BAD WEATHER [FSO]

Store managers get lonely during a snowstorm at the end of January or on the hottest day in August. Those are particularly good shopping months in any case, but if you are one of the few customers in sight on a bad day and are serious about buying something, ask about the price tag. On-the-spot markdowns are possible.

▶ BEWARE OF THE 90 PERCENT DISCOUNT

For as long as world-famous designers have shown their new collections at openings attended by the rich and the high-fashion elite, manufacturers with no intention of paying those designers a penny have initiated frantic efforts starting the next day to copy their lines.

This is perfectly legal. "Knockoffs" are an accepted part of the industry. In fact, many designers "knock off" their own high-priced designs in lower-priced lines of clothing, using less expensive fabrics and mass production methods but still producing good-quality garments.

What is not legal is counterfeiting, which is putting a fake label in a copy of an item of apparel or an accessory and then selling it as the real thing. In addition to being illegal, a counterfeit is nearly always a shoddily produced piece of merchandise.

If you see a $500 Gucci bag for $39.95 and think it is too good to be true, it is.

▶ THINK JANUARY AND JULY

Sales are routine year-round these days, but it is still true that stores are anxious to get rid of clothing that didn't sell during the Christmas shopping season. Doing some serious shopping during the first week of January can be especially rewarding. July is not only the slowest month of the year for stores in most areas, it is also when retailers are making room for winter lines and slashing prices on summer clothing.

▶ BUY "SLIGHTLY IMPERFECT" HOSIERY BY MAIL

So slight are the imperfections in the hosiery we've seen ordered from the free *L'eggs, Hanes, Bali, Playtex* catalog (800-300-2600; http://www.onehanesplace.com) that we'd probably use it even if it didn't offer an unconditional 100 percent money-back guarantee. With that guarantee, and the opportunity to save 50 percent on the brand we use (all the popular Hanes brands are available), the catalog is a basic annual resource.

If you prefer *No Nonsense* panty hose, the manufacturer offers "practically perfect" hosiery at 50 to 60 percent off retail prices. For a free catalog, call 800-677-5995.

▶ CHECK OUT SPIEGEL'S CATALOG

Spiegel (800-345-4500; http://www.spiegel.com) is a mail-order giant, but its clothing seems to be a cut or two above the competition's in terms of fashion. The web site offers special sales and the big Spiegel catalog ($3, money back with first order) includes much more than clothing; it is a good resource to check in other areas as well.

▶ BUY MEN'S DRESS SHIRTS BY MAIL

Paul Frederick (800-247-8162; http://www.menstyle. com) is a manufacturer of quality shirts that you will find in better stores, often with their private labels. The same shirts are available direct from the company for discounts that can be as high as 50 percent off store prices. Call for a free catalog or buy direct from the web site.

▶ BUY FROM LANDS' END OR L. L. BEAN

There are other good general mail-order catalogs, but we continue to find these two the most reliable for both men's and women's casual clothing. Discounts off retail prices can't be quoted because you won't find this clothing in retail outlets, but savings of from 20 to 35 percent off comparable apparel are likely.

Once you are on their mailing lists and buy even occasionally, you'll get seasonal catalogs. Both feature a few pages of marked-down, discontinued merchandise at very large discounts off previous prices. We nearly always find something to buy, and have never been disappointed. Both have outstanding web sites if you prefer to shop on-line.

Lands' End (800-356-4444; http://www.landsend.com); *L. L. Bean* (800-221-4221; http://www.llbean.com).

We have also been greatly impressed by the *Gap* web site (http://www.gap.com). There is a Gap store close to most of us, but the on-line catalog is superconvenient and features special sales.

▶ RENT INSTEAD OF BUYING

Want a knock-'em-dead evening dress for a once-in-a-lifetime occasion? At least check on what's available at rental shops in your area. Typically, you might spend as much as $250 to rent a $2,000 dress, and the odds get better every day that you won't be the only one at the affair with a money-saving secret. Check the Yellow Pages under "formal wear."

▶ CHECK OUT SAMPLE SALES

The *Sample Sale* web site (http://www.samplesale. com) lists current sales on clothing and jewelry in stores in New York City, Boston, Washington, D.C., Miami, Chicago, Los Angeles, and San Francisco.

▶ GET SENIOR DISCOUNTS

Sears offers a 10 percent discount to anyone fifty or over who joins a special shoppers' club. Many other chains as well as local stores offer discounts to senior shoppers, often limited to certain times of the week. If you are not sure, ask.

▶ MAKE A BUYER'S TRIP TO NEW YORK CITY [FSO]

Although not much clothing is actually manufactured in New York anymore, it is still the capital of the garment industry and a must stop for retail buyers from everywhere in the country. You can't get into the wholesale showrooms the buyers do, but savvy city shoppers know that not all of them are "for the trade only."

The *Bargain Hotline* (540-0123) is updated weekly (on Friday nights) and lists upcoming sample and overstock sales in garment-center showrooms—complete with what kind of merchandise is on sale at each showroom, their addresses, and information about what kind of payment will be accepted. The number can only be dialed from a phone within the New York metropolitan area (212, 516, 718, and 914 area codes) and the call will cost $1.95 for the first minute and 75 cents a minute after that.

Also check out the "Sales and Bargains" section in the back of the latest issue of *New York* magazine. It does a good job of keeping up with what stores and manufacturers have new and notable sales.

The famous Garment District (roughly between Fifth and Eighth Avenues from Thirty-fourth to Forty-first Streets) is filled with storefronts that say "trade only" or "wholesale only." But some of these places will sell direct. There are a number of showrooms in the area that welcome retail customers.

One of the best areas to explore for all kinds of discounted clothing is Orchard Street on the Lower East Side.

When you buy anything in New York, skip the city's huge sales tax by having your purchases shipped to your home.

▶ BUY MATERNITY CLOTHES BY MAIL

Mother's Place (800-829-0080) doesn't offer discounts, but it does offer a free catalog of its own-label maternity clothing at very attractive prices.

▶ BUY KIDS' CLOTHES BY MAIL

- *Olsen Mill Direct* (800-537-4979) sells the OshKosh line of children's clothing at factory outlet prices.
- *Chock* (800-222-0020) sells discounted pajamas and underwear.
- *Children's Connection* (516-798-0142) sells many top brands by the dozen as well as by the piece, always at large discounts.
- *After the Stork* (800-441-4775; http://www.afterthestork. com) sells quality kids' cottons at very competitive discount prices.
- *Lands' End* (see tip above), better known for adult casual clothes, has a terrific children's catalog.

The malls compete with mail-order operations quite successfully in this category. *Sears* (http://www.sears. com) and *JCPenney* (http://www.jcpenney.com) sell clothing for everyone, but their prices on good-quality children's clothes are especially hard to beat. They get stiff competition from the *Kids "R" Us* chain.

▶ DON'T JUST BUY CLOTHES, PLAN A WARDROBE

Impulse shopping in clothing stores is as dangerous as it is in supermarkets. To get the most from your clothing dollar year after year, you must discipline yourself. Certain styles of clothes and colors look good on you; stick to them. Never buy anything unless you can coordinate it within your basic wardrobe. A pair of shoes that goes with only one dress or a shirt that goes with only one sport jacket are expensive mistakes.

The best way to avoid impulse buying for clothes is to make up a very definite list of what you need. Keep this list in a small notebook that you can always carry with you, and update it constantly. It may be months before you find exactly the summer jacket you are looking for, but if you have a coordinated wardrobe it may be worth the wait.

See "Questions to Ask Before You Buy Anything" in

this chapter for a quick checklist to use before you make a final purchase decision on any garment or accessory. If you keep these questions in mind, you'll avoid a lot of mistakes.

▶ DON'T JUST BUY CLOTHES, INVEST IN THEM

If you always buy clothes to become part of an evolving but carefully coordinated wardrobe, you will need fewer items than if you buy the latest fashion fads or follow short-term trends. You will begin to think in terms of investing in clothes, not just buying them. While few of us can afford the very finest quality for every item in our wardrobe, investing in a few classic garments that fit that description becomes a realitic strategy.

You will seldom find the best for sale under signs that proclaim "60 percent off," but the exclusive specialty men's and women's stores all have sales, too. Look for their often sedate sale ads and stop in. There are clothing bargains at every price level, and the most satisfying in the long run may be the ones that were initially the most expensive.

▶ WORRY ABOUT BUTTONS

What happens if you lose one of the seven unusual buttons that "make" the outfit? Try to buy an extra button or two with the garment.

Alternatively, what if you find a quality garment compromised only by cheap buttons? It often pays to buy the garment anyway and purchase top-grade horn or natural buttons elsewhere.

▶ REMEMBER THAT "DRY CLEAN ONLY" COSTS EXTRA

A woman who dresses for an executive job in a city office fifty weeks of the year can easily spend $1,500 annually on dry cleaning. Buying some clothes that need to be dry-cleaned is unavoidable, but searching out summer blouses that can be washed is worth the effort.

As for clothes that must be dry-cleaned, avoid silk, because it is the most expensive fabric to have dry-cleaned as well as the most delicate, and pleated skirts and dresses of any fabric, because most dry cleaners will charge extra to press each pleat.

► LEAVE A NOTE FOR YOUR DRY CLEANER

If you know what caused a stain (even if you think it is obvious), pin a note over it when you send the garment to your dry cleaner. Helping him or her choose certain solutions and avoid others can make all the difference.

► BUT DON'T USE THEM TOO OFTEN

Dry cleaning isn't just expensive; it is also hard on fabrics and can fade colors. Unless the garment is stained, get it pressed instead—and save at least 50 percent.

► USE A SPRAY TIE PROTECTOR

Men who dress in a suit and tie every day often find themselves spending hundreds of dollars a year on what they wrap around their necks. Few have not had the experience of buying a $40 tie and seeing it destroyed at lunch the next day by an errant drop of sauce. Spray tie protectors actually work. Try a can on a couple of your favorites.

One more tip: If you water-spot a silk tie, wait for it to dry and then simply rub the spot with another part of the tie. Nine times out of ten, you'll remove the spot.

► USE SHOE GOO ON SNEAKERS

After a couple of months, an otherwise perfectly good pair of sneakers may begin to wear out in just one or two small areas of the sole. Instead of throwing them away, repair them overnight using an inexpensive tube of Shoe Goo, available in most sporting-goods and many hardware stores. You can easily triple the life of a pair of sneakers this way.

9

Dealing with Banks, Mortgages, and Credit

All of the services offered by your bank, credit-card company, or any other kind of lender are considered "products" by these organizations. Just like cans of soup on a supermarket shelf, these financial products—from checking accounts and home-equity loans to trust services and annuities—are conceived, priced, and marketed to make a profit.

Some people have trouble accepting this. After all, they trust their banks with their money, with their most precious and valuable documents if they have a safe-deposit box, and with their complete financial histories if they take out a loan. Banks have grave fiduciary responsibilities that make them more than mere marketers of different financial products.

While this is true, as it is true that banks are subject to strict regulation by both state and federal laws and agencies, it is also a fact that banks must make a profit to survive, and that fierce competition has eroded many traditional sources of profitability. So services that were given away to loyal customers in earlier generations have been turned into mini–profit centers.

To put it bluntly, your friendly banker of the new millennium is likely to do anything legal to part you from as much of your money as possible. You can't protect yourself against some abuses. All banks, for instance, make you wait longer than is actually necessary to draw on a check deposited into your account. If you can imagine how much they earn a year by having the use of billions of dollars for an extra day or two, you can understand why.

Keep these three principles in mind when dealing with banks, credit-card organizations, and other credit-granting organizations (department stores, auto dealers, etc.):

- Don't pay interest on a loan unless you have to. *The best way to earn 16 percent tax-free on your money is to pay off any 16 percent loans you have outstanding.* With the exception of a home mortgage and perhaps loans to start a business or invest in an education, it is always better (barring the return of double-digit inflation) to save first, then spend.
- Take advantage of the competition among banks and among credit-card organizations for your business. Shop around for the best deals you can get. A long-term relationship with one bank can be of some importance, but in these days of bank mergers and impersonal, computerized banking, it doesn't mean as much as it once did.
- Learn a few basics about how interest rates on loans are calculated. Tips in this chapter will help. Most important, make sure you understand all the fine print in a loan or credit agreement before you sign it.

▶ KEEP SHOPPING FOR BETTER BANKING DEALS

Differences in geography, state laws, and changing competition within markets make it difficult to set minimum standards that can be applied to all the different kinds of checking accounts available. But the easiest way for banks to increase profits from their retail operations is to raise the fees and minimum balance requirements of current customers. At the same time they are doing this, they may be advertising special introductory deals to attract new accounts. That's why it's a good idea to read the ads from different banks about minimum balances, fees, and services. At least once a year, make sure you review what you are paying versus what's being offered elsewhere. If your bank is involved in a merger, pay special attention to new fees and changes in services and balance requirements.

This isn't to suggest that you continually switch banks to save a dollar a month or to escape an extra $500 minimum requirement. But if you let your bank take your business for granted, it will. When you see a better deal elsewhere, get the details and show them to an officer of your current bank. Every bank gives its officers at least some flexibility to make fee and other concessions to good customers. If you are one of them, your bank won't want you to leave.

▶ COMBINE ACCOUNTS AT ONE BANK

The best way to eliminate most fees and become the kind of customer a bank wants to keep happy is to deposit enough extra money to be perceived as a significant customer. That may mean trading off an extra percentage point or so of interest on a couple of thousand dollars and keeping it in a bank's federally insured money-market deposit account, for instance, instead of a higher-paying money-market mutual fund.

Keeping that kind of money in such an account will usually mean you won't need a minimum balance in your checking account to escape fees. Since the very first rule of saving and investing is to have a minimum of three months' salary readily available for emergencies, a bank money-market account makes sense.

Another way to eliminate fees and become a more significant customer is to establish an IRA (Individual Retirement Account) with your bank. Many banks will now include IRA balances when determining what kind of deal you'll get on your checking account. It is perfectly legal to have more than one custodian for your IRA funds, so it is possible to keep just a small portion at your bank.

▶ CLOSE EXPENSIVE SAVINGS ACCOUNTS

How can a savings account be expensive, when it pays you interest? Simple. If your bank charges you a monthly fee or per-check fees for your checking account, you will nearly always be better off keeping in that account whatever minimum balance the bank requires for no-fee checking. If that means shifting funds out of a savings account, do it.

▶ SHOP FOR THE BEST CD RATES

Before you buy or renew a Certificate of Deposit at your bank, check its rates against the competition via *Banx-Quote* (800-765-3000; http://www.banx.com). It is easy to purchase a federally insured CD by mail, and rates vary significantly in different parts of the country.

Before you go to the trouble of sending CD money out-of-state, though, ask your bank's branch manager to match (or come close to) the higher rate. If you are a good customer and the bank wants to keep your business, it may be willing to negotiate.

▶ DON'T BUY CHECKS FROM YOUR BANK

Banks that once supplied good customers with free checks now mark up the checks they sell you by 300 percent or more over the price they pay their printers.

Deal direct with specialized check printers and save 60 to 75 percent. All they need is a sample check from you (write "canceled" on it before mailing) to match any bank's necessary computer codes. Among reputable sources to contact for catalogs and prices: *Checks in the Mail Inc.* (800-733-4443; http://www.checksinthemail. com) and *Current Checks* (800-426-0822; http://www. currentchecks.com).

▶ USE DIRECT DEPOSIT FOR YOUR SALARY CHECK

Not only is it a waste of time to stand in endless bank lines every week or two, you also get the use of your money faster when the company you work for sends your salary check to your bank electronically. If your employer offers direct deposit, have your salary deposited automatically into a money-market or interest-bearing account.

▶ BEWARE OF ATM SURCHARGES

If the bank you use now is charging you a fee to use its own ATM machines, transfer your account somewhere else. A bank that tries to get away with such fees is probably overcharging you for other things as well.

Also try to use a bank that doesn't add its own fee when you use another bank's ATM machine. If you do use another bank's machine, chances are you will be charged a fee by that bank. So stick to your own bank's machines whenever possible. When you are traveling, use your credit card whenever you can to cut back on cash needs. And avoid ATM machines in airports if at all possible. Fees there may be much higher than at the same bank's downtown ATMs.

There is a web site (http://www.surcharge-free-atms. com) where you can get statewide lists of ATMs that do not add a surcharge, but not all states were included when this edition went to press.

▶ CHECK OUT BANKING BY COMPUTER OR TELEPHONE

Atlanta Internet Bank (http://www.atlantabank.com), *Security First Network Bank* (http://www.sfnb.com), and

Salem Five Cents Saving Bank (http://www.salemfive.com) all offer no-fee checking accounts with very low minimum balance requirements, free ATM transactions, and free electronic bill payments. The major inconvenience of banking on the Internet is mailing your deposit checks. You can reduce the number of checks you must mail, of course, if you set up direct deposit of your salary and other recurring payments made to you. You can also use one of the many banks that offer free or low-fee electronic banking if you maintain a minimum balance and access the bank through either the *Quicken* or *Microsoft Money* software programs (See Chapter 10). Other banks will provide you with their own software.

What is it like to bank electronically? We have been using *Citibank Direct Access* for the past eight years. We pay 95 percent of our bills electronically, rather than with paper checks, thus avoiding postage costs. After the initial setup of recurring accounts, paying bills this way is much faster than writing a check and addressing an envelope. We transfer money from our interest-paying money-market account into our checking account only as needed. We access balances and send electronic messages to Citibank service people to do things like stop a check. And we do all of this from home, whenever we like.

Citibank doesn't charge its electronic banking customers any fees, but there is a hidden charge—the loss of the "float" on some electronic checks. When we write a paper check and mail it, a few days usually elapse before the check is deposited and the money is drawn from our account. When we make an electronic payment, our account is debited on the date we tell the bank to post that payment. In the case of payments to major stores, our telephone company, and our local utility, we post payments on the exact day the bill is due, because Citibank pays these companies electronically. In the case of smaller businesses we deal with, however, we must post payments a week or so before the amounts are due to allow for mail delivery of the check Citibank sends in our name.

This means that Citibank has the use of our money until the check clears. Nevertheless, we estimate that our savings in postage outweigh the cost of the float we lose. We also find banking this way wonderfully convenient. If you don't have access to a computer, many banks also allow you to pay bills by telephone. The plans we have investigated offer significant savings, essentially because a local telephone call is cheaper than a postage stamp and you can pay a number of bills with one call. Check out what your bank has to offer.

▶ JOIN A CREDIT UNION

Credit unions, which offer many of the same services as banks, are nonprofit organizations and often are able to offer members cheaper checking accounts and loans.

If your employer offers a credit union or you have a good community credit union in your area, you should certainly compare its prices and services with those of local banks. Many people use both, mainly because they can get a free checking account at their credit union. Some credit unions don't have automatic teller machines, however, a disadvantage if ready cash at any hour is a priority for you.

▶ DO YOU NEED A BANK AT ALL?

Quite a few people have given up banks altogether, and make use of asset-management accounts offered by most stockbrokers. Even some discount brokers are now offering free checking with asset-management accounts as well as free ATM access with debit cards they provide.

▶ THE PENNY PINCHER'S MORTGAGE

Unless you are certain you will own your home for only a few years and want to take a chance on changing interest rates, usually the best way to finance it is with a conventional fixed-rate mortgage amortized over as few years as possible. Since most people do sell their homes before the mortgage is paid off, make sure you or your accountant includes the points and origination fees in your calculations. A loan with a quarter-point higher rate might be preferable to a loan with high up-front costs.

ARMs (adjustable rate mortgages) shift the risk of interest-rate changes from the lender to you. Don't listen to expert opinions: No one knows which way interest rates are headed in the future.

There is no question that throughout the 1990s, interest rates declined significantly and people who had ARMs benefited. One reader of the second edition of this book, Joe Tufo of Alamo, California, showed us how well an ARM has worked for him. He bought his house in November 1991, got an ARM at a 7½ percent start rate, and renewed at 6 percent in 1993. If he had instead chosen a fixed-rate mortgage in 1991, he would have been paying over 10 percent. There is no question that Joe has saved many thousands of dollars so far. Also, since he intends to pay off his loan as quickly as possible and is rapidly prepaying his mortgage principal (see following tip), he feels comfortable with the risks of the ARM.

Of course, people who chose ARMs over fixed-rate mortgages fifteen years before Joe bought his house saw the opposite happen. In the 1970s, rates on some ARMs approached 20 percent.

Will that ever happen again? Nobody knows. Joe has convinced us that an ARM can be the preferred choice for some people. Nevertheless, even if you choose an ARM, we believe that if you are doing so because you can't afford a fixed-rate mortgage, you probably can't afford the house. Also, before you take on an ARM, make sure you work up a worst-case scenario to see what you would be faced with if interest rates go sky-high again. Make doubly certain you understand all of the small print in an ARM agreement.

Why pay off your mortgage as quickly as you can? Few people ever calculate just how much more interest is involved in longer-term loans. Here's one example, using a fixed-rate mortgage of $100,000 at 8 percent:

	15-year loan	25-year loan	30-year loan
Monthly payments	$ 955.65	$ 771.82	$ 733.76
Amount owed after:			
5 years	$ 79,193	$ 92,429	$ 95,169
10 years	47,131	80,985	87,872
15 years	PAID	63,959	77,001
20 years		38,579	60,806
25 years		PAID	36,677
30 years			PAID
Total Amount Paid:	$ 172,017	$ 231,545	$ 264,155
Total Interest Paid:	$ 72,017	$ 131,545	$164,155

The $221.89 difference in monthly payments between a fifteen-year and a thirty-year loan is significant to anyone with a $100,000 mortgage. But so is the $92,138 difference in the amount of interest paid. And if you can manage just another $38.06 in payments (the difference between twenty-five-year and thirty-year loans), you'll save $32,610 and be able to burn the mortgage agreement five years sooner.

For most people, most of the time, paying the highest monthly payments possible for the shortest period of time possible is a sound investment decision.

▶ IF YOU MUST BUY MORTGAGE INSURANCE

Unless you make a down payment of at least 15 percent on your house, the lender will insist that you buy private mortgage insurance (PMI). It may sound harsh, but we think anyone who has to buy mortgage insurance to buy a house would be better off waiting and saving until a 15 percent down payment is possible. If you do take out PMI, however, make certain before you sign any agreement that you will be able to cancel it after your equity in the house is more than 20 percent of its market value. The P stands for "private," not "permanent."

▶ RENEGOTIATE YOUR MORTGAGE

As a general rule, it pays to look into refinancing if you plan to stay in your house for a minimum of five years and if the rate on your current mortgage is at least one percentage point above the going rate for a thirty-year mortgage.

Depending on where you live, prevailing conditions, and the competition among mortgage lenders, you may have to pay up to 3 percent of the amount borrowed in up-front points and closing costs. Your present lender certainly isn't going to encourage you to cancel a loan whose terms are now very favorable to him. On the other hand, if your lender is convinced you are going to shop elsewhere, he may want to give you an attractive deal since he already knows you are creditwothy.

Here's an easy way to figure out how long it will be before it pays off to refinance. Just substitute your own numbers for those used in this example:

Suppose your present thirty-year $150,000 mortgage at 10.5 percent has a principal balance of $137,601 after exactly ten years. Your monthly payment is $1,372. It will cost you $3,000 in up-front points and penalties to refinance a twenty-year mortgage at 8 percent. Your new principal amount will be $140,601 ($137,601 + $3,000) and your new monthly payment $1,176. The numbers look like this:

Mortgage balance	$ 137,601
Plus points and penalties	+ 3,000
Total new mortgage principal	$ 140,601
Present monthly payment	$ 1,372
New monthly payment	− 1,176
Difference	$ 196

$3,000 refinancing costs
divided by $196 = 15.3 months.

If it takes 15.3 months before you pay off the cost of points and penalties, after that you will be saving the full $196 a month difference in monthly payments for the life of the mortgage. Total savings: $196 × 224.7 months (12 months × 20 years minus 15.3 months) = $44,041.

▶ PREPAY YOUR MORTGAGE PRINCIPAL

If you bought your home when interest rates were higher, prepaying your mortgage or adding to your monthly principal payments can make a lot of sense. Suppose you have a thirty-year fixed-rate mortgage of $200,000 at 9 percent. Your monthly payment is $1,609.25 and you will pay a whopping $379,328 in interest charges over the thirty-year life of the loan.

Now suppose that after five years, you raise your monthly payment to $1,800 a month, instructing the lender to apply the $190.75 difference to the principal of the loan. You can always change your mind when you voluntarily make such prepayments. But if you continue to make that relatively small extra payment, it will mean a saving of $95,506 in total interest charges and your mortgage will be paid off nearly eight years early.

One last calculation: If, instead of making that regular prepayment after five years, you saved $190.75 a month at 6 1/2 percent interest, tax-free, for the next seventeen years, you would have only about $56,678 in total savings.

An accountant can help you factor in all the variables that pertain to you, including the deductibility of mortgage interest on your income tax. A mortgage prepayment strategy shouldn't be considered until you have paid off any other debts, have at least three months' salary in an emergency account, and have adequate disability insurance. You should also make sure the strategy doesn't interfere with saving for retirement or future college expenses.

Finally, if you do make prepayments, watch your mortgage statements like a hawk. Many mortgage lenders haven't set up computer programs that easily handle prepayments, and have to be forced to credit them correctly.

▶ GET RID OF HIGH-INTEREST CREDIT-CARD DEBT

Probably the worst sin a penny pincher can commit is to get in the habit of using credit cards as a way to borrow money. The rates are exorbitant—typically 10 to 17 percent—and the temptation to keep adding to the principal amount gets millions of people in real trouble every year.

The only smart times to use credit cards are a) when you can't save money by paying cash; b) when you want to have recourse to a third party—the credit card company—to guard against the possibility of a merchant's not delivering as promised; c) as a way to take advantage of the "float"—the period of time between the date of purchase and when you have to pay the credit-card company the full amount in order to avoid any interest payments; and d) when you use a card that rewards you in some way for dollars charged on it.

If you are carrying credit-card debt, get rid of it as fast as you can. If necessary, and if you also have other high-interest debt such as a car loan, visit your bank or credit union and talk about one new "consolidator" loan at a lower rate that will enable you to pay off all your higher-interest debt. Homeowners can do this with home-equity loans, a particularly good deal because interest payments on home-equity loans are still fully tax-deductible. Just remember that you are putting your home up as collateral.

▶ IN TROUBLE? GET HELP

It's easy enough to give advice about staying out of trouble with credit-card and other debt, but if you think you are already there, get help immediately. *Consumer Credit Counseling Service* (800-388-2227) will tell you the location of the nearest regional office that offers counseling, sometimes at no cost and usually for a fee of no more than $10 a month.

▶ DROP "AFFINITY" CREDIT CARDS

Millions of people feel good about their Visa or Master-Card credit cards because they know that by using them, they are helping their favorite charity or their college alma mater. The fact is, though, that only a small percentage of your money actually ends up with the affinity organization and you can nearly always get a better deal on the card elsewhere. Besides, whatever donation you are making isn't tax-deductible. Write a check to your favorite cause instead.

▶ THE PENNY PINCHER'S CREDIT CARD

There are interesting bells and whistles attached to different credit cards. The tips following this one discuss them. But the single most important question you should answer before you decide which card is best for you is whether or not you are going to pay your full balance each month, thereby never incurring interest charges.

If you can do this—and it is a goal every penny pincher should have—you really don't *care* how high the interest rate on your card is set. You can concentrate on finding a card that a) has no membership fee; b) offers a twenty-five-day grace period from the time of billing until payment is due; and c) offers some valuable supplemental benefits.

We've switched, dropped, and added cards over the past few years, but we always keep those three features in mind. To us, a bank credit card is both a great convenience (it is easier to account for expenditures by budget category this way than by keeping track of cash expenditures) and a way to postpone putting out cash for from thirty to forty-five days (and thus get the interest on that money ourselves).

On the other hand, before some purchases, especially

in smaller stores, we ask how much we can save by paying cash. Green is quickly substituted for plastic when we like the answer.

What would we do if we were just starting out, couldn't get a low-interest bank loan, and had to buy a few high-ticket items before we had the ready cash to pay for them? First we would put off buying anything that wasn't absolutely necessary. Then we would pay the membership fee, if necessary, for a *second* bank card. Our first card, especially since it had no membership fee, might charge a high interest rate on unpaid balances. This second card would charge the lowest interest rates available. We would then use this second card *only* for the high-ticket items. Each month thereafter we would pay off as much as possible of the principal owed until we had no debt left. Finally, we would cut the second card in two, cancel it, and hope never to use it again.

If you haven't gotten to the point of cutting up your second card and still carry a balance on it, don't fall into the trap of thinking that interest rates on different cards are fairly consistent, so it doesn't make any difference which one you use. As this book went to press, rates ranged from 6 percent to over 19 percent. If you carry a balance of $2,000 a month, the difference in interest charges can add up to over $200 a year.

Barron's (a weekly financial newspaper) and *Money* magazine (a monthly) both list credit cards with the lowest current interest rates in each issue. *Bank Rate Monitor* (http://www.bankrate.com) is a first-rate web site that allows you to search its database of thousands of cards to find those with low interest rates, no annual fees, rebates, etc.

Fifth edition update: A disturbing new trend has been gaining ground among credit-card issuers. Some of them are either threatening to cancel the accounts of cardholders who pay off their balances each month or making them pay extra annual fees. Your account isn't profitable to them, it seems, unless you pay interest

charges. If this happens to you, use the sources above
to find other no-fee cards.

▶ THE FREQUENT FLIER'S CREDIT CARD

Paying no annual fee for a credit card isn't always the
best penny-pinching strategy. If you travel by plane
fairly often, charge more than $1,000 a month on the
card, and always pay off your monthly balance, you will
probably be better off with a card that awards airline
frequent-flier miles.

All of the major airlines, and many smaller ones, sponsor cards that give you one frequent-flier mile for every
dollar you spend. These frequent-flier miles can be combined with miles awarded for travel on the airline.

In a typical frequent-flier program, you need at least
25,000 miles to qualify for a free round-trip domestic
ticket. That ticket might cost more or less than $375,
but let's use that number to arrive at a value of 1.5 cents
for a frequent-flier mile ($375 divided by 25,000). Now
let's say you pay a $50 annual fee for a card and charge
$12,000 on it during the year. The 12,000 frequent-flier
miles you have earned are worth $180, so you are $130
ahead of the game.

This works only if you pay off your balance each month.
The airline cards never offer the lowest interest rates,
and if you pay their rates on unpaid balances, there is
no way an award of 1.5 cents per dollar will make up the
difference. Also, most airline cards require that the
miles you earn be used within three years. If you earn
only a couple of thousand miles a year through card use
and don't also earn a lot of miles by flying on the airline,
you may never get a chance to cash your miles in.

Among the airlines sponsoring Visa or MasterCards
are *American* (800-950-5114), *United* (800-537-7783),
TWA (800-322-8921), *Northwest* (800-360-2900), *US Airways* (800-732-9194), and *Continental* (800-377-0601).
Delta (800-759-6453) sponsors an American Express
card. If you fly on another airline frequently, call and
ask about any cards it might sponsor.

Diners Club and American Express both offer cards that allow you to accumulate points in a special account that you can transfer at any time to the frequent-flier program of an airline of your choice. The points don't expire as long as you are an active cardholder, and not being limited to one airline is an advantage. However, Diners Club (whose points can be transferred to the programs of all of the major U.S. carriers as well as some foreign ones) is not as widely accepted as Visa, MasterCard, or American Express. American Express points can't be transferred to all of the major carrier programs; neither American nor United, for instance, participate.

Finally, a number of banks sponsor cards that allow you to accumulate credits in an account maintained by the bank. When you earn enough credits, the bank will buy you a round-trip coach ticket on the airline and route of your choice. One major drawback is that these credits cannot be combined with frequent-flier miles earned on any airline. Look into *Chase Bank's Flight Rewards Visa* or *MasterCard* (800-720-0547) or *Bank of America's Travel Choices Visa* (800-349-2632).

▶ OTHER CARDS THAT OFFER AWARDS

Although airline mileage is the most popular credit-card award, there are also a number of cards that offer rebates of some kind. *General Motors* (800-947-1000) sponsors a no-fee MasterCard that gives you a rebate credit of 5 percent on all purchases charged to the card up to a maximum of $10,000 annually. That means you can earn $500 in one year that will be rebated if you purchase or lease a new GM car. The maximum rebate allowed is $3,500—the amount you might earn in seven years.

Amoco (800-858-3299), *Gulf* (800-677-6677), and *Phillips 66* (800-884-1930) are among the major oil companies that sponsor no-fee Visa or MasterCards that give cardholders rebates of up to 4 percent on gas purchases and 1 percent on other merchandise. *General Electric*

(800-437-3927) offers a no-fee card that gives users rebates of up to 2 percent a year on all purchases of GE products.

There are dozens of other rebate cards available, some that might be good choices for people with special interests or shopping habits, including *Toys "R" Us Visa*, *American Express Optima Golf Card*, and *TJ Maxx Visa*. Keep in mind that the interest rates on all cards that offer rebates are invariably higher than the no-frills cards issued by some banks. They make sense *only* if you pay off your balance each month. For an up-to-date list of major rebate and frequent-flier cards, visit the *Bank Rate Monitor* web site (http://www.bankrate.com).

▶ DON'T FALL FOR CREDIT CARD "INTRODUCTORY OFFERS"

The interest rates on credit cards can change at any time. Don't fall for the "introductory offer" rate often featured in huge type in the direct-mail promotions of various cards. You might be told that the introductory rate of 6 percent will be followed after six months by a "fixed rate" of 15 percent. The 15 percent "fixed rate" is meaningless. The card issuer can change rates however it likes simply by giving you fifteen days' notice.

▶ PAYING A FEE FOR YOUR CARD? MAYBE YOU DON'T HAVE TO

As competition escalates among card issuers, many of them offer no-annual-fee cards to new customers, but conveniently forget to do the same for existing customers. The next time you are billed an annual fee on your card, pick up the phone and ask the bank to waive it. It may very well be willing to do so. If you are still carrying a balance, a phone call may be all it takes to get an immediate reduction of the interest rate you are being charged. In either case, it does no harm to ask.

▶ WHAT ABOUT GOLD-CARD ENHANCEMENTS?

Do you really think you will ever use one of those "exclusive private clubs in London" offered as a reason to pay extra for a gold or platinum card? Do you really think your waiter will be impressed if you use a gold card?

Do you really care? Of course not. There are standard gold-card-enhancement packages on Visas and Master-Cards nationwide, and you may want to check them out (see information sources in previous tips). Most of us want only the enhancements that are also available on many standard cards—particularly automatic collision insurance when we use the card to rent a car and some kind of automatic extension of product warranty when we use the card to buy that product. Shop among them first before paying extra for a showy piece of plastic.

▶ WATCH OUT FOR TWO-CYCLE BILLING

If, despite all of our sermonizing, you do carry a balance on your credit card from time to time, make sure your issuer is not using "two-cycle billing." The insidious thing about this accounting dodge is that it doesn't affect the card's stated interest rate, but it can effectively increase the actual rate you pay dramatically. Cards using two-cycle billing retroactively impose finance charges on the *previous* month's balance when (even after many consecutive months of paying up in full) you decide to carry a balance.

Since even people who always pay full balances have been known to forget to mail a payment in time, every credit-card user should avoid cards using this billing method. Read the fine print on the back of your statement and call your card issuer if you are still not sure.

▶ YES. PILE ON CREDIT-CARD CHARGES

Only, *only* (the penny pincher's broken record) if you are *absolutely certain* you will pay the full balance every month. If you do, and you use an airline or other card that rewards you based on charges, why not use it wherever possible unless you can get a discount for using cash?

Many colleges accept credit cards for tuition bills. You can buy postage stamps with a card and make most of your charitable contributions that way. A very rich man named Eli Broad bought a painting for $2.5 million with his credit card a couple of years ago; he wanted and got a 2.5 million frequent-flier miles credited to his account. There are a lot of people sitting in free airplane seats because they used a credit card at supermarkets and at doctors' and dentists' offices. Where else? Before you use cash or your checkbook, ask.

▶ CANCEL OLD CARDS

When you do switch from card to card, don't just cut the old one up and throw it away. Make sure you write the card issuer telling it to terminate your account and to notify all credit bureaus that your account was closed in good standing. If you don't do this, a lender or credit-card company may check your records and turn you down because they see you have too many cards.

▶ DEBIT CARD OR CREDIT CARD?

When you use a debit card issued by your bank, whatever you charge is immediately deducted from your checking account. When you use a credit card, you have a grace period of at least twenty-five days before you have to write a check. Furthermore, a credit-card purchase gives you some protection if the merchandise you buy isn't delivered or is defective. For anyone who pays balances in full each month, a credit card (and even more so a frequent-flier or rebate credit card) is a better choice.

The exception is at an ATM machine, where a debit card is always a better choice.

▶ THE BEST SOURCE OF A LOAN

As a general rule, the worst possible source of a loan is the seller of the product. When you borrow money from an automobile dealer, the most common of many loans made by sellers of products, he gets a kickback (which you pay for) from the ultimate source of the money. Even if the seller is self-financing the loan, you can bet you'll be paying a far higher rate than you would had you borrowed from a bank.

Finance companies deal with the most unsophisticated borrowers, which is how they get away with borrowing money themselves and then relending it at a much higher rate.

The best source of a loan? Your own resources. If you've got $20,000 in a money-market fund and need to buy a new car, take it out of the fund and pay cash. You'll still have some emergency funds left over (you have no business buying a car for more than $15,000 if all you've got saved is $20,000), and no money-market fund is paying you as much in interest as you'll pay to a lender.

With that lecture over, a few other alternatives, none as good:

If you have a cash-value insurance policy, check out a loan from your insurance company. If you are fortunate enough to be a member of an active credit union, you will probably be able to get a low-cost loan there. You may also be able to borrow money from your profit-sharing fund at work; check with your benefits or personnel department. After that, banks are still your best choice. See the next few tips for what to look for and what to avoid.

▶ A ROSE IS A ROSE IS A ROSE, BUT A LENDER'S INTEREST RATE ISN'T

Your bank agrees to lend you $10,000 at 10 percent for one year. How much will you pay in interest?

The obvious answer is 10 percent of $10,000, or $1,000. The actual answer will almost certainly be different, and higher. Unfortunately, the interest rates quoted by lenders don't tell the whole story. The next few tips do.

▶ SIMPLE-INTEREST/SINGLE-PAYMENT LOANS

This is the least expensive way to borrow money. You pay interest only on the money you still owe. Using a single-payment method, you would take the $10,000 and at the end of the year make one payment to the lender of $11,000. You have had the use of the full $10,000 for the entire twelve months and have paid $1,000—10 percent—in interest.

Alternatively, if you pay off a 10 percent simple-interest loan in twelve monthly installments, your total interest payments will be only $550. Why? Because you will not have had the use of $10,000 for the full twelve months. Your first monthly payment of $879 would include interest charges of $83 and a partial payment of $796 on the principal. Your second monthly payment of $879 would consist of a smaller interest payment and a larger partial payment on the principal because you would now have the use of only $9,204 ($10,000 minus $796) of the principal. And so on, for each of the next ten months. As the amount of the principal still outstanding diminishes, so does the interest payment.

Either kind of simple-interest loan is highly desirable, but don't count on getting one from any lender unless you are a highly preferred or corporate customer.

▶ DISCOUNTED INTEREST LOANS

Still using our example of a $10,000 one-year loan at 10 percent, with this type of loan the lender deducts the 10 percent interest up front and therefore lends you only $9,000. At the end of the year, you will pay back $10,000 in a single payment.

Not so bad? Let's calculate your true interest rate. You have really borrowed only $9,000 and paid $1,000 in interest. When calculated ($1,000 divided by $9,000), this comes to a true interest rate of 11.11 percent.

It gets much worse. If you take the $9,000 and agree to make twelve monthly payments of $833.30 ($10,000 divided by 12), your effective annual interest rate on the money you have actually had use of comes to almost 20 percent!

You are beginning to understand some of the mysteries of banking. Read on.

▶ ADD-ON INTEREST LOANS

You may also be offered this method by a lender. The $1,000 interest on your $10,000 loan is added on to the principal in the beginning. Then you repay $11,000 in twelve monthly installments. True annual interest: almost 18 percent.

If you are quoted either an "add on" or "discounted" interest rate, the true annual interest you will pay will be almost *double* the percentage quoted.

▶ KNOW THE APR—AND MORE

Lenders can and still will quote you an add-on or discounted interest rate, but for the past seventeen years they have also been legally required to tell you the true annual percentage rate (the APR). Unfortunately, too many people still commit to overly expensive loans because the APR isn't mentioned until all the papers are about to be signed. Do not ever commit to a loan until you have seen—in writing, as federally required—the APR interest on it.

Even then, especially in the case of a complicated loan such as a mortgage, the APR quoted may not take into account some of the expenses you have to incur to get the loan (title insurance fees, credit-report fees, application fees, etc.). It gets very complicated indeed, but if you are repaying a loan over a thirty-year period, a difference of $1/2$ percent on a principal of $100,000 can amount to thousands of dollars. If you aren't comfortable doing it yourself, have a good accountant review the figures to arrive at your true loan costs.

▶ SECURED VERSUS UNSECURED LOANS

A secured loan means that you have given the bank some form of collateral as security. If you don't pay the money back, it gets to keep the collateral. Your home mortgage is a secured loan, but you can also secure a loan using stocks, bonds, a car, or any other hard asset as collateral.

An unsecured loan means the bank has extended credit to you without collateral. When you get an approved line of credit up to a certain amount at your bank and write checks against it, you are in effect taking out an unsecured loan. Banks are careful about the credit ratings of people approved for unsecured loans, but even so you will pay a higher interest rate than if the loan were secured by collateral. You've got to pay it back anyway, so why not secure the loan?

▶ BEWARE THE FLOATING RATE

Banks and other credit institutions love to shift risk from themselves to you. That's why you may be offered a "floating rate" loan, usually tied to the "prime rate" charged by banks to their best corporate customers. You might be offered a loan at "prime plus 3," for instance, meaning your interest payments would always be 3 percent over the current prime rate.

The danger here is the same as it is with an adjustable rate mortage. Avoid it if at all possible.

▶ THE PENNY PINCHER'S BANK LOAN

Despite the previous example of simple-interest/single-payment loans, you should know one thing about them: Banks rarely if ever offer simple-interest/single-payment loans to retail customers. Installment loans of any kind are more profitable. But you can at least try to negotiate. Here's how:

Dealing (ideally) with a bank officer you already know (your branch manager, perhaps), don't say anything about the single-payment method until after you have the bank's agreement on the amount and term of the loan as well as the APR. The bank, of course, will be planning to charge you monthly installments with a fixed monthly payment in which interest payments will gradually decline and payments to principal will gradually increase.

Once you have the commitment, tell your banker you will be willing to pay off the loan in monthly payments over the term agreed upon, and at the APR the bank has quoted. But you want the loan structured as a single-payment loan that allows monthly payments. In other words, you will pay the same amount each month toward the principal, as well as interest at the agreed-upon APR on the principal outstanding.

The result will be that you will pay more than you would under the usual installment method at the beginning of the loan, and less at the end. More important, you will pay less in interest over the term of the loan.

Your banker won't be thrilled with your suggestion, but you'll have a good argument: She has agreed to amount, to term, and to APR, and there's no additional risk to the bank. Why not do it your way?

▶ PAYING OFF EARLY: BEWARE THE RULE OF 78s

Although illegal in many states, some still allow lenders to use an accounting method called "the rule of 78s" when a loan is paid off early. If you decide to prepay a loan that uses this method—even if there is no prepayment penalty in your loan agreement—you will end up paying a much higher interest rate than the agreement calls for. Here's how it works in a loan with a one-year term:

The first month, you would pay $12/78$ of the interest,

the second month $^{11}/_{78}$, the third $^{10}/_{78}$, and so on down to $^{1}/_{78}$ in the final month. If you pay the loan off at the end of the sixth month, and the lender activates the rule of 78s, you will have already paid $^{57}/_{78}$ $(12 + 11 + 10 + 9 + 8 + 7 = 57)$ in interest—not half the amount owed, but nearly three quarters of the total.

When you read a loan agreement, look carefully for references to prepayment penalties, the rule of 78s, or the term "the sum of the digits." What you want instead is a simple-interest loan or an agreement that uses the actuarial method for computing interest due on prepayments. *Ask for it.*

▶ NO INTEREST CHARGES! BUY NOW! 24 MONTHS TO PAY!

And maybe you believe in the tooth fairy. The interest charges are hidden in the bloated price of the car or whatever else you are buying. It is still an installment loan, and the dealer can still sell it to a bank for a profit. In practice, because such offers are particularly attractive to unsophisticated borrowers and no APR need be declared, what you end up paying is higher than what you would have paid by buying the car for an honest price and paying interest on the loan.

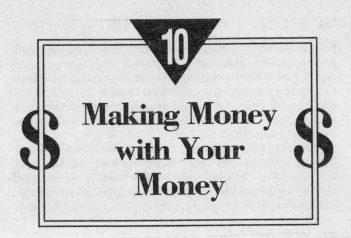

Making Money with Your Money

Penny pinching is easier when you have extra dollars to pinch. This chapter will suggest a few ways to make the money you earn work harder to make you more money.

The word "tip" has a deservedly negative reputation when it comes to investment advice. But unlike the tips your brother-in-law gives you about hot stocks, ours concentrate on the decisions you must make among saving and investing methods and techniques. (Tip #1: Avoid hot stock tips.) Or they suggest cheaper ways to make different kinds of investments.

As a brief checklist, they are useful. For complete investment advice, go elsewhere. Where? That's not an easy question, so we'll start with a couple of basic rules.

▶ DON'T BLINDLY TRUST EXPERTS

Yes, you can hire a financial planner to take complete charge of every aspect of your life that involves money—

your household budget, savings plans, investments, and retirement. You can take your allowance like a teenager and not worry about a thing. Naturally you will have less money to manage, since the fees for this kind of all-encompassing financial planning don't come cheap. And what happens if you choose an adviser who is inept, unlucky, or even dishonest?

Year after year, there are news stories about rich and famous athletes and show business personalities who lose millions or are even bankrupted because they trusted an adviser to make all their financial decisions. The media seldom report on the millions of middle-class people who rely on other people and end up paying big fees for terrible results.

The first and most important tip about saving and investing is to learn enough about the subject so that you can trust the one person who is ultimately responsible: yourself. You don't have to become an expert, but you have to know enough to decide what you want to hire experts for, how to choose good ones, and when it is just as effective—and cheaper—to do it yourself.

▶ GET INTERESTED IN YOUR MONEY

That's different from getting interest *on* your money. If you have enough penny-pinching instincts to save hundred of dollars a year by shopping wisely and saving on energy bills, you can't afford to skip the financial pages of your newspaper. What's happening to interest rates, federal budget deficits, the value of the dollar, and the economy has a direct bearing on your money and your future.

To get comfortable with the idea of being responsible for your money, first read the tips in this chapter. Frankly, if you have no background at all in money management, you're likely to be a bit confused, even though the tips may help you with specific questions or problems. So turn next to a book on basic investing principles. Among the good ones at your library, Andrew Tobias's *The Only Other Investment Guide You'll Ever*

Need is sensible, quite comprehensive, and more fun to read than most.

After you've read one or two books, begin spending a couple of hours a week reading newspapers (nothing beats *The Wall Street Journal*) and magazines (*Money* and *Kiplinger's Personal Finance Magazine* are fine, but working your way up to *Forbes* and *Barron's* is a reasonable goal).

Keeping up with a rapidly changing world and new investment possibilities is essential. The days of putting your money in "safe" investments and never worrying about them are over.

▶ BUY A PERSONAL-FINANCE SOFTWARE PROGRAM

If you have a computer, personal-finance software can be one of the best buys you will ever make. The top programs—*Quicken,* for Intuit, and *Microsoft Money*—cost less than $60 and offer comprehensive, well-organized ways to manage your money. You can use them to track your investments and your family budget, pay your bills electronically, figure out how much insurance you need, determine how much you'll owe in taxes, and much more. There is no better way to "get interested in your money" with a minimum expenditure of time and effort.

▶ SURF THE INTERNET'S INVESTMENT SITES

There are literally thousands of worthwhile sites for investors, and you can probably find advice and information on the Web about any investing question you will ever have. Use any full-scale search service such as *Yahoo* (http://www.yahoo.com) to see what sites are devoted to different aspects of investing. Many good sites charge subscription fees and you may want to consider using one or more of them. But start with these free sites:

- *Money Personal Finance Center* (http://pathfinder. com/money) directs you to other pertinent web sites and gives you access to many *Money* magazine articles and features.
- *Quicken* (http://www.quicken.com) may be too useful a site to remain free for very long, but it was when this edition went to press. You can load in your own portfolio and get automatic news alerts on securities you own. You can get profiles, overviews, and stock analysts' consensus opinions on any listed stock. You can even get immediate access to every form (10Ks, prospectuses, proxies) that public companies have filed electronically with the Securities and Exchange Commission since 1994.
- *Kiplinger* (http://www.kiplinger.com) features articles from *Kiplinger's Personal Finance Magazine* and some useful calculators.
- *Morningstar* (http://www.morningtar.net) offers detailed analysis of more than sixty-five hundred mutual funds.

▶ PLAY "WHAT IF" ON THE INTERNET

"How much do I need to save for retirement?" is one of the most important, and most complex, financial questions we must ever answer. There are so many variables involved that doing it the old-fashioned way, with pencil and paper, is hopelessly slow for most people. Personal-finance software is a big help. So are a few free web sites. Don't be scared away simply because they are sponsored by companies that would like to sell you something. The sell is very soft at the best sites, including:

- *Vanguard Mutual Funds* (http://www.vanguard.com) has a good retirement calculator and an even better calculator for those who are trying to decide between traditional and Roth IRAs.
- *John Hancock* (http://www.jhancock.com) has a more sophisticated retirement calculator that takes

into account other priorities you may have, such as saving for your children's college educations.

■ *Fidelity Mutual Funds* (http://www.fidelity.com) offers both an on-line calculator and a more extensive one that you can download free.

▶ PAY OFF HIGH-INTEREST DEBTS

It is silly to keep $2,000 in a money-market account paying 4 percent taxable interest at the same time you owe $2,000 on your bank credit card and are paying 17 percent in non-tax-deductible interest. The first way to get more income from your income is to pay off any high-interest debt—normally everything but your home-mortgage and home-equity loans, which are tax-deductible.

▶ OWN A HOME

Is this an investment strategy? And if so, is it still a good one? For decades, as residential real-estate prices in most parts of the country rose every year, it was virtually an article of faith among personal financial advisers that owning a home was the single best investment anyone could make. Then the end of the boom came. In the late 1980s, houses in some areas declined in value by 30 percent or more in one year. Even though most areas recovered in the 1990s, a lot of people were given good reason to question the old conventional wisdom.

The fact is, although there have been many periods of depressed real-estate prices in American history, in the long run prices have rebounded. In the long run, the odds are still high that the value of your home will at least keep pace with inflation.

But "in the long run" doesn't help much if you buy at a market high and are forced to sell in a depressed market a couple of years later. If you don't plan on staying in your area for a minimum of five years, renting might be safer. Otherwise, home ownership is still a sound investment. You have to live somewhere, and paying rent is a certain way not to build any equity. The one major tax shelter left to most people is the deduction of mort-gage-interest payments and real-estate taxes on their federal income tax returns.

Finally, if the real-estate market in your area is de-pressed, if the gloom and doomsday predictions are shared by just about everybody, you just may have the buying opportunity of a lifetime. Historically, the best buys are made when there are more eager sellers than buyers. Just as the best time to sell is usually when everyone else is jumping on the bandwagon to buy.

▶ TAKE ADVANTAGE OF TAX-DEFERRED INVESTMENT PLANS

You have certain investment goals—a new house, a wedding, redecorating, etc.—that probably can't be achieved with tax-deferred investments. That's because, with certain exceptions, the government assesses a big penalty if you withdraw money from a tax-deferred plan before you are fifty-nine and a half.

When your investment goal is a comfortable retire-ment, though, your first and best decision is to take maximum advantage of tax-deferred investment oppor-tunities. "Tax-deferred" means that no taxes are col-lected on the returns you earn on your investments until you withdraw the money in the account. By avoiding annual taxes for many years, a lot more of your money stays invested, earning interest and dividends and ap-preciating in value.

The Roth IRA adds another dimension to tax-defer-ment. Not only does your money appreciate free of taxes, you also owe no taxes on the money when it is withdrawn. Any personal finance guide will explain the ins and outs of IRAs (both traditional and Roth), Keogh plans, 401(k) and 403(b) plans, and SEPS (Simplified Employee Pension plans, which allow employers to con-tribute to employees' individual IRAs). These are all tax-advantaged ways to invest, and you should understand how each works. The next tip offers a few guidelines for people who have an employer-sponsored 401(k) plan.

▶ TAKE FULL ADVANTAGE OF YOUR 401(k)

If you are fortunate enough to have an employer who matches some percentage of your annual contribution to a 401(k) plan, take full advantage of your opportunity. Suppose your employer adds matching funds of 25 percent. Where else can you get an immediate, risk-free 25 percent return on your investment?

Take a look at how much you would save at various rates of return after thirty years of contributing to a 401(k) with an employer's matching funds equal to 50 percent:

Annual Employee Contribution	Rate of Return			
	6%	8%	10%	12%
$1,000	$118,587	$ 169,925	$ 246,741	$ 361,999
$2,000	$237,175	$ 339,850	$ 493,482	$ 723,998
$4,000	$474,349	$ 679,699	$ 986,964	$1,447,996
$8,000	$948,698	$1,359,399	$1,973,928	$2,895,992

In a 401(k) plan, you contribute pretax dollars, thereby reducing the income taxes you must pay that year. Whatever matching funds your employer puts into your account are also free of any tax that year. Then all of the earnings of these contributions compound free of any tax until you retire. At that point, you pay tax at normal rates as your money is withdrawn.

This is by far the best deal you will ever have to save and invest for a comfortable retirement. To take full advantage of it, do the following:

- *Start now.* Stop procrastinating, delaying, and dreaming about winning the lottery. The sooner you start, the better. The magic of compounding makes dollars you save at age twenty-five much greater nest-egg builders than dollars saved at forty-five. Given an annual rate of return of 10 percent, a twenty-five-year-old would have to save only $180 a month for the next forty years to have $1,000,000 at age sixty-five. A forty-five-year-old would have to save $1,392 a month to achieve the same result. A thousand dollars saved at twenty-five and compounding at 10 percent a year grows to $45,260 at age sixty-five. A thousand dollars saved at forty-five grows only to $6,728.

- *Save as much as your plan allows.* Putting every penny of your own money into a 401(k) is important for two reasons. First, because this is a way to save pretax dollars and to put them into a tax-deferred account. Second, because only this way can you take maximum advantage of your employer's matching amount.

- *Don't borrow from your plan.* The temptation is great when money is needed and you see that great lump sum that is all yours. But look elsewhere, a home-equity loan perhaps. Remember that any money you withdraw would no longer be compounding tax-free, and that interest payments would not be tax-deductible, as they would with the home-equity loan.

- *Don't play it "safe."* The biggest mistake made by most people when they look at the investment options offered by their 401(k) plans is to choose a Guaranteed Investment Contract or some other "safe" low-return short-term bond or money-market fund. When you have a lot of years left before retirement, history says you will be much better off investing in the stock market. Since 1926, long-term bonds had compound average total returns of about $5^{1}/_{2}$ percent, shorter-term treasury bills returned about $3^{1}/_{2}$ percent, and common stocks returned over 10 percent. Look at the difference over a thirty-year-period in the table above between a 10 percent and a 6 percent return, and you have to conclude that avoiding the stock market with long-term investments is not playing it safe at all.

This is not an argument for staking all of your 401(k) money in the most aggressive funds offered by your plan, or for investing all of it in the company you work for. The advice in the next tip applies to 401(k) investing as well as every other kind.

▶ NEVER BET IT ALL ON ONE SCENARIO

No one can predict the future. Not your brother-in-law with a hot tip about a stock that can't miss, not the chairman of the Federal Reserve Bank, not the most successful money managers in the world. Trust no one who is absolutely certain about what will happen to the stock market in the next few months, or where interest rates will be next year. *No one knows.*

In the long run (yes, again), although they may invest huge sums based on a predicted future scenario, most money managers who stay in business always diversify their assets in some form or another. They may think the economy will boom and the stock market will go up 2,000 points in the next year, but they don't bet everything on that one outcome.

Most of us should diversify our investments in two ways. First, we should own different categories of assets: real estate (perhaps just our homes), equities (stocks and stock mutual funds), fixed-income investments (bonds and certificates of deposit), and cash equivalents (money-market funds and savings accounts).

As a general rule, the younger you are the more heavily weighted your long-term investments should be in equities and real estate. That's because, historically, over a long period of time those investments have produced a greater return than bonds. If you are five years away from retirement, you may want to become more conservative, shifting some assets into investments that will pay you a fixed income and protecting yourself from the possibility of a long slump in the stock market. Even then, as a hedge against future inflation, you should own some equities or some real estate that may appreciate in value as well as produce income.

The second way you should diversify is within asset categories. Don't invest all of your equity money in one stock or buy the bonds of just one company. In fact, don't even invest in just one kind of stock or bond—the oil industry, for example, or computers or airlines. You will reduce your risks considerably by owning a portfolio that isn't completely dependent on one future scenario's coming true.

If you have $100,000 or more to invest and can establish a good relationship with a knowledgeable broker, you can diversify by investing in individual stocks and bonds. Otherwise, except for investments in U.S. Treasuries (see tip later in the chapter), your best alternative is to invest in mutual funds. The different types of funds give you a way to diversify categories (stocks or bonds) as well as to own widely diversified portfolios within those categories.

▶ HOW TO CHOOSE A MUTUAL FUND

Since four-hundred-page books are written on this topic and we cover the subject in about that many words, don't expect much detail in what follows. But there is an easy, three-step way to narrow your choices down from thousands of funds to a few that will meet your objectives.

(1) Exactly what are you looking for in a fund? Growth? Income? What kind of risk are you willing to take? Do you want a fund that invests all or part of your money outside the United States? Only you can decide what investment philosophy and strategies suit you best, although some of those four-hundred-page books may help you clarify your thoughts. There is no one mutual fund that is right for everyone, and if your portfolio is large enough, you should diversify into funds with different objectives and/or investing techniques.

When you feel comfortable with your objectives, it is time to go to the library. Take a look at the annual and/or quarterly mutual-fund issues of *Money*, *Barron's*, *Kiplinger's Personal Finance Magazine*, *Business Week*, and *Forbes*. Each uses somewhat different criteria in examining and ranking funds, but all include data about past performance, investment objectives, and 800 numbers to call for prospectuses. For the most comprehensive coverage of funds, ask the librarian for *Morningstar Mutual Funds*. By this point, you will be able to concentrate on the funds whose objectives match your own.

(2) Now narrow your choices to "no load" funds. All the magazines above tell you which funds are no-load. A no-load fund charges no commission on the up-front sale and no fee for the back-end redemption. There have been countless studies of the performance of no-load funds versus load funds, which can charge up to an 8.5 percent commission. None of them has yet made a compelling case that there's any difference in how the funds perform. There are many load funds with superior long-term records, but there are no-load funds that have performed just as well. An initial investment of $1,000 instead of $915 ($1,000 minus an 8.5 percent commission) gives you a head start.

(3) Finally, choose no-load funds with low fees. The best source of this information is *Morningstar Mutual Funds*. Or check *Money* magazine's annual mutual-fund issue (February) for a projection of expenses for the leading thousand or so funds. If your choice is between a fund with a terrible record whose five-year expenses per $1,000 are projected by *Money* at $50 per thousand and another with a superior record with projected expenses of $100, you might want to pay the higher expenses. But higher expenses don't guarantee better results, so if everything else is equal, why not opt for the savings?

By this point you will find your choices narrowed down to a very few funds. Get their prospectuses and read them. Remember that superior past performance is not a guarantee for the future. In fact, we suggest you stay away from the hottest funds of the previous year—the ones ranked at the very top for one-year performance. So much money is flowing into them that their managers may have a hard time investing it as wisely as they did in the past. Find a fund with a good long-term record over five or ten years, take the plunge, and monitor performance against the competition from then on.

You can skip a lot of this research if you use the next tip.

▶ BUY INDEX FUNDS

An index fund is a "passively managed" mutual fund that owns stocks that exactly replicate an index such as the Standard & Poor's 500 Composite Stock Price Index. That is, an S&P 500 index fund owns all 500 stocks in the index in exactly the same proportions as they are weighted in the index itself. The fund manager isn't trying to decide whether GE is a better buy than IBM or AT&T or Coca-Cola. He doesn't care. The performance of the index fund exactly tracks the performance of the index, less expenses incurred in running the fund.

Because the fund conducts no expensive research, its expenses are much lower than an "actively managed" fund, one in which the manager picks stocks he believes will outperform the market. Why would anyone choose to put money in a fund where nobody is even trying to "beat the market"? The answer, based on historical data, is that—in the long run—*very few actively managed funds outperform the indexes.*

Furthermore, in an example cited by John Bogle in *Bogle on Mutual Funds* (Dell Books, $12.95), the annual rate of return from the total stock market (which can be replicated by an index fund) was 12 percent between 1970 and 1992. For the average actively managed equity mutual fund, it was 10.8 percent. Remember, that is an average; *half of all funds did worse.*

Index funds are detested and reviled by many Wall Street professionals, but nobody can argue with the historical data. The reason index funds do so well, in addition to penny-pinching low expense ratios, has to do with the "efficient market theory" propounded by some Nobel Prize–winning economists. If you are intrigued, by all means read John Bogle's brilliant book, which explains all this and much more. All good libraries have a copy.

Many investors own one or more index funds as long-term cornerstones in their mutual-fund portfolios but also own actively managed funds to pursue specific asset-allocation strategies. This gets too complicated for a book about penny pinching, but you'll learn more from books like Bogle's.

One last word about index funds: If you buy one, pay special attention to how its expense ratios compare with those of funds tracking exactly the same index. Believe it or not, the annual difference can be as much as 300 percent. The *Vanguard Group* has always offered funds with extremely low expense ratios.

► WHY MARKET TIMING DOESN'T WORK

We added this explanation because dozens of readers of earlier editions questioned our brief advice in the previous tip about guessing which way the stock and bond markets are headed.

The appeal of market timing is understandable. If you could always buy when the markets are at their lows and sell when they are at their highs, you would never lose any money in a market decline. Your returns would be incredible. Doesn't Expert X on *Wall Street Week* predict an imminent collapse of the stock market? Why not sell everything on his advice?

First, because if you are a wise penny-pinching investor, you are not betting money needed in the short term in the stock market or in volatile bonds. You are investing for the long term. And in the long term, you are better off taking losses during a decline than you are trying to guess which way the market is going. Why? Because you can't know when the decline will halt and the market will rebound.

When the stock market does rebound, it tends to make a large percentage of its gains in a very few days. One study showed that a dollar continually invested in stocks from 1980 to 1992 would have grown to over $7. If you had taken your money out of the market and missed just the top 5 performing months in those years (out of 156 months total), your return would have dropped to below $3. Every study made of the stock market in the past fifty years confirms this phenomenon.

▶ CHECK OUT DRIPs

More than nine hundred U.S. companies, including many of the bluest of blue-chip stocks, offer Dividend Reinvestment Programs. DRIPs allow stockholders to automatically reinvest the dividends they earn in additional shares or fractional shares, without incurring brokerage fees. In addition, many of these corporations allow existing stockholders to make additional stock purchases directly from the company without paying brokerage fees, although some charge small fees of their own.

For long-term investors making regular, periodic investments in individual stocks, especially in odd lots of fewer than 100 shares, DRIPs are a great way to stretch every investment dollar. To find out if a company you are interested in offers a DRIP (and what its limitations and costs are), you can write or call its investor relations department at corporate headquarters.

Some companies (including Procter & Gamble, McDonald's, and Exxon) now sell shares direct to anybody, but most won't allow you into their programs unless you own at least one share. For more information, contact *Direct Purchase Plan Clearinghouse* (800-774-4117; http://www.enrolldirect.com). Remember that saving money by avoiding brokerage fees is a good strategy only if you would have bought the stock in any case. DRIPs are suitable only for long-term investors because you have less control over when or at what price you purchase more stock. Selling isn't easy, either; most companies take at least ten days to comply with a sell request. Finally, if you decide to use DRIPs in a major way, keep in mind the advice in a previous tip about the need for diversification.

▶ START A TEENAGER'S ROTH IRA

Putting money away for your child's college education and your own retirement are first priorities, but the long-term benefits of starting a Roth Individual Retirement Account as early as possible are so compelling that they should be considered by every investor with children.

If your child has any earned income, from a summer job or after-school work, she can start an IRA with an annual contribution equal to the amount earned up to $2,000. Suppose she earns $1,000 at age sixteen and you make a $1,000 gift to her that year, putting it into a mutual-fund IRA in her name. By the time she is sixty-five years old, that $1,000 will have grown to $133,000, assuming a growth rate of 10.5 percent a year. If she waits until she is twenty-five to make the same $1,000 contribution, it will grow to only $54,000 by the time she is sixty-five.

If you put $1,000 into her Roth IRA annually from age sixteen to twenty—a total of just $5,000—she will have a tax-free nest egg of $499,000 by the time she is sixty-five. Quite an inheritance from a farsighted penny pincher.

▶ ANYONE CAN OPEN AN EDUCATION IRA

Unless you or anyone else is funding a state-sponsored tuition plan (see next chapter) for your child in a given year, you can make a maximum $500 contribution to an Education IRA, naming your child as the beneficiary. Contributions are not tax-deductible in the year made, but earnings in the account accumulate free of tax and withdrawals are not taxed if used for college expenses.

Although higher-income parents cannot establish an Education IRA, they are allowed to give $500 to a third person who then establishes the account. Yes, even the IRS says it is legal.

▶ BUY U.S. TREASURIES DIRECT

Except for DRIPs, you don't have any choice when you want to buy stocks. You either pay a brokerage commission or you pay a mutual fund its annual fees as well as any up-front or back-end redemption fees it charges.

But why pay a broker—even a discount broker—as much as $10 to $90 each time you invest in supersafe U.S. Treasury bills, notes, or bonds? Unless you think you will want to sell the note before it matures, it is actually easier, more convenient, and completely free (except for the price of a stamp) to deal directly with the seller of the bonds—the U.S. government. Contact *Treasury Direct* (800-943-6864; http://www.publicdebt.treas. gov) to get an application to set up a personal Treasury Direct account. All you need is your Social Security number and a bank account where you want your future interest payments and principal deposited. From then on, using the very brief and easily understood forms provided, you can buy any denomination of new treasury offerings at exactly the same price a broker would pay.

▶ CHECK OUT OLD U.S. SAVINGS BONDS

Do you still have that $25 Series E U.S. Savings Bond Grandpa gave you for your birthday back in 1950 or 1960? If you do, you probably keep it in a safe-deposit box, glance at it once a year, and take for granted that it is still earning interest.

Holders of almost $2 billion in old savings bonds are presently making that mistake. Their bonds are no longer earning any interest at all because the bonds have reached final maturity.

Check the dates in the top right-hand corner of your bonds. If you have a Series E bond that is over forty years old, it has stopped earning interest. If your E bonds were purchased after November 1965, they will stop earning interest after thirty years. If you have a Series H bond that is over thirty years old, it has stopped earning interest.

What should you do? Once Series E bonds stop earning interest, you have a one-year period during which you can still exchange them for HH bonds, which are issued at full face value and pay regular semiannual interest. This allows you to defer reporting the interest earned on the E bonds until you redeem the HH bonds. If you miss the one-year deadline, or hold H bonds that have matured, of course you should redeem them (otherwise, it is like keeping cash in a mattress), but you'll have to pay taxes on the earned interest.

There are some other important facts to keep in mind about savings bonds. Each bond you own has a unique interest rate, increase schedule, value, and maturity date. Don't assume all of your bonds are the same; they're not. For instance, on most Series E and EE bonds, you can forfeit up to six months of interest if you redeem them even one day prior to a scheduled increase.

Although banks are supposed to have information about current values, timing issues (when specific bonds increase), interest rates, and dates of final and extended maturity periods, many don't. Others may not have accurate information. If you have questions about bonds you hold, your best source of free information is a Federal Reserve Bank (http://www.federalreserve. gov). A much easier way to get complete and accurate information is to contact the *Savings Bond Informer* (800-927-1091; http://www.bondinformer.com). For a small fee, this company will provide an easy-to-understand written statement outlining the timing issues, values, maturity dates, and interest rates for each of your bonds.

▶ COMPARE TAX-EXEMPT ALTERNATIVES

The interest on municipal bonds (bonds issued by states, cities, school districts, and other local and state authorities) are generally not subject to federal income taxation. If you live in the state in which they are issued, you also won't have to pay state income taxes on the interest. This can make municipal bonds and mutual funds that invest in them an attractive alternative to other fixed-income investments, especially if you live in a state with high income taxes.

The mistake many people make is to avoid taxes just for the sake of avoiding them. What you are interested in is the after-tax return, and there is a quick way to compare the after-tax return of a tax-exempt bond or fund.

Suppose you are in a 28 percent federal and 8 percent state tax bracket. Here's how you would analyze a yield of 5 percent that was tax-exempt in your state:

(1) Because state taxes are exempt from federal taxes, calculate your "effective" state tax. To do that, multiply the 8 percent state tax by 72 percent (100 percent minus your federal tax rate of 28 percent). That calculation is .08 × .72 = .057.

(2) Add your "effective" state tax rate to your federal tax rate. That calculation is 28 percent + 5.7 percent = 33.7 percent.

(3) Subtract 33.7 percent from 100 percent to get 66.3 percent.

(4) Divide the after-tax yield of 5 percent by 66.3 percent (.05 / .663) to get 7.5 percent.

All other things being equal, only if you can get a taxable yield of more than 7.5 percent are you better off than with the 5 percent tax-free yield.

Penny Pinching on Everything Else

College Expenses, Medicine, Cosmetics, Pets, Kids, and More

Here is a final grab bag of tips that didn't seem to fit under any of the previous chapter headings—in no particular order, and covering prescription drugs, cosmetics, college expenses, pets, kids, movies, lawn mowers, and more.

▶ DON'T TRUST ANYBODY'S BILLS

Keep good enough records of credit-card purchases to be able to check monthly bills for errors. Computers don't often make mistakes, but the people who punch in the numbers do.

▶ STRETCH REGULAR EXPENSES OUT

Many well-organized people get into a spending rut when it comes to certain regular expenses. If you get your hair cut every two weeks at $12 an appointment, that's $312 a year. If you stretch those fourteen-day intervals by just four days, you'll spend only $240 a year. One of us wears disposable contact lenses that have to be changed every week. By wearing glasses for two or three days in between lens changes, we use only forty weeks' worth of disposable lenses a year—reducing our annual costs by nearly 25 percent.

Reexamine every expense you make regularly. You may be surprised at how easy it is to cut back by stretching out.

▶ BUY HALF SHARES WITH OTHER PENNY PINCHERS

You use your lawn mower once a week and get it serviced once a year. If you buy your next one cooperatively with your next-door neighbor, it will probably last just as long, you'll still service it just once a year, and only one of you will be stuck with storing it. Most important, you'll cut your costs by 50 percent.

There are a number of things you need but don't use very often that can be bought cooperatively with trustworthy friends or neighbors. Garden tools are the most obvious examples, but sewing machines, magazine subscriptions, indoor power tools, and many other items are possibilities to consider.

▶ BARTER SERVICES WITH NEIGHBORS

A retired friend is an avid gardener with too small a yard to keep him happy. His accountant neighbor, who always hated any kind of gardening, now gets complete, loving care of his grounds—free. In return, he buys all the garden supplies for both houses and prepares the gardener's annual tax forms.

Given the increasing costs and decreasing availability of baby-sitters, you may also want to reach a barter agreement with other parents in the neighborhood. You'll keep their kids if they'll keep yours. Especially if your schedules are compatible (you have a class every Tuesday night, they bowl every Friday), this really does

work out and can save enormous amounts of money
over a year's time.

▶ TRY BARTER OPTIONS ELSEWHERE

If you like the idea of bartering, you don't have to limit
it to neighbors. It's anybody's guess how many accoun-
tants regularly barter free tax services with dentists for
free dental work, or how many garage owners barter
automobile maintenance for carpentry work on their
houses. Hundreds of millions of barter transactions take
place in the United States every year between people
who trade goods and/or services with no exchange of
money. Especially if you have a special skill, barter is
something to consider whenever you are buying goods
or services from an owner/manager or a professional.
Caveat: IRS regulations make most barter transactions
taxable.

▶ KNOW WHAT YOUR JOB SHOULD PAY

Should you ask for a raise? What should you ask for at
a job interview? What do other people doing your job
earn? The Internet has made it easier to find answers to
these important questions. *The Wall Street Journal* ca-
reer site (http://www.careers.wsj.com) lists current
median salaries in a number of job categories. *JobSmart*
(http://www.jobsmart.org), although primarily concerned with jobs in California, lists hundreds of links to
salary survey information in different industries. There
is an interesting calculator at *HomeFair* (http://www.
homefair.com) that allows you to adjust salaries by computing the cost-of-living differences among hundreds of
U.S. and international cities.

▶ GET FREE LEGAL ADVICE AND
FORMS

You can download a few common legal forms free of
charge, including a living will, promissory note, and a
financial power of attorney, at http://www.legaldocs.

com. And there is a lot of useful, basic legal advice and information available free at the *Nolo Press* web site, http://www.nolo.com.

▶ WAIT THREE MONTHS FOR MOVIES

Except for the biggest hits, most new movies are now available on video within three to five months. Renting a movie for $3 instead of paying $12 or more for tickets for two makes sense, unless there are special production values lost on the small home screen. Just as sensible: Borrow videos, particularly classic films, from your library, which also usually has records, cassettes, and CDs.

▶ FACE THE TRUTH ABOUT COSMETICS? NOT LIKELY

Deep down, you know the cosmetics makers sell hope, dreams, and fantasies. You know the ingredients in a $100 bottle of perfume may cost less than the $3 cost of the fancy bottle the perfume comes in. You know that nothing that comes in a box is really going to make you instantly beautiful, desirable, or younger.

So what? Life is not a matter of penny pinching alone. But even if you don't give up that expensive fragrance or switch to a cheaper brand of lipstick, perhaps you might consider the few money-saving tips that follow.

▶ DEEP-CONDITION YOUR HAIR FOR PENNIES

You can spend a lot of dollars on expensively packaged potions, but none will do a better job than this:

Beat together one egg and equal amounts—about a third of a cup each—of water and olive oil. Work the mixture into dry hair, leave on for one hour, then rinse thoroughly before shampooing and conditioning hair as usual.

▶ SAVE ON SKIN MOISTURIZERS

There is nothing a $20 skin moisturizer can do for you that won't be accomplished just as well by a $3 product. Or a 49-cent one—Vaseline petroleum jelly.

Perhaps you find the oil in some other moisturizer more pleasant. But all moisturizers contain some kind of oil, even those that claim to be oil-free; they are simply defining "oil" differently. The only thing that really moisturizes your skin is water, best applied through proper humidity in your house, by cutting back on hot water (which dehydrates the skin) in baths and showers, and by just splashing it on. All any moisturizer does is help hold water on your skin, and the only ingredient in any of them that does that is some form of oil.

If you want to use Vaseline, don't towel-dry after a bath or shower. Wait a minute or two and, while still damp, apply the Vaseline. Too messy? At least switch to something inexpensive that has a fragrance you like. And don't bother with different mixtures for hands, feet, elbows, neck, etc. They are interchangeable, but avoid using too oily a product on your face.

▶ SAVE ON ASTRINGENTS AND TONERS

The problem with penny-pinching advice about cosmetics is that nobody wants to hear it. The beautiful packages and ads insist that the $20, 8-ounce bottles of astringents or toners, used to clean and tighten pores after washing your face, perform some kind of magic.

Witch hazel ($1.99 a quart at drugstores) feels good, has no unpleasant odor, and works every bit as well. Some things haven't improved since your great-grandmother's time.

▶ GET FREE SAMPLES AT THE COSMETICS COUNTER

They are seldom offered, but when you buy something at a department-store cosmetics counter ask about free samples. The more you buy, the more generous the saleswoman will be.

Don't forget the ubiquitous "gift with purchase" offers either. Even if you refuse to give up those $20 moisturizers, at least you can get something free with them.

▶ BUY KNOCKOFF SCENTS

There is nothing illegal about copying a fragrance, and a company called *Parfums de Coeur* is doing exactly that with some of the world's most famous and expensive perfumes. You'll find their knockoffs in discount drugstores and chains such as Kmart. Even experts are fooled, and you'll pay a fraction of the cost of the real thing.

▶ SAVE ON DRUGS IN THE DOCTOR'S OFFICE

- Too many busy doctors still automatically use a brand name when writing a prescription. When you see your doctor pick up a pen to write your prescription, quickly ask if he will write it generically. Nine times out of ten, there's no reason not to save the money.
- Don't be shy about asking your doctor if she has any free samples of the drug being prescribed, especially if it is for very short-term use. The drug companies flood doctors' offices with samples and many doctors are happy to get rid of them.
- If the doctor is prescribing a daily 10-milligram pill, ask him if he will write the prescription for 20 milligrams. You can cut the pill in half, and the double dose will usually cost less than two single pills.
- Quite a few drugs are now sold over-the-counter that could be bought only by prescription until recently. The over-the-counter cost is always lower *unless* you have an insurance plan that covers prescriptions.

▶ JOIN THE AARP

Probably a majority of people celebrating (well, *observing*) a fiftieth birthday get what some younger friend thinks is a great joke gift—an $8 membership in the American Association of Retired Persons. The joke, of course, turns out to be that membership in the AARP (800-424-3410; http://www.aarp.org) is one of the great penny-pinching bargains of the century.

In addition to a quite readable magazine, *Modern Maturity,* membership entitles you to 10 to 15 percent discounts at many hotels and car rentals, excursion rates on some airlines, and discounts from florists and some cruise lines. You may also want to buy prescription and nonprescription drugs from the AARP's very efficient and very cheap discount mail-order pharmacy.

▶ BUY PRESCRIPTION DRUGS BY MAIL

You don't have to be an AARP member to use its pharmacy service. And there are other discount mail-order pharmacies whose prices you should check out, especially if you must take some medication over a long period of time. (Obviously, if your doctor prescribes an antibiotic, you can't wait ten days to have it delivered.) Because these companies buy in bulk quantities and have low overhead, they can offer prices on both brandname and generic drugs that are often lower than those of discount drugstores. All of the companies listed here also sell over-the-counter medications such as aspirin, sunblocks, and cold remedies at low discount prices. They will quote prices by mail and will also send you catalogs. Comparison-shop all of them before making a major purchase; prices vary greatly for different drugs. *AARP Pharmacy* (800-456-2226); *Diversified Prescription Delivery* (800-452-1976); *Medi-Mail Pharmacy* (800-331-1458).

▶ CHECK YOUR BENEFITS DEPARTMENT FOR DISCOUNT PRESCRIPTIONS

An increasing number of corporations have set up programs that allow employees to buy drugs at discounted prices from participating drugstores or from a special mail-order supplier.

However you buy a prescription drug, and especially if it is one that you will have to refill on a regular basis, compare prices from a number of sources. Then compare them again three months later. There are wide discrepancies even among discount suppliers, and prices are constantly changing. Finally, if you use a pharmacy regularly, ask it to match the best prices you find elsewhere.

▶ USE FLEX BENEFITS IF YOU HAVE THEM

If your company allows you to contribute pretax dollars, deducted from your salary, into a flexible benefits plan that reimburses you for all out-of-pocket medical expenses, sign up right away. Virtually everyone has some out-of-pocket medical expenses, even if they are just small copayments for drugs or doctor's visits covered by insurance. If these expenses are paid out of your flex account, instead of from your after-tax income, you have automatically saved 28 percent or whatever your tax bracket is. Be careful not to overestimate these expenses; you won't get back whatever isn't used at the end of the year.

▶ MAKE YOUR OWN FROZEN GEL PACKS

Applying a frozen gel pack to a muscle injury is easier than using an ice pack, but the blue gel packs sold in pharmacies are expensive. You can make your own for less than 25 cents. Partially fill a large heavy-duty plastic freezer bag with a mixture of $1/4$ rubbing alcohol and $3/4$ water. Seal and place in a second bag. Seal and put in freezer.

▶ CHECK OUT BABY BUSINESS ON THE INTERNET

Baby Business (http://www.sdx-tech.com/baby/index.html) is a nifty web site for parents looking for advice and bargains. It lists a number of sites (including Similac and Enfamil® baby formulas, Huggies and Pampers diapers, and Gerber and Beech-Nut baby food) that offer money-saving coupons and rebates.

▶ DON'T PREPAY FUNERAL EXPENSES

Millions of well-meaning people have bought "pre-need" plans that cover future costs of services, caskets, gravesites, etc. But too many of these plans, which are usually sold on a nonrefundable basis, have hidden fees that end up costing survivors more in the long run. There is also a risk that underfunded or unscrupulous plan operators may just disappear. Instead, make your wishes known in advance to family members and provide them with suggested low-cost mortuaries or reputable memorial societies. You can get a list of these from *Funeral and Memorial Societies of America* (800-765-0107; http://www.funerals.org/famsa).

▶ BUY READING GLASSES, SUNGLASSES, AND CONTACT LENSES BY MAIL

There are mail-order services offering prescription eyeglasses, but we prefer the convenience of trying on different frames at nearby discount optical stores. Reading glasses, sunglasses, and contacts are a different matter. If you need simple magnification, nonprescription reading glasses are available in our area either in discount drugstores, where we've never been able to find an acceptable style, or in optical stores, where even the "discount" prices seem inordinately high.

■ *Precision Optical* (for a free catalog: 507 Second Ave., Rochelle, IL 61068; 815-562-2174) offers a very good mail-order alternative. In addition to half frames, clear bifocals, and other magnifiers, it sells sunglasses and other nonprescription optical devices at very reasonable prices.

■ *Shades* (800-GO-SHADES; http://www.shades.com)

has a nice web site and a free catalog offering big discounts on Bausch & Lomb, Ray·Ban, and other brand-name sunglasses. Also check prices at *Shopping.com* (http://www.shopping.com).

■ *Lens Express* (800-666-5367) and *Lens Direct* (800-772-5367) will give you quick discounted price quotes on any contact lens prescription. Prices will vary; check both before ordering. Check your wholesale club, discount drug and optical stores, and Wal-Mart as well; all are aggressively discounting contact lenses.

▶ BUY FRAMED PRINTS ON THE INTERNET

ArtSelect (http://www.artselect.com) displays approximately two thousand prints, suggests appropriate frames, and sells the framed prints at discount prices—certainly less than we have seen at any of our local print galleries.

▶ GET PETS FREE

It is possible you will find a purebred cat or dog at an animal shelter. More likely you'll choose from mixed-breed animals. Either way, good shelters give away (sometimes charging a small fee or donation) healthy, vaccinated dogs and cats that are often in better shape than animals sold by pet stores.

▶ MAKE OWNING A PET LESS EXPENSIVE

It is easy to spend $1,000 a year on food, medical care, grooming, and other needs of a dog or cat. It is also easy to cut some of those expenses by ordering pet supplies from one of the national mail-order discounters. Among those that offer savings of from 35 to 75 percent:

■ *Pet Warehouse,* (800-443-1160; http://www.petwhse. com) Just about everything for owners of tropical fish, dogs, cats, birds, gerbils, etc. Good discounts and a very good catalog.

- *R. C. Steele,* (800-872-3773) Mainly a supplier for dogs—big savings and great service. Free catalog.
- *Doctors Foster & Smith,* (800-826-7206; http://www.drsfostersmith.com) Veterinary products and more, for cats, dogs, and horses.

▶ TRY STORE-BRAND FILM

The film with your discount drug chain's name on it was produced by a manufacturer that also markets under its own brand name. Same film, but the store brand will be 15 to 20 percent cheaper. Once you decide you like that film, buy it in multipaks and save even more. Just be certain you will use the film before its expiration date.

Whatever film you buy, you will pay more for higher speeds. If you are taking snapshots outdoors on a reasonably sunny day, you probably don't need more than 100-speed film.

▶ BUY GOLF AND TENNIS EQUIPMENT BY MAIL

There are a number of discount sources for golf and tennis equipment; they all advertise monthly in *Tennis, Golf Digest,* and the other magazines that cover these sports. Your best bet is to call a few of them for prices, because they constantly change.

▶ JOIN THE Y

Prices vary, and so does what is offered. But in many cities and towns across America, the Ys have wonderful facilities and offer incredible bargains to swimmers, runners, racquet-sports players, and fitness enthusiasts.

▶ EXERCISE AND DIET ON COMPANY TIME AND MONEY

More and more companies are offering exercise and diet programs to their workers, on premises and either free or well below the costs of comparable programs outside the office. If your company isn't one of them, you might canvass coworkers to build up interest and then talk to a benefits or personnel manager. The principle that healthier workers cost companies less is generally accepted today, so you may well get the program you want.

► CALL FOR HOUSEPLANT BARGAINS

Companies that rent houseplants to offices often sell those they can't use at a fraction of their usual retail price. If you are in the market for some new houseplants, check the Yellow Pages (under "plants") and make a few telephone calls.

► REDUCE A CHILD'S ASSETS BEFORE COLLEGE

More than 75 percent of students attending college today receive some kind of financial aid, and most of that aid is based on need. Even families with incomes over $100,000 a year can get financial assistance under certain circumstances, but they have to prove need based on what is called "Federal Need Analysis Methodology."

When you apply for financial aid, you will fill out a very complicated form that lays bare your income and assets as well as any assets your child has. It is important to know that only 5.65 percent of your assets are considered available for the costs of college, but 35 percent of your child's assets are.

What this means is that you have good reason to reduce any assets your child has *before* you file the financial aid documents. Buy the computer that will be needed in college—as well as clothes, airline tickets, etc.—using his or her assets, not yours.

If grandparents want to make gifts of money to your college-bound child, ask them to wait and instead pay tuition bills, or part of them, directly to the school. They can do this in any amount without incurring a gift tax.

▶ **PLAN WAY AHEAD FOR COLLEGE FINANCIAL AID**

The process of applying for and receiving grants and loans for a college education is always time-consuming and usually frustrating. But it is not as mysterious as it seems to those confronting all the forms and choices for the first time. Your library has books that tell you everything you need to know. If you don't have a home computer, your child probably has access to one at school, and information about financial aid is readily available on the Internet. One good place to start a search is at the Yahoo education site (http://www. yahoo.com/Education/). More specifically, you can get forms, advice on how to fill them out, and other information from the *Department of Education's Student Aid Information Center* (800-433-3243; http://www.ed.gov/ money.html).

Even if your child is years away from college, if you think you will need or want financial aid when the time comes, visit your library or the Internet now. What you learn may very well affect your saving, investing, and tax strategies in the ensuing years.

Here's one specific example: Suppose your child plans to enter college as a freshman in September 2000. The financial aid package he or she gets will depend on what your income was in 1999. That gives you a big incentive to defer income from that year (see Chapter 4).

Also, you want to be ready to file for financial aid as early as possible. Most colleges accept forms as early as January 1; mail yours the day after Christmas. The reason: Many colleges make grants (which you don't have to repay) on a first-come, first-served basis. The later you file, the more likely you'll be getting a higher ratio of loans (which you do have to repay) in your package.

▶ **FIND A SCHOLARSHIP**

High school guidance counselors have traditionally been the primary starting points for most people. There are also a number of good books about scholarships and financial aid. But the Internet has rapidly become the single most important source of information for most parents and students. One of the best sites we have seen is *fastWeb* (http://www.fastweb.com), a free service that helps you locate and apply for scholarships, internships, and loan and savings opportunities. You can set up a personalized scholarship search and get feedback about it on your own fastWeb mailbox. The site also has up-to-date information about financial aid and an on-line calculator that computes an estimate of a student's expected family contribution and financial need using the Federal Need Analysis Methodology. Finally, it has links to virtually every individual college and university scholarship, financial aid, and admissions office.

▶ CASH IN U.S. SAVINGS BONDS TO PAY TUITION

All the interest you earn on Series EE U.S. Savings Bonds is excluded from taxes when the bonds are redeemed to pay any part of your child's college tuition bills. This exclusion can't be claimed by higher-income families; if your adjusted gross income in the year bonds are redeemed exceeds a certain amount (currently around $75,000), the tax-free amount begins to be phased out and is phased out completely at around $106,000.

▶ START A STATE-SPONSORED COLLEGE SAVINGS PLAN

Most states now sponsor some type of college savings plan. Although the plans vary widely, there are two basic types. Prepaid tuition plans let you pay in advance—at today's prices—for college expenses that won't be incurred for a number of years. Typically, they give you a risk-free way to protect yourself against cost increases in state schools. If you live in a state that offers a prepaid tuition plan, you can defer federal income taxes on the money in your plan account until you withdraw it. Also, funds withdrawn can be used to qualify for Hope Scholarship tax credits (see Chapter 4).

State-run college savings plan trusts invest the money you contribute in state-operated mutual funds. No state taxes are owed on contributions and federal taxes are deferred until the money is withdrawn. Each state has a different cap on the amount that can be saved, and a minimum return may or may not be guaranteed. Unlike the prepaid plans, these savings plan trusts are not usually tied to attendance at in-state schools.

To keep up with developments in this rapidly changing area, the *College Savings Plan Network* has a web site (www.collegesavings.org) that is a good place to begin any research.

▶ START COLLEGE IN HIGH SCHOOL

One of the best ways to cut college expenses is to reduce the time period it takes to get a degree. The first way to do that is by enrolling in college-level courses while still in high school. To earn credits accepted by most colleges, you then have to pass an Advanced Placement exam administered by the College Board. High school guidance offices have full information.

▶ ENROLL IN AN ACCELERATED DEGREE PROGRAM

Many colleges have programs that make it possible to earn a bachelor's degree in three years instead of four. Such programs are arduous, demanding heavier course loads during the regular school year as well as summer school, but they can cut the cost of a degree by 20 to 30 percent.

▶ GO TO A COMMUNITY COLLEGE FIRST

You can cut the costs of a degree by as much as 40 percent if you spend the first two years at a local community or junior college and then transfer to a residential four-year college for your final two years. You'll save money by living at home; more important, the costs of a community college are usually at least 75 percent lower than those of a private four-year college.

▶ CHECK OUT COLLEGE DISCOUNTS

To attract good students, many colleges now offer various discounts on tuition. Among them: discounts if more than one family member attends the college at the same time; discounts for the children of alumni; older-student (twenty-five or over) discounts; evening and weekend discounts for classes held outside regular hours; and campus-activity discounts for certain student leaders.

▶ CHECK OUT COMPANY BENEFITS

Many corporations have assistance plans to help employees pay for their children's college educations. Ask your benefits department.

▶ STOP BUYING LOTTERY TICKETS

If you want to dream about being a multimillionaire, fantasize instead about an unknown relative dying and leaving his riches to you. It is a likelier scenario than a lottery win. State lotteries are nothing but another form of tax, and unfortunately this tax falls most heavily on those who can least afford it.

Here are some numbers to inspire you: Instead of throwing away $100 a year on lottery tickets for the next fifty years, invest that money in an aggressive growth mutual fund that averages a 16 percent return a year. At the end of fifty years, you will have $1,043,565 instead of a pile of worthless tickets.

▶ GET FREE CONSUMER ADVICE FROM THE GOVERNMENT

We've mentioned a couple of specific booklets available from the Government Printing Office in this book, but there are hundreds of them. Many are free and few cost more than a couple of dollars (unless you take into account the taxes you pay to write, produce, and print millions of copies a year).

One of the most useful is *The Consumer's Resource Handbook*. In addition to some reasonable (if not exactly streetwise) advice on how to be a smart consumer, this catalog lists addresses and telephone numbers of whom to write to at different corporations, including car companies, with a complaint. It also gives addresses and telephone numbers of different state and federal agencies, regulators, authorities, and commissions. It is a very handy book to have, and it is free.

The government will also give you advice on buying a used car (50 cents), choosing a nursing home (free), and traveling abroad ($1.25). It will tell you what to do about depression (free), asbestos in the home (50 cents), or a child with a speech disorder (50 cents). It has booklets on careers and education, exercise and weight control, federal programs, food and nutrition, health, housing, money management, parenting, small business, travel, and hobbies. You may not find every answer you want, but at these prices you may at least want to know what's available. You can get a free copy of the catalog that describes all the booklets, *Consumer Information Catalog,* as well as a copy of *Consumer's Resource Handbook* by calling 800-664-4435. You can also download them and hundreds of the booklets at no cost (http://www.pueblo.gsa.gov).

▶ KEEP SURFING

If ever there was a penny pincher's dream fulfilled, it is the Internet. We still subscribe to print magazines, but what we can get free from the web sites of thousands of magazines is astonishing. Confused about the new Roth IRAs, we found a web site developed for and by CPAs (http://www.rothira.com) where we got free information that would have cost us hundreds of dollars had we turned to an accountant. We download tax forms from the IRS site. We download recipes.

We constantly comparison-shop. Just one example: In the past month, a few of the tiny halogen bulbs used in our kitchen's under-cabinet lighting burned out. We'd last bought a couple of them a year ago at a specialty lighting store nearby for nearly $10 apiece. Demand for them is obviously low, so they aren't available at Home Depot or the other discount places where we normally buy lightbulbs. Two days ago, we went to http://www.yahoo.com, did a search for "halogen bulbs AND discount," and found *Sun Lighting Supply Company* (888-850-1556; http://www.sunlighting.com). It took us sixty seconds to find the lightbulb we needed—at $2.99 each if we ordered a dozen!

Perhaps savings this dramatic are unusual, but we are convinced that shopping the Internet, especially for unusual or hard-to-find items, is the penny-pinching wave of the future.

▶ LOOK FOR BARGAINS EVERYWHERE

They exist. No matter what you are buying, there are nearly always alternative sources and quick ways to find them. There are usually ways to negotiate better deals. Strategies that work in one area can often be adapted to work well in others. Use the tips you've read in these pages, but don't stop there.

If you are lucky, one of the things your taxes pay for is a good free library system. Use it. Ask librarians where to find information that will help you make major purchase decisions. Borrow cookbooks, travel guides, how-to references, and books on investing and saving. When you discover you are using a book constantly, go to a bookstore and buy it.

Start surfing. Even in its infancy stage today, the Internet is an incredible penny-pinching resource. It will soon become an indispensable one.

Things change. If you want to make your dollar go as far as possible, you've got to keep up. We know very well that the day after this book goes to press, someone will share with us a terrific new money-saving tip that should have been included. We'll keep looking. You should, too.

▶ PINCH PENNIES, NOT KIDS, FRIENDS, OR YOUR SENSE OF HUMOR

Saving money and not wasting any are worthwhile activities, but only if they don't interfere with the more important things in your life. Wasting a few dollars is better than jumping on your kids every time they forget to turn out the lights. And saving money should never get in the way of enjoying what you spend it on.

Keep things in perspective. Penny pinching is a rewarding means to an end, not the definition of a complete, well-rounded lifestyle.